The FBI and the Berrigans

Also by Jack Nelson

THE CENSORS AND THE SCHOOLS (with Gene Roberts, Jr.)
THE ORANGEBURG MASSACRE (with Jack Bass)

The FBI and the Berrigans

The Making of a Conspiracy

by Jack Nelson
and Ronald J. Ostrow

Coward, McCann & Geoghegan, Inc.
New York

SBN: 698-10464-1

Library of Congress Catalog Card Number: 76-187152

Printed in the United States of America

Acknowledgments

We are indebted to many persons for the help they gave in our research. But several deserve special thanks for granting numerous interviews, some of which lasted for hours. They include Professors Gene Chenoweth and Richard Drinnon, students Jane Hoover and Betsy Sandel and librarians Zoia Horn and Patricia Rom, all of Bucknell University.

Attorneys Ramsey Clark, Terry Lenzner, J. Thomas Menaker, Leonard Boudin and Paul O'Dwyer, and the legal secretary who worked with them, Vicki Dadurka, were extremely helpful. Justice Department officials William S. Lynch and Robert C. Mardian and several other federal and local law enforcement officials, who insisted on anonymity, provided considerable assistance. So did Congressman William R. Anderson and Tom Buck.

Robert and Mig Hoyt provided some research material, as did a number of newsmen: Bryce Nelson of the Los Angeles *Times*; James Wieghart and Mike McGovern of the New York *Daily News*; Loye W. Miller of Knight Newspapers; Bill Burkett of the Harrisburg *Evening News*; Jane Shoemaker of United Press International; William Eaton of the Chicago *Daily News*; Robert Sanford of the St. Louis *Post-Dispatch*; Robert Shogan and Nicholas Horrock of *Newsweek*; and Champ Clark of *Time Magazine*. Frank Wilson typed our manuscript and made helpful suggestions, as did Patricia Curran Ostrow.

We are deeply grateful to two editors for helping us avoid pitfalls and assisting our efforts to make the book the documentary we intended. They are Peggy Brooks, senior editor of Coward, McCann & Geoghegan, and Edwin O. Guthman, national editor of the Los Angeles *Times*. Any pitfalls we failed to avoid are our own fault.

Contents

CHAPTER ONE

The "Incipient Plot"

J. Edgar Hoover strode purposefully down the hallway of the Capitol, a briefcase under his right arm, his old enfeebled friend and top aide, Clyde A. Tolson, limping along a respectful half-step behind. It was a familiar scene in Washington, the two of them walking that way, both clad in sharply creased dark suits, white shirts and conservative ties, folded white handkerchiefs showing from their breast pockets. Both tight-lipped and stern looking.

This day—November 27, 1970—Hoover's expression seemed even sterner than usual, his mouth only a slit on the massive, bulldog face that had been a favorite subject of news photographers and cartoonists for almost half a century. For most of his brilliant career as director of the Federal Bureau of Investigation he had been virtually sacrosanct, a towering symbol of American virtues, impervious to what little criticism had come his way. But lately, some political leaders had severely criticized his administration of the FBI and questioned whether he had stayed too long as director. Moreover, the press, which had helped make him a living legend in American law enforcement, had been unusually critical in recent months, and public opinion polls had shown that faith in the FBI was dropping away among those under thirty-five.

Hoover was prepared to tell Congress that the FBI was just as efficient as ever, that it could cope with the subversion of the 1970s as it had with the saboteurs of World War II and with John Dillinger and other gangsters of the 1930s. Although he often talked about such historic accomplishments and the FBI emphasized them in its public relations program, Hoover also took enormous pride in contemporary FBI activities. In fact, whenever testifying before Congress on behalf of FBI appropriations, he stressed that the FBI was working overtime in keeping close tabs on the Communist Party, which he considered a serious threat to internal security, and on other radical groups, including the Bl..ck Panther Party, the militant antiwar movement, and what he termed New Left extremist groups, "notably the so-called Weatherman." Today he would testify that the FBI needed additional agents because of the increased work load of investigating such groups.

Hoover was an old hand at such congressional appearances. He had been director of the FBI for more than forty-six years, serving under eight presidents.

He would be seventy-six on January 1. Under the Civil Service Retirement Act he had faced compulsory retirement at age seventy, but President Lyndon B. Johnson had exempted him by executive order. And President Richard M. Nixon, a friend and admirer for many years, had perpetuated the order. Hoover's constant companion for more than forty years, Clyde Tolson, had been failing in health for several years and had suffered a stroke which affected his walk and speech. He had turned seventy on May 22, but at Hoover's behest was exempted from mandatory retirement by order of Attorney General John N. Mitchell.

President Nixon and Mitchell had said Hoover had their complete confidence and could remain in office as long as he was physically able. Hoover and Mitchell, who shared a "law and order" philosophy, enjoyed a close working relationship, a sharp contrast to the gulf between the FBI director and such attorneys general as Ramsey Clark and Robert F. Kennedy. Hoover and Mitchell agreed that domestic subversives posed a serious threat to national security, and to meet the threat Mitchell beefed up the Justice Department's Internal Security Division, which his predecessors had let grow quiescent.

Hoover long had been a leading law and order symbol because his iron-handed rule had transformed the FBI from a scandal-ridden agency into one of the world's most respected law enforcement agencies. But in the past year there had been recurring criticism that he had stifled needed change in the FBI and that instead of correcting its mistakes, he merely had covered them up to avoid embarrassment.

In addition, FBI agents had been accused of using agent provocateurs in several cases and of having lied to Justice Department attorneys to cover up for state patrolmen who had fatally shot three black college students and wounded twenty-seven others in Orangeburg, South Carolina. Hoover himself was accused in 1970 of having used a transcript of electronic eavesdrops of alleged extramarital activities by Dr. Martin Luther King, Jr. to blackmail the civil rights leader into toning down his criticism of the FBI's handling of civil rights cases.

Ramsey Clark, in his book *Crime in America*, wrote that Hoover put personal glory above effective crime control and allowed "his self-centered concern for his reputation" to affect his judgment.

A professor at John Jay College of Criminal Justice in New York and another at American University in Washington, whose students included more than a dozen FBI agents and clerks, criticized Hoover's rule by "personality cult." And in New York one of the agents, ex-Marine Captain Jack Shaw, wrote a lengthy letter to the John Jay College professor, a detailed criticism of Hoover's rule. ("We are not simply rooted in tradition. We're stuck in it up to our eyeballs. And it all revolves around one key figure—the life and exploits of J. Edgar Hoover.")

Hoover, always extremely sensitive to any criticism, struck back at critics with what the St. Louis *Post-Dispatch* described as his "waspish reaction to any hint of FBI infallibility."

He ordered FBI employees attending John Jay College and American University to drop out of the schools. He accused Shaw, an agent with an unblemished record, of "atrocious judgment," then forced his resignation, which he accepted "with prejudice," a black mark that effectively blackballed Shaw from employment in the law enforcement field for several months. (Shaw later filed suit against Hoover and the FBI and won an out-of-court settlement—$13,000 in back pay and elimination of the black mark from his records.)

Hoover excoriated Clark as a "jellyfish" and in the same newspaper interview denounced Robert F. Kennedy who had been assassinated two years earlier, as the first attorney general to cause the FBI trouble.

There had been other criticism of Hoover and the FBI, too, all of it extremely embarrassing to a man who still had strong official support and a loyal public following. Perhaps nothing had been more embarrassing than the actions of the Berrigan brothers—Philip, a Josephite, and Daniel, a Jesuit. The priests were vociferous theorists and the most dramatic practitioners of a loosely knit group of radicals, mostly Roman Catholics, who destroyed draft board records and engaged in other acts of civil disobedience to protest American involvement in the Vietnam war. The so-called Catholic Resistance numbered no more than several hundred, plus several thousand sympathizers, among the nation's 47,000,000 Catholics. Although the great majority of the activists were Catholic laymen and priests and nuns, or former priests and nuns, there were a few Jews, non-Catholic Christians and atheists and agnostics.

Members of the Catholic Resistance prided themselves on individual acts of conscience and while they admired the Berrigans, they considered neither them nor anyone else to be leaders per se. It was not the Berrigans who launched the first draft board raid, but a nineteen-year-old Minnesotan, named Barry Bondhus. His eleven brothers and machinist father in Big Lake, Minnesota, helped him prepare for the 1966 action by collecting material he would use. In some ways, Bondhus' choice of symbolism has never been surpassed. He dumped two buckets of human feces into a Selective Service filing cabinet, rendering unusable hundreds of 1-A draft records. Although the protest, known as The Big Lake One, drew little press notice, it was credited as "the movement that started the movement."

It was more than a year later—October 27, 1967—that Philip Berrigan and three others destroyed draft board records at Baltimore. From that point on, the Resistance claimed responsibility for the destruction of Selective Service records in more than twenty-five locations. At least fifty-five persons were tried, convicted and sent to jail for the raids. In the beginning, the raiders would wait for police or FBI agents to arrive at the scene of the crime and to arrest them. But as the Vietnam war dragged on, the movement sought a broader impact. The raids were staged at night, and the raiders no longer waited to be arrested. Prominent university faculty members and other professionals were enlisted to "surface" and proclaim their "responsibility" for the illegal protest, which complicated the mission of the FBI.

Both Berrigans were now serving time for destroying draft board records—Philip for his part in the Baltimore raid and both he and Daniel for their part, along with seven others (the Catonsville Nine), in burning records with homemade napalm at the Catonsville, Maryland, Selective Service office. The brothers had been prime irritants of the FBI, especially Daniel who had managed to elude agents as a fugitive from the Catonsville case for more than four months. Daniel had taunted the FBI by giving underground interviews, popping up at hurriedly called press conferences, making impromptu speeches at small gatherings, and once escaping from the clutches of scores of agents at Cornell University. In one of the interviews, he referred to FBI agents as "Keystone Kops."

Even behind bars the Berrigans had remained a source of irritation, sending out antiwar messages, recruiting convicts to their cause, and staying in contact with the Resistance through mail and visitors to the prison. Moreover, when Hoover went to the Capitol on November 27, 1970, he was known still to be smarting over Daniel Berrigan's antics as a fugitive.

In his briefcase Hoover carried prepared testimony for the Supplemental and Deficiencies Subcommittee of the Senate Appropriations Committee. His lengthy testimony ostensibly was designed to substantiate the FBI's request for an extra $14,500,000 to provide 1,000 additional agents (boosting the total to 8,350) and support personnel and related equipment "to handle the increased work accruing under the Organized Crime Control Act of 1970 as well as for the additional work being required in New Left, racial extremist and aircraft hijacking matters."

Not that Hoover ever really needed to substantiate a request for appropriation of additional funds. Whatever Hoover wanted from Congress, Hoover got. Only twice since 1950 had the FBI not received the exact amount of its budget requests. On those two occasions, the FBI received more than it had requested.

Traditionally, Hoover restricted his Capitol appearances to the House side. But this day was different; he had a sensational internal security threat to report.

Awaiting the FBI officials in the ornate, chandeliered Room S-128 of the Capitol was a long-time Hoover admirer, Senator Robert C. Byrd of West Virginia, chairman of the subcommittee, a man very much like the FBI men in appearance—dark suit, white shirt, conservative tie, hair combed straight back with scant sideburns. Hoover and Byrd shook hands, then sat on leather chairs facing each other across a long mahogany table with green felt top, bare except for several glasses and gleaming silver water pitchers. Since it was a holiday weekend—the day after Thanksgiving—only one other subcomittee member, Senator Roman L. Hruska (R. Neb.), also a longtime Hoover admirer, was present. Hruska sat beside Byrd, facing Hoover and Tolson and John P. Mohr, sixty-one, assistant to the director, who had made the trip over from FBI headquarters with them in Hoover's specially constructed $28,000 armor-plated Cadillac. Hoover's habit of buying a new armored car annually was about the only thing that ever caused any Congressional mail critical of FBI appropriations. Some tax-payers objected to the fact that Hoover built up a fleet of the vehicles for his use around the country at places he frequently visited, such as Miami and Southern California, where he and Tolson took in the horse races.

The FBI officials brought with them about fifty copies of Hoover's twenty-seven-page prepared statement. Before the closed-door session began they turned over the copies to Thomas J. Scott, clerk of the Senate Appropriations Committee, for immediate distribution to a group of reporters.

Rapidly reading his statement to the subcommitte, Hoover cited numerous statistics as he always did in testifying that his agents, although overworked, were efficient and effective. He said overtime "totaled over 4 million hours during the fiscal year 1970, an average of over 2 1/2 hours every workday." His critics would argue that he failed to relate the fact that agents were under standing orders to work overtime to make the FBI look good at appropriations hearings. And some agents would complain privately that they frequently remained on duty unnecessarily, without meaningful work to do, just to establish the overtime record.

Hoover read on for sixteen pages, citing other statistics, outlining the FBI's increased duties under the Organized Crime Act, and describing what he considered to be a mounting danger of subversion by the New Left. He said such groups, "notably the so-called Weatherman," had stepped up terrorist activities in 1970.

This group originally belonged to the Students for a Democratic Society but separated because it did not consider the SDS to be sufficiently militant and violent in its actions. The Weatherman claimed credit for an explosion at a New York City Police Department facility on June 9, 1970, which caused $150,000 damages and eight injuries. The group apparently was involved in earlier abortive efforts to dynamite targets in Detroit. Three underground Weatherman activists were killed in a New York City explosion in March, 1970. The Weatherman group now is completely underground and in May, 1970, Bernardine Dohrn, one of its leaders, declared a state of war against the United States on behalf of the group. Over 20 Weatherman militants are currently fugitives, including Dohrn, who is one of the FBI's "Ten Most Wanted Fugitives," arising out of indictments on anti-riot charges and violations of Federal bombing and gun control statutes during the past year.

And now Hoover reached a section of the statement that would overshadow everything else he had to say that day:

Willingness to employ any type of terrorist tactics is becoming increasingly apparent among extremist elements. One example has recently come to light involving an incipient plot on the part of an anarchist group on the east coast, the so-called "East Coast Conspiracy to Save Lives."

This is a militant group self-described as being composed of Catholic priests and nuns, teachers, students, and former students who have manifested opposition to the war in Vietnam by acts of violence against Government agencies and private corporations engaged in work relating to U.S. participation in the Vietnam conflict.

The principal leaders of this group are Philip and Daniel Berrigan, Catholic priests who are currently incarcerated in the Federal Correctional Institution at Danbury, Connecticut, for their participation in the destruction of Selective Service Records in Baltimore, Maryland, in 1968.

This group plans to blow up underground electrical conduits and steam pipes serving the Washington, D.C. area in order to disrupt Federal Government operations. The plotters are also concocting a scheme to kidnap a highly placed Government official. The name of a White House staff member has been mentioned as a possible victim. If successful, the plotters would demand an end to United States bombing operations in Southeast Asia and the release of all political prisoners as ransom. Intensive investigation is being conducted concerning this matter.

Despite the sensational nature of Hoover's allegation, neither Byrd nor Hruska asked him any questions about it, not even the identity of the "possible victim." But Byrd did ask a question about the Communist Party that drew from Hoover a reply that the FBI was well aware of "what is going on" with all militant groups and was prepared to take steps to prevent violence. Byrd asked him if he saw evidence that the Communist Party was stronger and more effective in the United States than it had been in recent years "by virtue of the fact it can move in and does move in on these dissidents' activities and does reach into the Black Panther Party, and it does apparently reach into the colleges and universities of the country, and into the churches and news media, I assume?"

Hoover replied that Byrd was correct despite the fact that actual party membership had been decreasing. He said, "They have also tried to clean out of their groups any they suspect might be Government informants and informants of local authorities. I have heard the statement made by some of the jackals of the press that if all of the FBI informants left the Communist Party, it would completely collapse. That is absurd and an untrue statement."

When the FBI director had completed his testimony Senator Byrd said, "Mr. Hoover, we are delighted to hear your statement today. It has been an extremely good one and we have appreciated your presence . . . we will give every consideration to your request as we always do."

As Hoover hurriedly left the Capitol, reporters also heard him say the Black Panthers were involved in the kidnap-bombing conspiracy. The Chicago *Tribune*, a staunch Hoover supporter, reported:

"Rushing out of the Senate appropriations subcommittee hearing room where Hoover made the charges, reporters who had not yet read the prepared statement asked the FBI director, 'Who was involved—Black Panthers?' 'Yes, yes,' Hoover replied and pushed past them."

Inside the FBI, some officials grumbled among themselves that the man they knew as "Mr. Hoover" or "the director" had jeopardized an ongoing investigation. And outside the bureau, critics accused him of violating Justice Department guidelines on pre-trial statements. The guidelines, embodied in the Code of Federal Regulations, provide that "disclosures should include only incontrovertible, factual matters, and should not include subjective observations."

Actually, Hoover's comments before Senator Byrd's subcommittee marked the third time he had briefed Government officials on a kidnap-bombing plot and the second time he had made on-the-record accusations against the Berrigans and the East Coast Conspiracy to Save Lives. He had given the same testimony eight days earlier, before a House Subcommittee on Appropriations, but it was not released to the public at that time. Despite the furor that developed over the release of Hoover's Senate testimony, however, the FBI printed for distribution to the press and others on December 11 a booklet containing the testimony before the House subcommittee. It included a cover letter from Hoover saying it was "a reprint of my on-the-record testimony" and "it is my hope that through this document a better understanding will result of the work and problems facing the FBI."

Long before any of the testimony, Hoover, in a secret conference with White House officials and Republican Senate leaders, said such a conspiracy existed. On September 22, he told the President and the GOP leaders that an additional 1,000 FBI agents were needed and a major reason was that radical groups were devising violent plots, including some that would endanger high Government officials. He stressed that the East Coast Conspiracy to Save Lives was behind a kidnap-bombing conspiracy and said other groups planning violence included the Weatherman and the Black Panthers. President Nixon supported Hoover's request for additional appropriations and asked Congress for legislation authorizing the FBI to investigate immediately any arson or bombing on the campus of any college receiving Federal aid. Congress eventually enacted both proposals.

Word of Hoover's briefing of White House and Congressional leaders made the front page of the New York *Daily News* in mid-October, more than a month before the FBI director testified before the Byrd subcommittee. The story reported that Hoover had warned that the East Coast Conspiracy to Save Lives planned to disrupt the Government with political kidnappings and assassinations and to cripple communication, transportation and sanitation locations. Hoover, the *Daily News* reported, cautioned senators to avoid congregating in large numbers or traveling together so as not to present an inviting target.

The story caused little stir around the country. But six weeks later Hoover's testimony about the Berrigans dominated the news on the Thanksgiving weekend. The newspaper, television and radio reports fell like a thunderclap on some of the priests' closest allies who often had discussed illegal antiwar activities in group sessions. Among them were five zealots who were to play leading roles in an unfolding drama of Hoover and the FBI vs. the Berrigans and the Catholic Resistance:

--Sister Elizabeth McAlister, thirty-two, a New York nun whose close personal relationship with Philip Berrigan included discussions of possible marriage. The clandestine plotting of antiwar activities seemed to thrill her; she wrote of some of the plans in grandiose terms in letters smuggled into prison for

Philip Berrigan. Some of her friends thought that in her extreme dedication to the Resistance they discerned an urge to project a Joan of Arc image.

--The Reverend Joseph Wenderoth, thirty-four, of Baltimore, a member of the East Coast Conspiracy to Save Lives, which had publicly taken responsibility for destroying draft files in Philadelphia and records of General Electric Co., a big defense contractor, in Washington. Powerfully built, he was known as a "quiet jock" during seminary days when athletics provided the only major diversion from rigid religious training as a Josephite.

--The Reverand Neil McLaughlin, thirty, of Baltimore, who as a member of the New York Eight took public responsibility for stealing draft records in the New York City area. McLaughlin, short and frail, knew Wenderoth at the seminary and now they roomed together. Both worked among poor blacks and, like other members of the Catholic Resistance, they linked poverty, racism and other domestic ills of the Nation to America's involvement in the Vietnam conflict.

--Anthony Scoblick, thirty, of Baltimore, an ex-priest who was married to an ex-nun, Mary Cain, also an antiwar activist. As members of the Boston Eight before their marriage, both took responsibility for destroying draft files at Jamaica Plain, Dudley, Uphams Corner and Copley Square in Boston. Scoblick, dark and muscular, had met Mary Cain, as well as Wenderoth and McLaughlin, while working as a Josephite in a Baltimore ghetto.

--Eqbal Ahmad, forty, a Pakistani and a non-Catholic, a jocular, but also intensely serious student of guerilla warfare, the self-described "odd man out" of the group of Resisters. Short and dark, he was a loquacious but articulate activist who had helped direct the underground strategy that had prevented the FBI from capturing Daniel Berrigan for more than four months. He was a fellow at Chicago's Adlai Stevenson Institute for International Affairs.

Sister Elizabeth was driving alone in Baltimore about 12:30 P.M. en route to the Gambrile, Maryland, home of her twin sister, Kathleen Brigham, wife of an Army major who was a Vietnam war veteran, when news of Hoover's testimony two hours earlier blared over the car radio. She later recalled: "I almost went into a stupor. I thought, 'What is this? My God what is this?' I kept the radio on for three hours and it came on again and again and again, about every fifteen minutes—'FBI Director J. Edgar Hoover charged . . . ' I said to myself, 'This is terrible, Dan and Phil are in jail and can't answer the charge, the lawyers should answer it.' It was like carrying on a dialogue with the radio. Finally, when I was almost at my sister's house the radio quoted Bill Kunstler and Bill Cunningham as saying it was a far-fetched spy story and I thought, 'Wow, the lawyers are on it already.' "

She remembered her thoughts suddenly shifting to a convict at the Lewisburg Federal prison— Boyd Frederick Douglas, Jr.— who had smuggled messages between her and Philip Berrigan when the priest had been imprisoned there. She hoped that prison authorities had not learned of his role as courier.

Sister Elizabeth frequently wore mini skirts and with her long shapely legs, her smooth complexion, oval face and almond-shaped blue eyes, she looked younger than her thirty-two years, despite a sprinkling of gray in her long brown hair. She had a master's degree in art history and was a professor of art history at Marymount College, Tarrytown, New York.

As she drove toward her sister's house, she wondered whether any of the messages Douglas had carried had fallen into the wrong hands. Some of the letters between the priest and the nun contained expressions of love which she figured "might blow the minds of some people."

In one letter she had written: " . . . put it on another level— this heart and form, these eyes long for the sight, sound, & touch of you (however briefly or subtly) . . ."

And in a letter to the nun, Phil Berrigan wrote: "Have been mulling over your suggestion (made with half seriousness, I guess) that the future ought to include a dye job, a cover operation, a coupla kids (adopted), and our own movement. I guess, Liz, we'll be called upon to make many critical decisions, but then we'll have the strength to make them, and make them right . . . "

In other letters, the two discussed illegal antiwar actions—past and proposed. In fact, one of Sister McAlister's letters to Berrigan had suggested that future strategy include a non-violent "citizen's arrest" of a government official, perhaps

Henry A. Kissinger, President Nixon's national security advisor. In the letter, she mentioned that at a meeting in Connecticut "Eq outlined a plan for action" that included kidnapping—"in our terminology make a citizen's arrest of—someone like Henry Kissinger." Berrigan had replied—also in a letter smuggled by Douglas—that the plan was grandiose but could be carried out, and he proposed that the terms of releasing such a hostage should be halting of American bombing of North Vietnam.

In Baltimore, Wenderoth, McLaughlin and Scoblick also heard radio news reports of Hoover's accusation. Although none of them had attended the Connecticut meeting at which Eqbal Ahmad, Sister Elizabeth and several others had talked of such a strategy, all three had participated in Resistance discussions that included talk of "citizen's arrest." In fact, the day of Hoover's charge, Wenderoth had gone down to Broadway Center in Baltimore to check with a legal services attorney about the law of citizen's arrest in Maryland.

When Wenderoth heard the news, he had just returned to the row house in the East Baltimore black ghetto where he and McLaughlin had been living for the previous several months— ever since they had been banished from their parishes by the prelate who had ordained them, the Most Reverend Lawrence Cardinal Shehan of the Baltimore Archdiocese—after they claimed responsibility for destroying draft board records.

"Good God," Wenderoth later said he thought. "What a hell of an imagination Hoover has." Hoover's charges about the East Coast Conspiracy to Save Lives, Wenderoth said, "blew my mind—I hadn't even seen any of those people for months. Not only that, but I knew the Berrigans were not members of the East Coast Conspiracy and had no connection with it." Wenderoth had reason for concern, however, for he was a member.

McLaughlin had just returned from spending Thanksgiving Day with his mother when he heard the news. "My first reaction," he said later, "was that it was just an attempt to get back at the Berrigans. I thought it would be a big splash and that would be the end of it."

Scoblick, who the previous June 27 had married Sister Mary Cain in an ecumenical ceremony, also felt the matter would blow over. But he had reason to be apprehensive for he knew FBI agents had frequently tailed him to meetings with other members of the Catholic Resistance and even had disrupted his wedding ceremony on grounds they were searching the church for a fugitive—Daniel Berrigan.

The most mysterious figure of the five, Eqbal Ahmad, was in Paris appearing as an antiwar critic on "The Advocates," a National Educational Television program, when he read of Hoover's accusations in the International *Herald Tribune*. "It sounded so ridiculous to me," he later recalled. "I knew I had brought up the matter of a 'citizen's arrest' but the discussion came to nothing. We talked about a lot of ideas that were rejected, like massive communications tie-ups for example. I was worried about Hoover's accusations, but more amused than anything else. I couldn't figure out how the hell the FBI knew about the Connecticut meeting—maybe electronic surveillance. But I thought that nobody could make a case out of that."

As soon as Ahmad finished the filming, he flew back to New York, then took a cab to the Sacred Heart of Mary convent at 137 West 85th Street where Sister Elizabeth and seven other nuns lived. Ahmad had been a friend of Daniel Berrigan since 1968 when both were on the faculty at Cornell University, but he had only met Philip Berrigan twice. However, Ahmad had become good friends with Sister Elizabeth, who, according to Wenderoth, "turned to Eq as a strong person, one with political analysis and strong insights, a man with background and experience who knew what the Government was trying to do in Vietnam and Cambodia and what it was doing to try to stop the peace movement. She often turned to Eq for advice after Phil was sent to prison."

Ahmad had become part of the circle after Philip was captured. He used his contacts with Sister McAlister and Fathers McLaughlin and Wenderoth as a means of throwing the FBI off the trail of his good friend, Daniel Berrigan. Realizing the FBI suspected him of the role of architect of Daniel Berrigan's underground, Ahmad thought that frequent meetings with the Catholic Resisters would lead the FBI to tail them rather than the network of persons outside the ranks of the Catholic radicals that actually hid Daniel. Before Daniel went underground, Ahmad had worked with other members of the Catholic left, but his link to them had been Daniel.

Of course, there were other antiwar organizations Ahmad could have joined. But as he later said of the Catholics: "These good, primitive Christians at least had a constituency and a vision. So many other groups—women's lib and men's lib and a lot of ad libs—took the view that you couldn't change the war until you changed America. The Catholics had roots and they focused on the issue, the war, rather than on something else."

Ahmad was greeted at Sister McAlister's convent by the provincial superior, Sister Jogues Egan, who also had participated in antiwar strategy sessions, including the meeting at Connecticut. She explained that Sister Elizabeth, her secretary, was expected shortly. Ahmad had never heard of Boyd Douglas, but Sister Jogues knew of him and his courier role and his name had occurred to her immediately upon hearing Hoover's accusation. "Oh Lord, Boyd must have something to do with this," she thought.

Sister Jogues, fifty-two, white-haired and pleasant looking with a smile that crinkled her face and brightened her eyes, knew that her distinguished visitor would be more than slightly upset upon learning that a convict had been trusted to smuggle messages containing discussions about illegal antiwar activities.

"I tried to break it to Eq gently about Boyd," recalled Sister Jogues, who was a visiting scholar at Columbia University and former president of Marymount Manhattan College and of Marymount College, Boca Raton, Florida. "He was furious at first. He raged around, fuming, 'Fucking Catholics, Goddam stupid Christians! Liz had been riding on a wave of adulation in the peace movement and when she comes in here I'm going to tell her what I think. I am going to really let her have it.' "

But when Sister Elizabeth walked in nervously wringing her hands and smiling faintly, Ahmad rushed to her, threw his arms around her in a tight embrace and exclaimed, "Ah, Liz, how are you? Do not worry about it. It will be all right!"

Ahmad himself was worried, however, for now he had evidence that the Catholic radicals he loved and held in such high esteem were as naïve as he had suspected. Two of them even committed to paper such suggested strategy as a political kidnapping. Later he learned that Sister Elizabeth had even written of the plan: "This is in utter confidence and should not be committed to paper." Ahmad declared, "It's insane—writing this on paper to a man in prison, then saying don't commit it to paper—and giving the letter to another prisoner!"

If Ahmad had had any religious faith, it would have been sorely tested. But he professed little or none, although he indicated to friends that one day he would return to Pakistan and enter politics and list himself as a Moslem, the faith in which he was raised. He always prided himself on using common sense and good judgment ("He argued facts and strategy while we argued moral questions," Wenderoth said) and he felt the FBI would not have captured Daniel Berrigan had the priest not ignored Ahmad's advice to stay away from known friends in the movement. "My God," Ahmad would say at times in his pronounced Pakistani accent, "I am dealing with children."

He had come to the United States thirteen years earlier on a Fulbright grant, had earned a PhD from Princeton and later taught there, at the University of Illinois and at Cornell. A prolific writer, Ahmad served as editor of *Africasia*, a French news magazine about Third World affairs, and he wrote extensively about revolutionary and guerilla movements and government responses to them. He was married in 1969 to Julie Diamond, daughter of a Jewish businessman in New York, in a ceremony performed by Daniel Berrigan. Since 1968 he had been a fellow at the Adlai Stevenson Institute.

With Philip Berrigan behind bars, Ahmad had become a theoretician and analyst for the group. He would, on the one hand, analyze bombing tonnage figures and discuss the meaning of the Cambodian invasion. On the other hand, he would counsel on the futility of more draft board raids, urging the activists to turn to organizing antiwar GI coffee houses.

There was a significant difference between Ahmad and others in the circle. The eager activists considered themselves firmly dedicated to non-violent social and political change. Ahmad was ambivalent on violence. While regarding violence personally distasteful, he said he would support violent revolution under the right circumstances. His distaste for violence could be traced to his childhood. At the age of four, sleeping alongside his father, Ahmad was awakened by assassins chopping his father to death with crude instruments. The senior Ahmad was a reformist landlord in the state of Bihar, and it was believed his killers were angered by his land reform efforts.

Few who knew the Berrigans and other members of the Catholic Resistance believed that any of them would consider resorting to violence. Foolish and grandiose talk, perhaps, but nothing that would include serious planning of violent acts that might endanger human life.

Philip Berrigan first heard of Hoover's accusation in the yard of the Federal Correctional Institution at Danbury, Connecticut. Other inmates had heard radio reports of Hoover's testimony and relayed them to Philip. He later said his first reaction was that the movement "had greater effectiveness than we thought. They wanted to bury us in prison for the rest of our lives."

In New York, two attorneys, William M. Kunstler and William C. Cunningham, the latter a Jesuit, reacted on behalf of the Berrigans saying Hoover should either prosecute them or retract the allegation. After a visit from the lawyers the Berrigans released a statement, which said:

> On Friday, Mr. Hoover singled us out as leaders of an East Coast Conspiracy to Save Lives. We are happy to agree that such a conspiracy of conscience does exist; in a far more extensive form than Mr. Hoover recognizes. There is also a West Coast Conspiracy to Save Lives, a Middle Atlantic and a Southern Conspiracy to Save Lives. There is, in fact, a Worldwide Conspiracy to Save Lives and "to demand an end to U.S. bombing operations in Southeast Asia."
>
> Mr. Hoover, however, is overgenerous. At Danbury we have neither the facilities nor personnel to conduct such an enterprise. Nor do we have access to government funds. We have already been tried and condemned by Mr. Hoover's remarks, and we should have an equal opportunity to answer his charges. He ought, in view of the seriousness of the allegations he has made, either to prosecute us or publicly retract the charges he has made.

Kunstler and Cunningham, who had represented the

Berrigans at their trials, earlier had termed Hoover's testimony "a far-fetched spy story" fabricated to support the FBI's request for additional funds.

In Washington, the Reverend Joseph Wenderoth held a press conference along with five other members of the East Coast Conspiracy to Save Lives—the Reverends Peter Fordi, thirty-two, of Woodstock, Maryland, and Richard Bidwell, thirty-nine, of Boston, both Jesuits; Sisters Susan Cordes, thirty-two, of Grand Rapids, Michigan, and Susan Davis, thirty, of Baltimore; and John Finnegan, twenty-two, of Philadelphia, a Catholic draft resister and former student at Pennsylvania State University. They denied any complicity in a kidnap-bombing plot and said the Berrigans were not leaders or even members of the group. They also circulated copies of a February 24, 1970, pamphlet and news release which identified them and five other antiwar activists as the only members of the East Coast Conspiracy to Save Lives. The pamphlet, which included a group photograph of the members, claimed the group had destroyed draft files in Philadelphia and General Electric files in Washington.

In a prepared statement, the group said,

> Since that time, we have continued active unarmed resistance. We have spoken to others about the reasons for our action and the need for more of the same. We have attempted to bring others to a better understanding of the irresponsible and dangerous misuse of power by those in positions of power in America. . . . We here claim that while we are friends and deeply respectful of the Berrigans, they are not our leaders. We say that Hoover's charge against us is an attempt to instill in us and others a paralyzing fear, and we refuse to be so paralyzed. We reaffirm our commitment to a radical restructuring of our society by attempting to awaken the conscience of America. We invite others to support us against Mr. Hoover and the FBI. . . .

Others identified as members of the East Coast Conspiracy to Save Lives were Nancy Assero, twenty-two, of Baltimore, a student at Mt. Saint Agnes College; John Theodore Glick, twenty, of Lancaster, Pennsylvania, who had refused induction and was a draft resistance organizer; Charlotte Lacey, eighteen, of South Philadelphia, a part-time art student and graduate of Cardinal O'Hara High School; Mike Panella, twenty-four, of South Philadelphia, draft resister and organizer; and the Reverend Philip Linden, twenty-eight, a Josephite from East Baltimore, one of the few blacks in the Resistance.

The Berrigans also had an unusual defender—and an extremely staunch one—in a Democratic Congressman from Tennessee, William R. Anderson, forty-nine, World War II hero and former commander of the atomic submarine *Nautilus*. A hawk-turned-dove, he had helped expose the tiger cages for political prisoners at Con Son after going to Vietnam in June, 1970, on a "fact-finding" House mission. Later, reading up on the dissident side of the war, he came across the works of the Berrigans and was so impressed that he decided to visit them in prison. He became convinced of their total commitment to non-violence.

After Hoover's accusation, Anderson again visited the Berrigans, then wrote a letter to Hoover expressing confidence in their dedication to non-violence and declaring, "If there is any substance to your allegations . . . I respectfully submit that it is your duty to arraign them before a federal grand jury to seek an indictment. If on the other hand, there is no substance . . . then certainly we should expect an explanation, if not an outright retraction."

Anderson, who released copies of his letter to the press, went on to say that the matter transcended the Berrigans and added to "a growing tendency on the part of our executive branch to employ the tactics of fear and to be less than candid in dealing with the public."

Hoover, in a letter dated December 2, replied: "Today I have received your observations regarding my testimony before the Senate Appropriations Subcommittee concerning Fathers Daniel and Philip Berrigan. I was surprised to observe that your letter was released to the press prior to its receipt by me. You may be assured my testimony was predicated on the results of careful investigation. All information developed regarding this matter is being furnished the Department of Justice which has the responsibility for initiating prosecutive action."

The FBI once again violated Department of Justice guidelines on release of prejudicial information by distributing copies of Hoover's letter to the press. A week later, Anderson, in a lengthy House speech, accused Hoover of resorting to "tactics reminiscent of McCarthyism" and said: "The verbal assault by Mr. Hoover on Fathers Berrigan is the climax of a series of events during the past several months which, when taken as separate incidents, are shocking and unbelievable, but when related one to the other, emerge as an outrageous pattern of fear and repression."

The Nixon Administration's official reaction to Hoover's testimony was guarded with the President himself sidestepping a question that Dan Rather, a White House correspondent for CBS, asked at a nationally televised news conference on December 10. "Mr. President," Rather asked, "as a lawyer and as his immediate superior, do you approve of the following actions of FBI Director J. Edgar Hoover? One accusation which has been made public—accusing two men of conspiring to kidnap Government officials and/or blow up Government buildings as an antiwar action before any formal charges had been made and a trial could be arranged for these gentlemen. And continuing to call the late Martin Luther King a liar. Do you approve of those actions?"

President Nixon replied: "I have often been asked my opinion of Mr. Hoover. I believe that he has rendered a very great service to this country. I generally approve of the action that he has taken. I'm not going to go into any of the specific actions that you may be asking about tonight with regard to the testimony, for example, that you referred to. The Justice Department is looking into the testimony that Mr. Hoover has given and will take appropriate action if the facts justify it."

A spokesman for Attorney General John N. Mitchell said that Mitchell did not know that Hoover had planned to testify about the investigation and was surprised that he had. Privately, Mitchell was infuriated and baffled that Hoover would compromise an ongoing investigation. And Mitchell was known to have had words with Hoover about it.

In testifying about the alleged kidnap-bombing plot, Hoover

had acted against the advice of other FBI officials. While
reviewing in advance a copy of Hoover's prepared testimony,
Charles D. Brennan, an assistant director in charge of the
Domestic Intelligence division, had spotted the section about the
plot and had written the director a memorandum urging that it
be deleted because it would damage an ongoing investigation.
The memo carried the written endorsement that his position was
supported by all officials of his division, the largest in the FBI.
Other top FBI officials also supported Brennan's position.

Hoover kept the fact that he had acted contrary to the advice
of other officials a closely guarded secret. And after he was
publicly criticized, he blamed the officials. "Mr. Hoover had seen
every memorandum on the case and knew as much as anybody
about it," one of the officials later said in an interview for this
book. "But he would never accept responsibility for anything
that went wrong. He accused us of not keeping him sufficiently
informed of the investigation and said if he had known more
about it he would not have testified about it. He also said he did
not realize his testimony would be made public, but he knew
copies were being released to the press. He just wanted the
publicity. He acted quite angry about the whole thing and Clyde
Tolson was there as he always was, like a parrot, repeating
everything the director said. Mr. Hoover was just mad because
he ignored advice that turned out to be good and it backfired on
him. He could not stand bad news. It was like the story of the
despot cutting off the head of a bearer of bad news."

Hoover, a master of public relations, may have stubbed his toe
in testifying about the Berrigans. But he also had accomplished
his mission at the Capitol, grabbing page one headlines and
chunks of newspaper space and radio and television time on a
holiday weekend that produced little competing news.

Now determined that the case would be prosecuted, he took a
personal hand in the investigation. On his orders, several
hundred agents from Washington, Philadelphia and New York
were thrown into the massive probe. In the margins of investigative reports that reached him he would write in blue ink
such orders as "expedite" and "pull out all stops" and "push
this hard." One of the FBI officials involved in the investigation

said, "A cryptic blue-ink notation was all that was needed. When the director made a blue-ink notation, it was more powerful than a long legal memorandum."

"To clean his own skirts, as he always did," the official said, "Mr. Hoover made a blue-ink notation that other officials had failed to keep him properly informed about the case prior to his testimony. That way not even history could ever blame him."

CHAPTER TWO

What Manner of Men

Who were these Berrigans that they could so anger the director of the Federal Bureau of Investigation and prompt questions that made the President of the United States engage in artful sidestepping?

The answer requires a glance at the Catholic Church in America in the early 1970s, which had been experiencing unprecedented turbulence. Daniel and Philip Berrigan were not the source of that turbulence. But they were among the more visible manifestations of it, they helped keep it astir and without it they could not have found the receptive audience they did.

Much of the ferment was generated by Pope John XXIII's liberalizing moves: His Pacem in Terris encyclical in 1963 which rejected war as an alternative for nations to consider in the nuclear age, his opening the door to altering church practices that had remained unchanged since medieval times and the Ecumenical Council Vatican II meeting from 1962 to 1965 which lifted partway the fence of parochialism that had restricted the church for so long.

In the late 1950s and early 1960s, Daniel Berrigan was in the vanguard of American priests seeking to revamp the church's liturgy and make it more meaningful to the young. Philip Berrigan was a leader among those Catholic clerics trying to involve the church more deeply in the number-one social issue of the time—equality for the black American.

But, in the mid-1960s, the nation became increasingly involved in Vietnam. It was an involvement that siphoned off money and energies the Berrigans thought should be devoted to rooting out poverty and attacking discrimination. More important, they viewed the war as inhumane and counter to the spirit of Pacem in Terris. Their mounting opposition to the war conflicted with the unswerving support the church and its members had given in previous American wars. A leading theory of American Catholic super-patriotism had it that members of the faith expressed their loyalty to country so positively because of hostility and suspicion from Protestants who dominated the American scene.

The church's "just war" doctrine, which permitted Christians to fight inhabitants of another country if certain restrictive conditions were met, converted a civil obligation into a morally binding religious obligation, and justified the taking of a human life in the course of a just war. (However, attempts by Catholic war resisters to use the same doctrine as a basis for refusing induction while the United States was waging what they regarded as an unjust war in Vietnam have been rejected by the Supreme Court.)

Catholics provided such unquestioning support to the wartime state in the past that members of the faith rarely sought exemption from combat military service as conscientious objectors. In World War II there were only 223 Catholic conscientious objectors in the United States, according to a graduate study by Paul Riley of Temple University. This was out of a Catholic population of 20,000,000 males and compared with the total of 53,354 COs of all faiths.

Through World War II, the American church hierarchy gave no support to Catholics who questioned the morality of war. Thus in 1943 the only Catholic conscientious objector camp was closed, partly because it annoyed the Bishop of Manchester, New Hampshire, in whose state it was located. He told selective service headquarters that "a person could not be a Roman Catholic and a conscientious objector at one and the same time."

Placed against this backdrop, the Berrigan brothers' proclaiming the Vietnam war to be evil and scaling the ladder of protest—from visiting Congressmen to demonstrating on the doorsteps of the homes of military leaders and, finally, destroying draft board files—offended the state as well as a sizable segment of their church.

The Berrigans, to be sure, were not the first American Catholic pacifists. In a letter to Representative William R. Anderson of Tennessee, Daniel cited Dorothy Day, founder of the Catholic

Worker Movement, and the late Thomas Merton, a Trappist monk, as having shaped his non-violence. Recalling that he and Philip attended a 1964 retreat conducted by Merton on the "spiritual roots of protest," Daniel said: "I wrote him once that I could still remember the article of his in the Catholic Worker that turned me from damp straw to combustible man . . . . He got us started, after Dorothy Day. The consequences are not theirs, but ours."

Berrigan told Anderson that Merton was shocked when he and Philip joined in burning draft records. He said he thought Merton "suffered the kind of electric shocks that come to a man when his friends take him literally."

There is a key difference between the Berrigan protest and that of Merton and Miss Day, who promoted pacifism from the Spanish civil war throught the Vietnam conflict. The Berrigans finally moved outside the system, breaking laws that nurtured a war they considered immoral and then attempting to escape the punishment. Miss Day and Merton remained inside the system.

A novelist sketching the early life of a pair of revolutionary priests would have to look no farther than the actual experiences of the Berrigans. The two youngest of a family of six brothers, headed by an authoritarian father who was a militant labor organizer, they knew what it meant to be hungry. Their father's rough handling was offset by their mother's gentle touch. No matter how low their larder, the Berrigan door was always open to the hungry, penniless passerby, and they had many such visitors during the depression years.

Pinpointing what prompted Daniel and Philip Berrigan to buck both church and state depends on the observer you talk to. Jerome Berrigan, the oldest of the three younger brothers, and Corita Kent, a former nun who is a close friend of Daniel's whose silk screen designs have been used for the covers of his books, pointed to the Irish revolutionary spirit as a dominant force. Philip, the youngest in the family, cited his father and his earliest memories of the hard times on the iron range of Minnesota and later a small farm outside Syracuse, New York, as the shapers of his rebelliousness.

Daniel has recalled treatment at the hands of his father's spinster sister, Aunt Maggie, who moved in during the year their mother was hospitalized with tuberculosis, as a cause of "a lot of our kookiness and aggressiveness." He said Aunt Maggie starved the children, pleasing his father's sense of economy, but the children's pinched cheeks helped hasten the mother's recovery and brought her back to feed the flock.

The father, Thomas William Berrigan, who died in 1969 at the age of ninety, was born in Syracuse a few years after his parents gave up farming in Ireland during the potato famine and came to the United States. After two years of college, he headed west via a succession of railroad jobs. He put down roots in the great Mesabi Iron Range of northern Minnesota, where he drove locomotives for the mining companies.

There he met and married Frieda Fromhart, a German-born, devout Catholic. As a teenager Tom Berrigan had moved away from the church because it did not support trade unionism, his prime interest. His gentle wife brought him back to the church. As Frieda gave birth to their six sons, the family moved often from one worn, small, company-owned cottage to another.

Tom Berrigan was irascible, domineering, certain of his convictions, and he ran the family with a stern hand. Family stories differed on why the Berrigans moved back to Syracuse, the father's hometown, in 1926. Some say it was his union activism and socialist convictions that cost him his locomotive-driving job. Others claimed he was fired for reading poetry on the job. He was a great lover of poetry—Yeats, Shakespeare, Shelley and his own, a fondness not shared by publishers, much to his disgust.

Another explanation for the return to Syracuse was that the Mesabi Iron Co. shut down operations in Babbitt, Minnesota, and Tom Berrigan found himself out of a job, with six children ranging in age from three to fourteen. Philip was three at the time of the move, Daniel five.

Tom Berrigan rented a sixty-year-old house that had been left to the Catholic diocese of Syracuse. It was near Galesville in the rural outskirts of Syracuse. With it came ten acres that he and his sons farmed to supplement his income from such jobs as tending the furnace in a Catholic orphanage. The father reveled in physical labor and expected his sons to do the same. In addition to the farming, there was much to be done. The house had no central heating or plumbing. The sons often collected wood from the countryside for the fireplaces and stoves and hauled drinking water in buckets from a public tap a half-mile away.

Some of the father could be seen in the sons: The love of poetry in Daniel, the love of physical exertion in the strapping Philip who was a star athlete in high school, and, in both sons, support for the unfortunate who had less.

Despite Tom Berrigan's militant labor organizing and his prodding the church to take up for the have-nots, he was remembered by his son, Jerome, as "quite authoritarian." The son told a newsman that his father "was very inclined to cooperate with anyone else in authority—the church, the school, the law. We were brought up to totally accept church rules and school rules and all the rest of it."

The lesson apparently stuck with the older of the Berrigan brothers, Thomas and John, who have voiced strong disapproval of their younger brothers' actions. Thomas, a foreman at the same Minnesota mine where his father used to work, has described their antiwar activities as "a waste of two promising Catholic priests."

"I deal with everyday problems, heavy equipment, working men," he said, adding that "a great block" separated him and his two younger brothers. "I'm no lover of the establishment, but I don't believe in overthrowing it with nothing to replace it. To my mind they are visionaries—fuzzy-minded and not very practical," Thomas Berrigan said. "I have no sympathy at all for their methods. They are alien to my nature."

John Berrigan, two years younger than Thomas, was equally critical. In a letter to the Minneapolis *Tribune* after Philip and Daniel were behind bars for burning draft board files, John wrote: "Who do they think they are to take the law into their own hands?"

Later, he explained: "I decided to say something because I got tired of seeing letters and statements supporting my brothers. They were drivel. I don't go along with all this destroying draft records and all the stuff they've done."

John, a winter watchman for a deserted summer resort in northern Minnesota and a summer crewman on Great Lakes ore boats, said that when his brothers began the priesthood, "they were conscientious priests. We were all proud of them. Now they're breaking the law by destroying property. What they are doing is against the best interests of the United States."

Thomas Berrigan was not totally surprised that his brother Daniel took the path he did. "Because of his slight physique and frail health, Dan was rather sheltered as a child. And I think that continued for him in the Jesuits, whom I also consider sheltered and impractical," Thomas said, ignoring Daniel's extensive travels and service for the Jesuits in South America, Europe and Asia.

"I wouldn't have expected it of Philip," Thomas said. "He has had far wider experience than Dan and always seemed like a very solid person."

The third member of the older trio of Berrigan brothers, James, grew far more sympathetic.

As Jerome Berrigan said: "James went to Vietnam as a civilian engineer in 1966 and he came out with many misgivings. He returned to the United States during the radicalization of my brothers, and he came to be totally supportive of them." After working in Syracuse, James moved to the Virgin Islands.

The father of the clan had little reaction to his younger sons' radicalism because it evolved while his health was failing. "He already had a number of falls and was somewhat senile," Jerome said. "I know how he would have approached their views, however—a careful listening to everything they had to say for all sorts of reasons. And his general attitude would have been one of agreement because he had such love and respect for his sons that he would have deferred to their consciences and their sense of what was right."

Their mother, gentle and devout, had a major role in shaping Daniel and Philip. Her love of mankind, her insistence that her boys be good and compassionate and devout Catholics, and, most of all, the steady hand at the rudder she provided to offset the father's moods and outbursts had great impact on her sons.

(Her concern for her boys and her tendency to interpret conditions in the best light still shone as brightly as ever when she visited them at the drab Federal Correctional Institution at Danbury, Connecticut, in the summer of 1971. Accompanied by son Jerome and his wife, Carol, the eighty-five-year-old Mrs. Berrigan noted with pleasure that prison had taken some pounds off Philip's large frame, expressed concern that it had done the same for Daniel, but concluded that the authorities must be treating both her sons well because both were tanned.)

The mother's influence was heaviest on Daniel because his physical fragility often kept him inside the house where he helped with her chores, a fact that did not sit well with the authoritarian father. Daniel was the most devout of the boys and constantly worried about the suffering in the world, she recalled.

The Berrigan brothers attended St. John the Baptist Parochial High School, a two-mile walk from their home. Of all the brothers, only Daniel was remembered by the sisters there as a brilliant student. He wrote poetry and led cheers while his brother, Philip, two years his junior, starred at baseball and basketball. The teachers recalled Philip as an average, but extremely cooperative student.

At age seventeen, Daniel and a friend applied to the Jesuits, whose cool detachment impressed them. Other orders had responded to their inquiries with brochures that featured swimming pools among the enticements. Daniel later recalled that "the Jebbies just had a couple of tight little quotes from St. Ignatius in a very stark pamphlet." Because his family lacked the money to send him to college, he spent an extra year at St. Joseph's polishing his Latin before beginning the thirteen years of training required of priests in the Society of Jesus.

Philip, upon his graduation, worked for a year scouring soot-caked locomotives at the New York Central yards to earn college money. He spent a semester at St. Michael's College in Toronto before he was drafted in 1943. Army service was the first installment in his radicalization. He underwent field artillery training in the Deep South—Fort Gordon, Georgia, then Florida and North Carolina—where he saw close up black poverty and second-class citizenship, an experience that influenced his postwar life.

A myth surrounded Philip's overseas service in the military. The tale apparently was supposed to illustrate either that a man who could take to the World War II battlefield with genuine gusto could later embrace non-violence without reservation, or that a man who experienced war horror would be converted into an apostle of pacifism.

Sympathetic biographers, such as Francine du Plessix Gray who wrote so movingly about the Berrigans in the *New Yorker* magazine, helped propagate the myth. In her book, *Divine Disobedience*, she quoted an unnamed friend of Berrigan as saying: "Philip Berrigan is like Saint Paul, an exceptionally gifted warrior. Before his conversion he could kill men more enthusiastically than most soldiers can."

Mrs. Gray reported that Philip fought in the field artillery in France and Germany, then switched to the infantry and was commissioned a second lieutenant in France. "It is a period of his life which he dislikes to discuss," she wrote.

Similarly, Jim Forest, a co-worker in the Catholic peace movement and an admirer of the priest, capsulized Berrigan's wartime experiences in *The Berrigans* this way: " . . . and then the war in Europe, the seeing of gutted cities, the experience of death and of death-making; a battlefield commission in the artillery."

Actually, according to Philip's own account, on file at the Baltimore headquarters of his religious order, Society of St. Joseph, he saw no combat, though he underwent officers' training in the infantry in hopes of seeing some action.

"Went overseas with a field artillery unit as a sergeant," he wrote in describing his forty months in the Army. "While in Germany, volunteered for officers' training in the infantry in the futile and foolish hope of seeing some action. But by the time I was commissioned, the war had ended."

At the Catonsville Nine trial, Philip described himself as "an enthusiastic participant in World War II—in contrast of course to my present attitude which arose because of the influence of people who have surrounded me."

He noted that he had spent about a month in the British Isles, seeing such bombed-out cities as Bristol, Coventry, Sheffield and London.

Discharged from the Army in 1946, Philip enrolled at Holy Cross College in Worcester, Massachusetts, a Jesuit school, where he caused little stir academically or otherwise. He managed to score some Bs in his major of English, but he flunked calculus as a senior and had to take a second examination to pass Catholic theology.

The Reverend John P. Haran, a religious ethics professor at Holy Cross, has pondered whether Philip's rapt attention during discussion of the Catholic "just war" doctrine gave a signal of what was to come.

While Philip studied and played intramural sports with what his classmates remembered as vigor, Daniel was in the final years of his Jesuit training at a seminary in nearby Weston, Massachusetts. This gave the brothers the opportunity to reestablish the relationship they had enjoyed before the war, and they had long discussions on the weekends.

Their brother next up the ladder, Jerome, also had decided on the priesthood, but he had entered a Josephite seminary, an American order founded after the Civil War to help Negroes. Graduating in 1950 from Holy Cross, Philip followed him into the Josephites.

When family members wondered why he had not joined Daniel in the more rigorous Jesuit order, Philip explained: "I haven't got time." The Jesuits would require thirteen years of training, but the Josephites credited his college years, allowing him to be ordained in five years.

Daniel, however, seemed to have wielded more influence with Philip than any other family member. Philip dedicated his first book, *No More Strangers*, a study of the psychological roots of racism: "To my brother, Father Dan, S.J., without whom neither my priesthood nor this book would be possible."

In manhood as in childhood, the two brothers were virtually opposites in physical appearance. Daniel was slight, and his hair was dark and closely cropped. He often had a bemused smile, like a person who saw something humorous in a situation that escaped others. His world travels, particularly his years in France, had polished his speech and manner. He looked like the poet he was, one who had just emerged from a garret following an exhausting, all-night session of wrestling with a manuscript.

Philip was a big man who expressed himself in highly physical ways—a booming voice, crushing embraces for men and women alike. His personality was more mercurial than Daniel's, his ups and downs more apparent. His gray hair made him appear the older of the two. Philip's physical manner spilled over into his writing style, so that broad, sweeping statements abound in his books and letters.

Daniel was ordained in 1952, and the next year the Jesuits sent him to France for a year's study. There he encountered a segment of the church that had been radicalized partly through participation in World War II resistance, and he was exhilarated by the French worker-priest movement. The priests of that movement dropped the traditional barrier between priest and penitent and spurred the workers on in their quest for better pay and working conditions.

The worker-priests, Berrigan later wrote, "gave me, for the first time, a practical version of the church as she should be."

But the worker-priests stepped on too many toes to suit Rome. Pope Pius XII ordered the movement disbanded, much to the shock of Daniel Berrigan. Another event that drove a lesson home while Berrigan was in France was the French defeat at Dien Bien Phu. "My French friends woke me up to the evils of colonialism," he later said.

Returning to the United States in 1954, Berrigan was assigned to teach French and theology at a Jesuits' preparatory school in Brooklyn. His extracurricular interests in those years centered on combating poverty and achieving the rare kind of relationship between layman and priest that the worker-priest had sought. His rare rapport with the young began to manifest itself, and he served as chaplain for a chapter of the Young Christian Workers, a religious harbinger of the Students for a Democratic Society.

In 1957, he was named a professor of religion at LeMoyne University in Syracuse, which brought him back together with his parents and his older brother, Jerome, who had quit the Josephite order a year before ordination.

Jerome later explained that he left the order because of his "general feeling that I was not cut out for the priesthood. It was just a matter of conscience. I had expressed doubts to Phil several months before, and he counseled my waiting. Having waited, I made my decision."

Meanwhile, Philip Berrigan, ordained in 1955, had been assigned to teach high school in New Orleans after a year as an assistant at a ghetto parish in the District of Columbia. At Saint Augustine High School, about a mile from New Orleans' French Quarter, Philip was remembered by some of the all-black school's graduates as a teacher who was heavy on the reading-list assignments, provocative as a discussion leader and questioner and rough on the basketball court.

More than anything else, his contagious energy and industriousness were recalled by those who studied under him and taught alongside him. After a day of teaching, he would join the school's black janitor in cutting the lawn, repairing and painting, followed by an evening of voracious reading and clipping of a wide range of public affairs material.

Disgusted by the hostility of Louisiana priests outside the Josephites toward desegregation, Philip became a potent civil rights leader within the order. Under his tutelage, one of his students became the first black to be employed by the Western Electric Co. plant in New Orleans. A tactic that became a Berrigan favorite was to send squads of blacks to a mass officiated over by a segregationist priest.

His charismatic flare for leadership was demonstrated when he and four other priests sent 300 of their students from door to door collecting food and other donations for the poor, which the students then distributed. In one year, the team distributed $15,000 worth of food, furniture and clothing.

During these years, the two Berrigan brothers began to work as a team. Daniel, teaching at LeMoyne, helped Philip with scholarships for Saint Augustine graduates to study at the university, and Philip drew upon Daniel's supply of idealistic young to assist with good works in the South during summer vacations.

In 1963, Philip and Father Richard Wagner, a fellow Josephite, planned to conduct a sit-in at the Negro waiting room in the Jackson, Mississippi, airport terminal. As they boarded a southbound plane at New York, a press release was issued announcing their intention. The news flew faster than the airplane. The priests were changing planes at Atlanta when Philip

Berrigan was summoned to a terminal telephone. The Very Reverend George F. O'Dea, Josephite superior general, was on the line ordering the priests to scratch their plans.

It was learned subsequently that the Bishop of Jackson, the Most Reverend Richard Gerow, was infuriated by the priests' plan for witness and had warned O'Dea that if the priestly sit-in occurred he would ban Josephites from his southern Mississippi diocese.

The incident was one in a series that caused Philip to regard his order as an Uncle Tom organization that merely sought to comfort blacks instead of prodding them into action to better their existence. Philip bristled at the restraint as his superiors barred him from moving too far too fast.

Like Daniel's bitter disappointment when Rome crushed the worker-priest movement, the experience drove home to Philip the lesson that the institutional church would often side with the repressive elements in society to maintain the status quo. But the incident also taught Philip the value of publicity as news of the priests' aborted odyssey was published throughout the country. Priest and nuns flocked to subsequent civil rights demonstrations in ever increasing numbers.

About this time, Philip began to see a relationship between America's treatment of the Negro and the nation's reliance on nuclear might. He expressed this theory in his book, *No More Strangers*, which he worked on in 1963 and 1964 during a year's leave of absence from Saint Augustine's to raise funds for his order in the New York area. He wrote:

I submit that the two phenomena, segregation and the arms race, are very much connected and that the vicious seeds of one help to promote the other.

. . . we have internationalized our attitudes of injustice and exclusivism, our determination to preserve our status quo of privilege and possession. And this to such an extent that we are still creeping toward that apex of irresponsibility in which nuclear war appears more and more logical as the bold sanction of our national integrity.

In connection with his fund-raising mission, Berrigan

arranged for a consulting firm to study the Josephites and submit recommendations on how the order could better fulfill its mission. The consultants proposed that $2 million be raised to enable the Josephites to play a more prominent role in the fast developing civil rights revolution. But the order's ruling council rejected the proposal, a setback that finally convinced Berrigan he could best accomplish his goals by working outside the confines of the order instead of trying to change the organization.

His goals and Daniel's began to merge rapidly. Like Philip, Daniel had demonstrated a special quality for inspiring students at LeMoyne, getting them to reexamine concepts they had learned by rote and channeling their energies outside the classroom into work for the underprivileged.

Both Berrigans used the technique of forming sodalities, groups that rigorously worshiped daily and took the gospel literally, curbing their own material hunger and working tirelessly for the poor. Inspirational and demanding leadership was required to win any following for such literal translation of the words of Jesus and the Apostles. The Berrigans provided it, leaving some of their priestly colleagues in awe.

What most irritated the church hierarchy, however, were Daniel's efforts toward liturgical reform, controversial steps to make the church less obscure and more relevant. It was an activity that little interested Philip. ("If liturgical renewal doesn't change people's hearts about war and racism, to hell with it," Philip later said.)

Stripping elements of obscurity from the liturgy and bringing the priest in closer contact with his congregation, Daniel Berrigan turned the altar in his off-campus chapel around to face the congregation and delivered part of the mass in English. The acts were a precursor to the Vatican Council which approved altering what had stood for centuries. Berrigan described the greater contact with the congregation and the use of language that all could understand as "pizzazz" aimed at reaching the young.

That kind of change did not sit well with his superiors, and the Jesuits sent Daniel Berrigan back to France on a year's sabbatical. The trip further radicalized him. He went a full-faced, impeccably neat cleric attired in the priest's standard Roman collar and black suit and returned a hollow-cheeked man who wore a turtleneck sweater, a beret and a ski parka.

He traveled to Eastern Europe and Russia and talked to Catholics there whose faith he hailed as "purified by persecution." He spent nearly two weeks in South Africa. While experiencing what he described as "intense exposure to a segregationist police state," Berrigan voiced a philosophy that was later to be used repeatedly in explaining why the Catholic Resistance risked imprisonment in protesting the Vietnam war.

It occurred at a meeting in Durban when the priest was asked: "What happens to our children if things go so badly that we have to go to jail?"

"I remember saying," Daniel wrote, "I could not answer that question not being a citizen of that country, but I could perhaps help by reversing the question. What happens to us and our children if we do *not* go to jail?" (Italics his.)

(Daniel Ellsberg used a variety of the same theme in 1971 in explaining why he leaked the Pentagon Papers to the press. "Wouldn't you risk jail if it would help end the war?" he asked.)

Daniel Berrigan attended a Christian Peace Conference in Prague in the summer of 1964. It drew delegates from Communist and non-Communist countries, and Father Berrigan wrote that the conference discussed matters "that diplomacy and power and the military were not talking about. That is to say, how can we survive as human beings in a world more and more officially given over to violence and death. I think the imperceptible movement of my conscience was pushed forward by that experience."

Delegates condemned the limited but growing role of the United States in the Vietnam war. "From Japan to Cuba, Christians were assailing us, extremely embittered at the course that even then seemed to be written in our stars," Berrigan said.

Daniel returned to the United States in the summer of 1964 and was assigned to edit and write for the Jesuit Missions magazine in New York. Now he and Philip were only sixty miles apart. The Josephites had transferred Philip to teach at the order's lower seminary, Epiphany Apostolic College in Newburgh, New York.

With the Josephite hierarchy well aware of Philip's propensity for organizing armies to do battle on behalf of the have-nots, Newburgh was a surprising assignment. The John Birch Society thrived in the highly conservative city where the nation's reverses—foreign and domestic—were automatically thought to be the work of Communists. A few years before Philip's arrival, the city began to focus the nation's attention on the welfare problem when City Manager Joseph Mitchell tried to pare the relief rolls drastically. Mitchell's crude welfare reform was blocked when state authorities obtained a court injunction barring the move.

Philip wasted no time in stirring things up. Reacting to the squalid condition of Newburgh's black slums, he assigned his seminarians to wards and directed them to visit all the poor families in order, among other things, to check for building code violations. While this hardly won the hearts of the town's slumlords, it was a minor irritant compared with Philip's booming denunciation of America's escalating role in Vietnam. The predominantly Catholic city gave the kind of allegiance to the nation's overseas adventures the Roman church usually gave the state.

In 1964, before his transfer to Newburgh, Philip had been named one of four co-chairmen of the Catholic Peace Fellowship, a group formed to offset the super-patriotic strain in the American Catholic church by supporting conscientious objectors and winning converts to non-violence. Philip lectured frequently and stridently in the Northeast, attacking the nation's moves in Vietnam and condemning his church for its failure to speak out against what he viewed as brutal aggression.

Philip's lectures, drawn from his extensive reading and clipping, were so fact-laden that his audience at times seemed inundated. His anger, amplified by his zest, sometimes gave his speeches the ring of dogmatism and the speaker the tone of one who would consider no other viewpoint.

In February of 1965, after President Lyndon B. Johnson took a crucial escalatory step, ordering retaliatory strikes against North Vietnam, Philip and Daniel Berrigan were the only American Catholic priests to promise total "non-cooperation" with the nation's Vietnam policies by signing a "declaration of conscience." Among the other signers were Dr. Martin Luther King and Bayard Rustin from the civil rights movement and Dr. Benjamin Spock from the antiwar movement.

The following month Philip took part in an antiwar forum at Mount Saint Mary's College in Newburgh, which exploded as some members of the audience shouted down the panel of scholars who were so critical of the war. Philip had organized the group, Emergency Citizen's Group Concerned About Vietnam, that sponsored the forum. The Newburgh *Evening News* described the session as "the long application of propaganda advanced by the Kremlin," a description that did nothing to mollify the community's mounting anger with the brash priest.

Father O'Dea summoned Philip to the Josephites' Baltimore headquarters and ordered him to resign from the Emergency Citizen's Group and to stop talking about the war. Aside from the pressure that Newburgh Catholics were exerting on Epiphany Apostolic College, the head of the Josephites did not see the same direct link between racism and American moves in Vietnam that Father Berrigan did. Despite his superior's order, less than a week later Philip decried the evil of the Vietnam war during a civil rights lecture at the Newburgh Community Affairs Council. This time, the Newburgh *Evening News* charged that Philip was alienating "those good and loyal Americans who dearly want to help the Negro but who are reluctant to put themselves beside individuals actively serving Communist objectives." The school was warned that if Philip were not sent packing, the parents of the students would receive letters notifying them that their sons' English teacher was a Communist.

Philip was reassigned to Baltimore and the Church of St. Peter Claver in the midst of the ghetto. Initially he obeyed the orders to keep mum on the war and, instead, organized blacks to challenge mistreatment by landlords with picketing and other protests.

Meanwhile, Daniel was having his share of troubles with the Jesuit hierarchy. He had joined with three other churchmen to establish Clergy and Laymen Concerned about Vietnam in 1965. The organization, which eventually grew into the largest single peace group in the nation, banded together more respected antiwar opinion-leaders than any previous group.

Daniel Berrigan's role in the formation of Clergy and Laymen angered Francis Cardinal Spellman of New York whose annual Christmas trips to the troops in Vietnam symbolized rock-ribbed Catholic support for the military legions against Communism.

Spellman's displeasure grew when Daniel delivered a memorial sermon for Roger Laporte, a Catholic peace militant who immolated himself on the steps of the United Nations to protest the war. Daniel's sermon contained no censure for Laporte for taking his own life.

"New York was not an auspicious place to be a peaceable Catholic priest," Daniel wrote in *The Trial of the Catonsville Nine*, recalling that period.

In November of 1965, the Jesuits gave in to the pressure, chiefly from Spellman's chancery, again unknowingly furthered the radicalization of their best known priest. They sent him to Mexico. "As one of my friends expressed it," Daniel later wrote, "sending me to Latin America was a little like tossing Br'er Rabbit into the briar patch."

During the four-and-a-half month trip, he visited ten countries, talking with students, slum dwellers, government officials and church leaders. He discussed American involvement in their political and social life. The experience underscored his feeling that the United States was squandering millions on a foreign adventure in Vietnam, while ignoring opportunities to alleviate misery and injustice in its own hemisphere.

Back home his exile touched off a volume of protest that is rare within the church. A hurriedly formed Committee for Daniel Berrigan enlisted thousands of priests, nuns, seminarians and laymen. Protests erupted at Jesuit colleges throughout the nation, and the liberal segment of the Catholic press was highly critical of the forced sabbatical.

The Jesuit order finally relented, while maintaining all the while that the now famous priest was on an ordinary trip abroad. He returned in March of 1966 and told a press conference that he planned to engage in more militant peace protests than ever.

It was Philip, however, who began to increase the risks taken by the protesters. He found that he could never reach the blacks he ministered to with the message that they would benefit from reversing the nation's Vietnam involvement. In the fall of 1966, with fellow clergymen, united under the banner of the Baltimore Interfaith Peace Mission, Philip first tried meetings and debates with some of Maryland's United States congressmen.

By the end of December, the protesters took more direct action, picketing the homes of Secretary of Defense Robert S. McNamara and Secretary of State Dean Rusk. Rusk afterwards contacted Philip and met with him and two of his fellow demonstrators for nearly two hours. The session succeeded only in angering Philip who quoted Rusk as stating that he would "leave all morality up to you clergymen."

From January through June of 1967, the Berrigan-led protesters turned their attention to the homes of the Joint Chiefs of Staff at Fort Myer, Virginia, across the Potomac River from Washington and bordering Arlington National Cemetery. There they knelt in prayer symbolizing the need for divine intervention against the nation's military policies. Although they were physically hustled from the grounds by military police in incidents with comic opera overtones, they failed to achieve what Philip had voiced as a primary goal: Either establish a precedent for peace protesters to enter government property, or be arrested—"That will be just the kind of witness I want to offer," Philip said.

In the wake of that failure, the demonstrators took a further step up the ladder of protest—this time, destruction of government property. Over the summer of 1967, Philip and the close circle of activists around him debated what kind of property would be appropriate. They discarded, among other ideas, the suggestion to destroy an unused part of the Green Beret training camp at Fort Howard, Maryland.

Finally, they settled on destroying draft files. To heighten the symbolism, the destructive agent would be blood, the symbol of purity in the Catholic faith. Some of Philip's associates, such as Father Richard McSorley of Georgetown University, counselled against the tactic. They reasoned that the symbolism would be missed—if not resented—by most persons, and that the participants would likely be imprisoned, removing them from the ranks of peace activists.

Philip and his three colleagues would not be turned back. The raid was staged against the draft board in the Baltimore Custom

House on October 27, 1967. It was the first of as many as thirty
such raids by teams mostly of Catholics, until the Camden, New
Jersey, fiasco in August of 1971 when a score of raiders were
caught in the act by a beaming band of FBI agents.

Joining Philip in the Baltimore raiding party, which became
known as the Baltimore Four, were David Eberhardt, the
agnostic son of a Protestant clergyman; Thomas Lewis, an artist
and the son of a corporation executive; and James Mengel, a
minister of the United Church of Christ who had served as an
Army chaplain in Korea.

The Baltimore Four struck only six days after the massive
antiwar demonstration at the Pentagon where Daniel, who had
joined the Cornell University faculty as co-director of Cornell
United Religious Work, was arrested with several of his students
for demonstrating after their permit ran out. Thus, both
brothers, by then widely known symbols of clerical opposition to
the war, sat in jail because of their resistance.

By this time, critics of the war cut all through American
society. Voices that had remained still while the Berrigans and
their associates preached and demonstrated joined the chorus of
protest. Philip and Daniel, however, regarded protest that
stopped short of the Baltimore Four tactic as too little and too
late. They offended a good many allies in the winter of 1967-68.

Jim Forest, whom Philip had persuaded to scrap school plans
and devote fulltime to the Catholic Peace Fellowship in 1964,
recalled Philip's attitude after the Baltimore raid. " . . . some of
us who had been on pilgrimage year upon year suddenly
seemed in the B.C. division of his new commitment," Forest
wrote in *The Berrigans*.

In a letter to Forest, who participated in the Milwaukee
Fourteen draft board raid the following year and was convicted
and spent a year in federal prison, Philip condemned antiwar
work that he rated "safe, unimaginative, staffish and devoid of
risk or suffering."

Philip wrote that he and Daniel "have been led to different
roads, ones which seem to us more at grips with this awful war
and the insanity of our country. To stop this war, I would give my
life tomorrow, and I can't be blamed if I have little time for those
who want to run ads in the New York Times . . . . Both Dan and

I are seriously dealing with clergymen and laymen, professionals and family people, who have come to the point of civil disobedience and the prospect of jail, and are even foundering with convictions beyond that point. As Johnson continues to have his war, and that means the probability of invading North Vietnam, we will either witness from jail, or we will go ahead with social disruption, including non-violent attacks against the machinery of this war . . . .

"In a word, I believe in revolution, and I hope to continue a non-violent contribution to it. In my view, we are not going to save this country and mankind without it . . . . "

Putting the declaration into action, Philip began to recruit a team to join him in another draft board assault before the slowly grinding legal machinery could take him out of circulation for the first.

Meanwhile, Daniel was exploring a tactic of his own—a trip to Hanoi. Accompanied by Professor Howard Zinn of Boston University, Berrigan flew to Hanoi in January of 1968, responding to a North Vietnamese invitation to retrieve three captured American pilots.

"I have always believed that the peace movement must not merely say no to the war," he said in explaining his decision to go. "It must also say yes to life—yes to the possibility of a human future. We must go beyond frontiers—frontiers declared by our country or by the enemy," he wrote in *The Trial of the Catonsville Nine.*

"So I thought it would be important to show Americans that we were ready to risk our lives to bring back American prisoners because we did not believe that in wartime anyone should be in prison or should suffer separation from families, simply we did not believe in war. And so we went."

The trip led Daniel to label Vietnam "the land of burning children," a phrase the Catholic Resistance was to employ repeatedly in explaining why they chose to set fire to draft records. ("So I went to Catonsville and burned some papers because the burning of children is inhuman and unbearable," Daniel wrote.)

Daniel felt betrayed by the government's handling of the journey, however. He said that William H. Sullivan, U.S. ambassador in Laos, had reversed an agreement the three pilots had to return to the United States by commercial rather than military aircraft.

The distinction was important, Berrigan maintained, because the North Vietnamese "connected the whole enterprise with the American peace movement, and the relations slowly built up over the preceding two years with Americans who had come to Hanoi. So they were understandably anxious that the trip be a symbol of independent peace action, taken at the initiative of North Vietnam and responded to by Americans who were resisting the war in their own country," Berrigan wrote in *Night Flight to Hanoi*, a diary of the journey.

" . . . there was no reasonable doubt in the minds of the three airmen, as they recounted their impression to us, that the Vietnamese would connect their decision with the fate of other prisoners." Although a commercial flight would take twenty-four hours longer than a military jet and would expose the pilots to the news media, they elected to fly commercial "out of compassion and thought for their fellow prisoners," Berrigan reported.

After fifty minutes of what Berrigan described as "heated and close" discussion with Ambassador Sullivan, the ranking officer among the prisoners, Major N.M. Overly, an Army career officer said: "Any least indication of the will of my superiors is a command to me."

To Father Berrigan, "it was the most ominous sentence I had yet heard in a war whose daily currency was groundless rhetoric, duplicity, body counts and murderous ideology. Yet I must confess that the sentence also had a kind of untouchable platonic perfection. As an expression of the system from which it issued, the sentiment was virtuous beyond praise."

By the time Daniel returned, Philip had recruited most of those who would accompany him May 17, 1968, to the second-floor offices of Local Board No. 33 in a Knights of Columbus hall in Catonsville, Maryland. Others approached Daniel about participating, but he was non-committal. Philip then went to his older brother, and after what biographer Francine du Plessix Gray reported was a nearly all-night discussion over a bottle, Daniel enlisted.

"I went to Catonsville and burned some papers because I had gone to Hanoi, because my brother was a man and I must be a man," Daniel wrote. " . . . Although I was too old to carry a draft card, there were other ways of getting in trouble with a state that seemed determined upon multiplying the dead, totally intent upon a war the meaning of which no sane man could tell."

Joining the two Berrigans were Tom Lewis from the Baltimore Four; George Mische, a former Alliance for Progress and peace movement organizer; David Darst, a Christian brother who was killed in an automobile accident after the trial; Mary Moylan, a nurse and former nun; Thomas and Mary Melville, an ex-priest and his wife, both Maryknoll missionaries who were expelled by the American ambassador from Guatemala for their ties to anti-government guerrillas; and John Hogan, who was booted out with the Melvilles for the same reason.

Consulting a Special Forces' handbook for instructions, the protesters concocted a batch of homemade napalm. They entered the Selective Service office and, after a slight scuffle, packed 378 files from the 1-A Qualified drawer into a trash basket, took them outside and burned them with the napalm, praying all the while.

Reporters and photographers, notified in advance of the daytime assault, recorded the action, and a photograph of the raiding party, praying while the records went up in flames, was published throughout the nation.

The trial became the peace movement's biggest success at dramatizing the clash between the man who would violate a state's law that he felt violated a higher law and the state which argued that such lawbreaking would end an ordered and just and civilized society.

"There is, in the government's mind," Prosecutor Barnett Skolnik said in his summation to the jury, "a fantastic arrogance that goes along with the sincerity of these people. They hold their views so sincerely and so deeply that they feel they have the right to impose their views upon people who disagree. Now that, ladies and gentlemen, is not just sincerity. That is an arrogance which the people of this country simply cannot abide."

Philip Berrigan: "Your honor, I think that we would be less than honest with you if we did not state our attitude. Simply, we have lost confidence in the institutions of this country, including our own churches. I think this has been a rational process on our part. We have come to our conclusion slowly and painfully. We have lost confidence because we do not believe any longer that these institutions are reformable."

Upon conviction, the defendants received various terms: Philip, three and a half years to run concurrently with the six-year term he drew for the Baltimore Four conviction, and Daniel three years. But next they took a much bigger step away from the American system.

Casting aside the principle of civil disobedience followed by Thoreau, Gandhi and Martin Luther King—that one who civilly disobeys the law because he thinks it or the policy advanced by it unjust must pay the price—the Berrigans went underground.

Scheduled to surrender April 9, 1970, at the Baltimore courthouse, after the Supreme Court refused to hear their appeal, they failed to appear.

Daniel Berrigan, interviewed by Paul Cowan of the *Village Voice* while he was on the run from the pursuing FBI, recalled that he decided to defy arrest when he was talking with friends at Cornell about the spring festival to be held at the university to honor him in April.

"He wanted to reexamine the whole concept of going to jail," Cowan wrote, "to see if it was possible to survive in an underground, particularly an underground based on nonviolence."

Said Berrigan: "I wanted to confront the mythology of the good guy whose goodness depends on his willingness to go to jail, the sort of idea that spread with the civil rights movement and Martin Luther King. All that's over now. The important thing is to keep working.

"This whole thing is really an experiment," Berrigan said. "Is it historically ready? Can the resource of community and shelter be devised, and not just community and shelter but appropriate action? I don't know. But certainly exploring those questions through my actions makes more sense than going through the unending ritual of crime and punishment."

Earlier, Daniel had given readers what may have been a hint of his eventual decision to flee, in the introduction to his book, *The Trial of the Catonsville Nine,* written in the summer of 1969:

Indeed it cannot be thought that men and women like ourselves will continue, as though we were automated heroes to rush for redress from the King of the Blind. The King will have to listen to other voices, over which neither he nor we will indefinitely have control: voices of public violence and chaos. For you cannot set up a court in the Kingdom of the Blind, to condemn those who see; a court presided over by those who would pluck out the eyes of men and call it rehabilitation.

Daniel viewed the underground as a means of amplifying—not muting—his propagandizing through media, which would be more likely to publish and air the words of a fugitive priest than those of a cleric not on the run. He also saw his fugitive status as a way to involve more and more middle-class people in a much deeper commitment to the peace movement than they otherwise would make.

"I see myself as somebody who, from, let's say, a geography of personal jeopardy, is opening up new ways for other people by way of invitation—they're invited in new directions as a result of my presence," Daniel said in a National Educational Television interview. "They're invited to respond to this in a way that is really concrete, in the lives they're leading, whether within their family, within their profession, within their church or synagogue . . . .

" . . . It's an effort not merely to talk to many Americans through the media, but really to get to people I live with, people who harbor and who aid and who keep me afloat and keep me in communion with others, to raise exactly those questions—that is to say: What is the virtuous man today, and what, especially, is his attitude toward the law when the law is being used by those in power to break the law of humanity?"

CHAPTER THREE

A Massive Manhunt

On April 13, 1970, four days after the Berrigan brothers went underground, the Catholic Resistance distributed a press release announcing that Daniel would appear at a Cornell peace rally on April 19 and that Philip would attend a similar rally at St. Gregory the Great Church on Manhattan's Upper West Side two evenings later.

"Federal Marshals are expected to haul the two priests away in chains at these occasions," the release stated.

Daniel Berrigan showed up for the Cornell rally wearing a motorcycle helmet and goggles. A huge crowd of admiring and protective students surrounded him. While at Cornell, Berrigan had served as associate director of Cornell United Religious Work and had counselled students about risking jail by resisting the draft as an act of conscience. Now he had taken a risk, and some 10,000 students were there to honor him and witness the outcome.

The rally was part of a weekend celebration the students called "America Is Hard to Find." Before going underground Berrigan had helped plan the event. The evening function was called a "freedom Seder"—for the traditional feast that Jews have in connection with their festival of freedom holiday, Passover, which was about to begin.

Daniel, in a statement carried by the Cornell *Daily Sun*, said he hoped to be able to speak before being apprehended by federal authorities.

Scores of FBI agents mingled with the thousands of students, lest their quarry attempt to slip away after speaking. To ringing cheers and thunderous applause, Daniel Berrigan delivered an impassioned plea for resistance, then sat down while a rock band took over.

Over the din of electric guitars and a pounding bass drum, Dan heard a voice whispering in his ear. "Do you want to split?" the voice asked.

The priest looked surprised, hesitated and said: "Give me ten minutes to think about it." In half that time he had made his decision. "Why not?" he told the voice.

The voice was that of a friend of Eqbal Ahmad, who formerly served on the Cornell faculty with Berrigan. Ahmad had suggested an escape plan to the friend, whom he would not identify.

The friend told Daniel that a confederate would douse the lights and he was then to step into a huge papier-mâché figure of an apostle, one of the props in the pageant. In the darkness Daniel walked as quickly as he could manage in the awkward figure to a panel truck waiting outside. The truck sped off immediately.

By the time the lights went back on, the agents realized what had happened and gave chase. They located the truck in ten minutes. But Daniel had already been transferred to a car, and the agents lost his trail.

Two days later at about noon, five FBI agents appeared at the front door of the Sacred Heart of Mary convent, a five-story brownstone at 137 West 85th Street in New York. Several other agents remained outside, keeping the front and rear entrances under surveillance.

Sister Jogues Egan, the mother superior, thought the agents at the door "looked like good Irish Catholics." An agent named O'Toole told her they wanted to search the convent, the home of Sister Jogues, Sister Elizabeth McAlister and six other nuns. He said they were looking for a fugitive.

"I can assure you no one is hiding here," Sister Jogues told him.

She later recalled: "I asked if they had a warrant to search the convent and Mr. O'Toole said they didn't need one because they were searching for a fugitive—Father Phil Berrigan—and they had a bench warrant. Mr. O'Toole said, 'After all, you are Berrigan sympathizers.' "

Sister Jogues followed them as they searched the convent, going through all the bathrooms and bedrooms, peeking under beds and looking in closets. She said they were obviously uneasy about the religious setting and glanced warily at the peace symbols and prints on racism and poverty that competed for wall space with religious pictures. A large poster quoted from Alan Paton's *Cry the Beloved Country*, in which an African minister, reflecting on racial separatism said: "I have one great fear in my heart that one day when they turn to loving we are turned to hating."

On the living room wall was a framed serigraph of page one of the August 14, 1965, Los Angeles *Times* extra chronicling the Watts riot with the headline: "Eight Men Slain; Guard Moves In." And in the ground floor bathroom, distinguished by a black-and-white commode seat of psychedelic design, a bigger-than-life-size picture of Cuban Premier Fidel Castro caught the agents' eyes.

"They searched everything," Sister Jogues recalled, "right up to and including the roof. When they entered the chapel, one turned and whispered, 'Is the Blessed Sacrament here?' and I said, 'yes,' and they kneeled and crossed themselves—very reverential, very courteous. They were nervous about the whole idea of searching the convent. After they finished, Mr. O'Toole got me to sign something saying I had let them search. He didn't have a form, so I wrote it out for him on a piece of Provincial Headquarters stationery. Of course they didn't find him because he wasn't there."

Philip Berrigan and David Eberhardt, a fellow fugitive from the Baltimore Four conviction, were only a few blocks away, however, at the rectory of St. Gregory the Great Church on West 90th Street. They had slipped into the rectory before dawn and with friends had rehearsed an escape route.

The two fugitives had proclaimed in a press release their intention to surface at an 8:30 P.M. event at the church, appropriately called "Up from Under."

And for most of the day, FBI agents, stung by Daniel Berrigan's public escape, had been keeping an eye on the red brick building that housed the church, school and rectory of St. Gregory the Great. About 5 P.M. they closed in.

Several agents led by Tom Walsh entered the rectory where he told the pastor, the Reverend Harry Browne, a classmate from Fordham, that they were searching for the Berrigans.

"Father Dan, Father Phil, are you in there?" Walsh called out as agents carried on the search. When the pastor refused to open a locked study, the agents smashed down the door. They found Philip Berrigan and David Eberhardt in a closet and handcuffed them. Before leading them away, Walsh apologized to his old classmate for coming before the rally started. "I'm only one of the Indians," he said to Father Brown, who wept in frustration.

That night at the rally FBI agents waited in the sacristy and lined the back of the church hoping to catch Daniel Berrigan also. Scores of agents were outside. The FBI later acknowledged that 100 agents were assigned to cover the rally, which accounted for one-fifth of the total crowd.

Instead of Philip Berrigan and Eberhardt, the meeting heard from their allies, including Eqbal Ahmad, who had engineered Daniel Berrigan's escape. Ahmad read from a statement Philip Berrigan had scribbled while hiding in the rectory closet.

Entitled "Under and Up" the statement described the priest's experiences in the "limbo" between sentencing and jail. Explaining why he had chosen to go underground, Berrigan wrote: "Our salvation had to be won again."

The audience of 500 showed its support of the break from traditional ways of civil disobedience. Howard Zinn, a Boston University professor and early opponent of the Vietnam war, won a standing ovation when he referred to "the nice game of civil disobedience," and said: "You don't surrender that easily to real evil. Wherever Dan Berrigan is, I hope they never get him."

The bonds that the Berrigan brothers had forged with the most outspoken of the political and economic have-nots were apparent at the rally. Felipe Luciano, a leader of the Young Lords, a Spanish Harlem political group, screamed at the audience: "You are not defending Dave and Phil. You are not defending Dan Berrigan. You are defending your own fucking lives . . . . Fascism is not creeping. It's galloping right up your behinds."

While those at the rally tried collectively to soothe their sorrow over the capture of the two men, Philip Berrigan and David

Eberhardt bedded down in the federal house of detention in New York, awaiting a hearing the next morning and a move to an institution for longer-term residents.

They were sent to Lewisburg Federal Penitentiary, usually a way station for prisoners convicted of war resistance acts. Once processed at the maximum security prison, most of such inmates were then transferred to the minimum security Allenwood Farm about eighteen miles away or to the Lewisburg Farm a half-mile over the wall.

Father Berrigan and Eberhardt, however, were kept at Lewisburg. They contended that prison authorities were holding them hostage for the missing draft board raiders, particularly Daniel Berrigan. The officials denied the allegation, noting that both prisoners had been in "fugitive status" before being sent to Lewisburg and thus were more of a security risk than the standard war resister.

The day after Philip Berrigan's capture, Agent O'Toole led a team of agents back to the Sacred Heart of Mary convent. Sister Jogues was not there at the time. Sister Dymphna Leonard answered the door. This time, they said they were looking for Daniel Berrigan, and Sister Dymphna asked if they had a search warrant.

She quoted O'Toole as saying: "We don't need one. We've got a bench warrant. It will be much worse for you if you don't let us search the house."

After the fruitless search, she said she resisted signing a form stating she had permitted it. But she finally did after the agents told her Sister Jogues had signed one the day before.

The agents were on solid ground in claiming that a bench warrant for Daniel Berrigan constituted authority for them to search the convent and other places they had reason to believe Daniel was hiding. The bench warrant is a command by the court to a law enforcement officer to produce the person named in the warrant. Unlike a search warrant, the bench warrant is not issued for a particular place. It covers any place the fugitive may be hiding.

Courts, including the Supreme Court, have given wide latitude to the officer searching for a fugitive. There is no parallel between the bench warrant and the search warrant which has come under critical scrutiny by the courts in recent years. Evidence gathered by police who lacked a search warrant or who overstepped the warrant's authority has been excluded by the courts in line with Supreme Court rulings. But this has not been the case with bench warrants for fugitives.

The fact that the agents sought signatures from the nuns attesting that they did not object to the searches probably indicated the FBI men felt they had to step gingerly in dealing with a religious house. The signatures would make it difficult for the nuns later to bring suit against the bureau claiming that the search had violated their Fourth Amendment protection against unreasonable searches and seizures.

Although they didn't know it at the time, the FBI agents were only a few steps behind the fugitive priest. The next weekend, April 26, 1970, the New York *Times* published an interview with Berrigan, who, the newspaper reported, "was relaxing with his legs curled up on a couch in a Manhattan walk-up apartment where some friends had arranged for the interview."

"My arrest would take a great burden off my friends," Berrigan told the interviewer. "But it is proper that they should share my business if my burdens are useful. They're not just sitting up with a cancer patient. Maybe they're sitting in a delivery room, midwifing the future.

"My being outside must radicalize my friends. They can't help me without putting themselves in legal jeopardy. I don't long for arrest. I long for one more useful day."

The interview, like several others the priest was to give over the next months, jabbed sharply at the FBI. "Antiwar Priest Sought by FBI Says He Will Continue Defiance," proclaimed a two-column headline over the story.

The following month, *Saturday Review* featured Berrigan writing on the twenty-fifth anniversary of the death of Dietrich Bonhoeffer, German Lutheran clergyman executed on Hitler's orders for his role in the resistance inside wartime Germany.

"Daniel Berrigan, S.J., wrote the above prose-poem while a fugitive from imprisonment for his actions in protesting the war in Vietnam," the magazine noted in italicized type.

In early June, the target of the FBI search was heard on the local NBC evening news in New York, interviewed by Edwin

Newman. The FBI stepped up its hunt. When Berrigan's eighty-five-year-old mother was hospitalized with a broken hip later that month, agents staked out the hospital in Syracuse 'round the clock.

Commenting on this attempt by the FBI to nab him, Berrigan said in a *New Yorker* interview: " . . . they were sure I'd go to see her. They're not aware of my high degree of discipline. Everyone except the FBI knows that I'm disciplined to stay away from the people I love the most—the Jesuits, my family, my closest friends.

"One of the reasons I'm doing this is to break down the myth of the omnipotence of the people in power—to prove the power of powerlessness. I must say that the FBI are the politest bloodhounds I've ever had on my trail. A disproportionate number of them are Catholics, and they never lose their Catholic manners. I hear that they're still doing the round of the convents, peeking under the nuns' beds and saying 'Father Dan? Are you there, Father Dan?' "

Such taunts were felt at FBI headquarters. The fervor of the FBI hunt can be gauged from the bureau's performance at the June 27 wedding of Anthony Scoblick, the ex-priest, and Mary Cain, the ex-nun. The wedding was held at St. Augustine's Lutheran Church in Baltimore because Scoblick had not been dispensed of his priestly vows by Rome and could not arrange the ceremony at a Catholic church.

Shortly before the ceremonies, several cars carrying agents pulled up to the church. Some FBI men entered the church and others carrying walkie-talkies remained outside. More cars with agents arrived. Estimates by wedding guests put the number of agents inside the church between twenty and thirty, with at least that number outside.

Sister Elizabeth McAlister sat in a back pew of the church, with two agents wearing sports shirts sitting on either side of her. Before entering, she heard one of the agents outside communicate over his walkie-talkie: "The place is covered now."

During the eucharist, one guest, Sister Kathleen Contino, hugged one agent and offered him what she called the kiss of peace. Flustered, he backed off.

While the ceremony was underway, several agents remained at

the rear of the church while others searched rooms and closets, apparently recalling how Philip Berrigan had been nabbed. After the ceremony, the federal agents lined the staircase to the reception room beneath the church. The bride, exasperated by the uninvited guests, asked them to leave.

She asked their identities and one said: "We're from the FBI."

"Who invited you?" asked the new Mrs. Scoblick.

"We invited ourselves," the agent replied.

The agents retreated to their cars nearby and waited for the wedding party and guests to depart. Several of the guests had planned to gather elsewhere after the ceremony, but they gave up, they said later, because of being followed by the ubiquitous FBI.

Writing about the wedding in a letter smuggled to Philip Berrigan, Sister McAlister said the "federal presence" at the ceremony ran second only to the St. Gregory the Great rally April 21 when the FBI sent 100 agents to nab Daniel.

"Rather than lead the gentlemen right to a session we split and regrouped at 8:30," the nun recounted. The group headed for a motel but "the gentlemen checked the register straight away."

The FBI had counted on catching Daniel Berrigan at the wedding, which attracted many other participants in the radical Catholic peace movement. But he stayed far away, heeding the counsel of Eqbal Ahmad, a prime architect of the underground system, to keep away from persons known to be his friends. Ahmad went to the church, but spotting the numerous FBI agents decided not to go inside. The FBI also figured Daniel would show up in Los Angeles, at the August premiere of his play, *The Trial of the Catonsville Nine.* First-nighters included a good many FBI agents, but Daniel Berrigan was nowhere in the playhouse.

FBI frustration over the failure to capture Daniel Berrigan was made all the more acute by the poet-priest's frequent interviews and articles in newspapers and magazines while he was on the run. Often he would take a verbal poke at the FBI. In the *New Yorker* interview, for example, he was asked how he had prevented the bureau from discovering his whereabouts.

"Because the FBI are overtechnologized and dehumanized,"

he answered. "It's like the U.S. Army, which, with all its material, can't win against the North Vietnamese people, who have a passion for their land and their community. You could say that my survival is a triumph of the love and humanity of the people who shelter me over the FBI, who are merciless but extraordinarily unimaginative men."

The bureau, which has a large percentage of Roman Catholic agents, found such a gibe from a fugitive Jesuit priest especially grating. The FBI had always regarded Catholic colleges, with their emphasis on authoritarianism, fertile hunting ground for agent recruits. A Jesuit priest who criticizes the church and his state runs against the grain of all the bureau holds holy.

Daniel Berrigan's taunts were infuriating Hoover, of course. In the margins of investigative reports on the FBI's search for him, Hoover would scrawl in blue ink, "This subject must be apprehended at the earliest time possible" or "Why aren't we making more progress on this?"

To other FBI officials, that meant putting more manpower on the case and they did. "When he wrote in blue ink in the margins it was one of two things," one of the officials involved in the investigation said in an interview. "It was either an order, as in the case of the Berrigans. Or it was an intemperate remark about somebody. He wrote intemperate remarks about a lot of people—Presidents, Vice Presidents, cabinet members, senators, congressmen. That was why some of us believed he would insist on dying in office. He would not want to be alive to be embarrassed by possible disclosure of some of these remarks by his successor. Some of the things he wrote were incredible. We used to joke in the bureau that he was like an embezzler in a bank who couldn't take a vacation."

As Daniel Berrigan's flight stretched into four months, he grew bolder. His most daring stroke came on August 2 in Germantown, Pennsylvania, a suburb of Philadelphia.

The congregation of the First United Methodist Church had expected a guest minister to deliver the sermon that warm August day in 1970. So it came as no surprise when John C. Raines, assistant professor of religion at Temple University, stepped up to the raised altar.

But Raines, whose credentials as a committed theologian included several arrests for civil rights activities in the South in the 1960s, had a different surprise for the congregation.

"We live in extraordinary times, and in extraordinary times we must be ready to take advantage of suddenly emerging possibilities," he said. "So it is with us this morning. We have a visitor. For reasons that become obvious with a little reflection, it was not possible to anticipate his arrival amongst us in advance. For reasons that are equally obvious, he will have to leave directly following the sermon . . . .

"As a person, I'm sure he'd like to stay all afternoon and in the long hours of the morning. But we no longer live in a time and a place where that is possible. Perhaps, some day, it will be possible once again in this nation.

"So, now, if you would join me in welcoming our guest, our visitor, Father Daniel Berrigan."

The elfin-like, goateed priest, wearing a dark suit and white shirt and tie, then did what he wanted to do when he went underground nearly four months earlier. In the medium of a sermon, he attempted to convince a predominantly middle-class group that "a Christian can confront the law of the land, that law which protects the warmakers even as it prosecutes the peacemakers."

For twenty minutes Berrigan encouraged the members of the congregation to reexamine themselves to see if they could strip away some of the insulation from their lives to help stop their countrymen from killing humans in another land.

"The Christians can refuse to pay taxes," Berrigan told the congregation, some of whose members appeared to be scanning their memories for a news item or two they dimly recalled about the fugitive priest. "They can aid and abet and harbor people like myself, who are in legal jeopardy for resistance, along with AWOLs. They can work with GIs on bases, helping these young men to awaken to the truth of their condition and their society, in coffee houses, or in hospitality in their own homes. They can organize within their professions and neighborhoods and churches, so that a solid wall of conscience confronts the death-makers. They can make it increasingly difficult for local draft boards to function."

Strong medicine for a Sunday sermon, even for a church accustomed to messages supporting the crusade for social justice. But the words were little different than those Daniel had conveyed to the families that had been harboring him in Midwestern and Eastern cities. By the time his odyssey would end—nine days later—the families would number 37 in all. About 200 people assisted in making arrangements, he estimated.

"We have chosen to be powerless criminals in a time of criminal power," he told the congregation. "We have chosen to be branded as peace criminals by war criminals . . . .

"There are a hundred non-violent means of resisting those who would inflict death as the ordinary way of life. There are a hundred ways of nonviolent resistance up to now untried or half-tried or badly tried.

"But the peace will not be won without such serious and constant sacrificial and courageous actions on the part of large numbers of good men and women. The peace will not be won without the moral equivalent of the loss and suffering and separation that the war itself is exacting."

A minute later, Berrigan ended his sermon and left hurriedly. His appearance and sermon at the church were publicized widely.

Two days later, Philip Berrigan told Sister McAlister in a smuggled letter: "The Germantown affair was an audacious stroke—and 20 min. Once people got the drift, someone could have run for the phone. The place was alive with rumors here—suspicions had it that the bruv had been captured. In fact, I fully expected that to be true until the chargé [a term Berrigan often used for Boyd Douglas, the prisoner who smuggled messages for him] came on hand to reassert a little reason. I'll be much more reluctant to snap at the bait next time."

The FBI was getting closer to the priority quarry, however. Agents closed in on 201 Dean Street in Brooklyn, where Eqbal Ahmad and his wife Julie lived—only minutes after Daniel left the three-story brownstone.

The Ahmads were out of town at the time and had left their second-floor apartment in the care of friends, Mr. and Mrs.

Ferez Ahmed. Ahmed, also a Pakistani, had been a sociology professor at East Carolina University in Greenville, South Carolina, for more than six years.

When an agent rang the doorbell to the Ahmad apartment, Ferez Ahmed was talking on the telephone. His wife answered the door. Later, he recalled: "Two men who identified themselves as FBI agents asked for Eq, and when my wife told them he was not there they rushed on in. I put the telephone down and asked who they were and they told me they were FBI agents and wanted to search for a man named Berrigan and that they had reason to believe he could be hiding there.

"I asked if they had a warrant to search, and they said they didn't need one because they were searching for a fugitive. I told them I could not prevent them, but that I did not like somebody else's home being searched without their presence and without any legal paper. They searched the closets and bathroom and everywhere and of course he was not there. And they searched the neighbor's apartment upstairs, and he was really scared. But he didn't know what was going on. When they left, they tried to apologize and tell me it might have caused some inconvenience, but it was their work and they had to do it. I signed nothing saying I permitted them to search because I didn't permit them. When Eq came home I told him what had happened, he called up the FBI to protest and they told him I was cooperative. I wasn't nasty but I wasn't cooperative."

Charles Lynch, a black who lives in a third-floor apartment, was "a little nervous" when he answered his doorbell and the agents said, "We have reason to believe a fugitive is hiding here." Lynch recalled that they showed him a photograph of a man they identified as Father Dan Berrigan.

"I let them in," he said, "but I told them I understood they were supposed to have a warrant to go through my apartment. They said they didn't need one because they were looking for a fugitive. They let me know I could be in trouble if I had knowledge of Berrigan being in the building and didn't tell them. One agent said I was guilty if I knew anything and didn't tell them. I didn't know anything."

Daniel Berrigan rejoiced in the close calls when he wrote his imprisoned brother a letter that Boyd Douglas smuggled in. "There have been hilarious alarms and close hair-breath hairy escapes from injustice which I won't regale you with," he said. "It'll make good wheelchair guff for our old age."

Much of Daniel Berrigan's time underground was spent trying to prompt others to rethink their values and take a risk of their own in the struggle for peace.

"The outside scene," he told his brother Philip in the smuggled letter, "is just as badly lighted as the inside, just as much in need of illumination . . . . Just as imprisoned, and more so, I should say. So I cling to small meetings in homes, trying best to sock it to them, to help read headlines and small print, very much encouraged and then not so—a kind of fever chart of the days and nights . . . .

"The main thing is that I begin to see something that hasn't been tried, a nonviolent underground-above-ground act which keeps in touch with the media and with people up close and makes hay in the rain and sun . . . .

"The proof that one can stay responsibly and nonviolently at large is a small crack in the inviolability myth that governs thinking about the powers; the idea ridiculed and discredited by the Vietnamese themselves, that the U.S. always gets its man."

At times, Daniel would encourage the host family to invite friends they knew well—and trusted— to a weekend retreat. "The purpose of our meeting was to consider how we and others like us could play a part in creating a new society—one which would be free of war and exploitation, of racism, and of the systematic dehumanization of persons to which we knew that the routine of our lives contributed," wrote a member of one of the host families.

According to the anonymous account, published in *The Berrigans*, the participants at this particular retreat were "middle-class, liberal and intellectual families predominantly Jewish." The writer said that although the retreat did not lead him or her to "walk away from life and commitments I have made," it did instill "a new quality" to that life. "For I cannot return to it uncritically or unquestioningly."

Other times, Daniel would blend into the family's regular

daily routine, entertaining the children, talking to the mother while she performed her household chores, but frequently questioning and talking about commitment.

Father Anthony Mullaney, convicted of destroying draft board files as a member of the Milwaukee Fourteen, assessed the influence of Daniel in interpersonal relationships.

"If you allow yourself to really listen to Berrigan—and that's not an easy thing to do, because he's a threat—but if you allow yourself to listen to him, then you begin sharing what he's experienced and, before you know, you're saying something like this, 'How do I respond to this type of thing?' And you find yourself getting deeper and deeper into resistance."

Daniel, in the National Educational Television interview that was filmed while he was underground, was asked whether he felt his ideas had altered the lives of individuals with whom he had contact.

He replied, "I think really the first evidence of anything really occurring in the lives of others is some evidence that some change has occurred to oneself, you know, and I'm quite certain that that has occurred."

Berrigan said that based on the intensity of discussions he had with various groups during his flight he was "reasonably confident" that they found the steps taken by him and his brother to be moving. "That means something to them, and they're willing to follow through on it."

After nearly four months of shuttling from one family to another, of growing tense over such ordinarily routine acts as calling from a public telephone and of constantly prodding his hosts and mass audiences to rethink their existences, Daniel grew weary and longed to spend time with old friends.

Sister McAlister first told Philip of Daniel's plan to hide out with an old friend in a letter that Boyd Douglas carried into Lewisburg a week before Daniel made the move. Relating her frustrations over the difficulties of arranging a "surfacing" following a draft board raid, the nun wrote: "Stringfellow may not be useable because he is part of bruv's next move."

In the same letter, she confessed to reservations over the tight security measures surrounding Daniel Berrigan's movements. "I

begin to feel at cross-purposes with bruv as we have con-
scientiously avoided anyone involved with him."

The nun referred to Stringfellow in a subsequent smuggled
letter, telling Philip: "Stringfellow still plans on trying to get to
you I think but he's now or soon will be mixed up with
bruv . . . ."

Daniel Berrigan, spurning Ahmad's advice to steer clear of
known associates, had gone to the estate of his longtime friends,
William Stringfellow and Anthony Towne, both forty-two and
both noted Episcopal laymen and writers. It was located on
Block Island, twelve miles off the coast of Rhode Island, between
Newport and the tip of Long Island.

There he would follow a regimen of three earlier visits before
he became a fugitive and would go off by himself much of the day
to meditate and write. The product of his labor, *The Dark Night
of Resistance*, a combination of prose and poetry that probed
"the fate of human goodness in a bad time," was published after
Daniel was behind bars. It carried the dedication: "To Bill and
Tony, for I was homeless and you gave me shelter."

Towne later said that Berrigan roamed throughout the seaside
acreage, wearing a bright yellow slicker and thus could be seen
easily by the occupants of several nearby houses.

In the evenings, he would rejoin his friends. Stringfellow
would retire soon after dinner. He suffered severe digestive
problems that required him to rest more than half of every day.
Daniel would stay up and watch a late movie on TV. Towne, who
later shook his head over the Grade B films which he said Daniel
enjoyed thoroughly, sat with the priest.

About ten thirty the morning of August 11, Daniel's fifth day
on the island, he had not come to the yellow ranch house from
the shed at the rear of the house where he slept and worked. The
shed, called the Manger because it had served as a one horse stall
for a previous owner, had been remodeled into a studio.
Bookshelves lined the walls, and a large bay window looked out
on the fields and sea. Daniel slept there on a cot so his 2 A. M.
typing would not disturb his hosts.

Winds had climbed to thirty or forty miles an hour, and rain
seemed imminent as a northeaster storm moved in. Towne,

peering through the kitchen windows for sight of a green parrot that had recently joined less exotic birds dining at the feeders he had put up, spotted the parrot. As he studied it, his eyes were diverted to a flash of bright orange—in thick shrubbery 200 yards away, near the stone wall that lined the property.

The night before, Towne had commented on the three large fishing boats that seemed to be blocking Old Harbor which the house overlooked. Perhaps they were seeking refuge from the oncoming storm, but he noted that they were the biggest boats he had ever seen in the harbor.

He and Dan Berrigan speculated that the boats were FBI blockaders, sealing off escape routes. They claimed the flags the ships flew were fake Costa Rican standards—a sure giveaway.

Now the evening joke lost much of its punch. The orange flash, Towne was certain, was a man's slicker. Remembering that his friends poked fun at his paranoid nature, he called Stringfellow to confirm his find. Yes, a man in orange, with field glasses dangling from his neck, like a bird watcher. But neither mid-morning nor August are the times to spot birds on Block Island, especially with a storm breaking.

Stringfellow went to wake Dan Berrigan but found him already outside, sampling the day. He led him back inside to the kitchen window.

"What an odd color for an FBI agent to wear on duty," said Dan.

The rain had begun to pour. Berrigan had talked Towne out of driving the car down the road for a closer look at the man in the underbrush.

"No, that's too risky," the priest said. "If it is the FBI they might think it's me in the car trying to escape and shoot."

Stringfellow donned a slicker and headed for the intruder. As he walked out the gate onto the road, two cars full of men zoomed by him up the driveway. The man in the orange slicker, emerging from the undergrowth, first said he was birdwatching and then showed Stringfellow his FBI identification.

Berrigan appeared at the front door. "I suppose you are wondering who I am," he said. "I am Daniel Berrigan."

The agents—about twelve had gathered outside the house—responded by putting the priest up against one of the automobiles and frisking him. They handcuffed him and waited while Towne ran to the Manger for Berrigan's glasses and cigarettes and a pair of pants and sneakers to add to the Bermuda shorts, T-shirt and slicker he was wearing.

In the rear seat between two husky agents, Berrigan raised his manacled hands and touched his fingertips together. "God bless," he said.

Berrigan recalled that on the way to the Coast Guard station for the boat ride back to Port Judith on the mainland, one of his captors told him he was a Jesuit boy and that he took particular satisfaction in his capture.

"He told me, 'I said to myself when we took you, A.M.D.G.' (Ad Majorem dei Gloriam—To the Greater Glory of God, the Jesuit motto)," Berrigan said.

Stringfellow said he and Towne realized they were "in jeopardy" because the priest was found in Stringfellow's home. "I suppose everybody's in jeopardy nowadays," Stringfellow said.

"A Christian does what he must do as a Christian," Towne and Stringfellow said in a joint statement. "Daniel Berrigan is our friend and always welcome in our home. A visit from him is an honor for us because he is a priest of uncommon conscience, he is a citizen of urgent moral purpose and a human being of exemplary courage."

Even after capture, Berrigan remained the skilled propagandist. A photograph of him being taken from the Coast Guard station, his manacled arms held firmly by two grim-faced, determined-looking agents, one still sporting his bird-watching costume, was published in newspapers throughout the Nation. In contrast to the agents' scowls, Berrigan was beaming, his head tilted back as if to proclaim a triumph.

Robert McAfee Brown, Stanford University professor of religion, later wrote in a special issue of the *Holy Cross Quarterly* devoted to the Berrigans:

. . . one looked at this picture and asked, "Who is truly free?" And the answer was that the man who was going to prison was the man who was truly free, while the man who was sending him to prison was the man who was truly bound. All the normal assessments of our society were challenged by the spontaneous gaiety of a man about to spend three years in jail.

On December 17, 1970, a federal grand jury in Providence, Rhode Island, indicted Stringfellow and Towne on charges they unlawfully harbored and concealed the fugitive priest. The indictment also charged that they had become accessories after the fact to the action of the Catonsville Nine because they had hindered his punishment. The maximum punishment for harboring a fugitive was five years imprisonment and a $5,000 fine, while the accessory count in this case carried a two-and-a-half-year maximum sentence.

The Justice Department also gave serious thought to tying up what the FBI regarded as loose strings remaining from Berrigan's four-month success at eluding the bureau. George Beall, United States attorney for Maryland, commented on the day Berrigan was captured that his office was considering contempt and bail-jumping charges against the priest. His assistant, Barnett D. Skolnik, expressing concern about any precipitous action, added: "We don't want to go off half-cocked on this . . . . We'll consult the appropriate sources and make a decision.

"The FBI has had egg on its face in this one. Starting the day he got away at Cornell, they've been embarrassed," Skolnik said. Additional charges were never filed.

Daniel Berrigan's capture changed the day-to-day existence of his brother, Philip, almost as dramatically as it altered his own. Daniel was sent to the Federal Correctional Institution at Danbury, Connecticut, on August 12, and his brother was shifted there thirteen days later.

Danbury, designated a medium security facility, had the reputation of being the "country club" of federal prisons. Lewisburg, where Phil had been held, was a maximum security penitentiary that could have been the model for those "Big House" prison movies of the thirties and forties—red brick construction, rounded archways that ran from floor to ceiling like those that led to medieval dungeons and a high wall surrounding the prison. It was the only federal prison with such a wall, a barrier that constantly reminded those inside that they were severed from society.

During their four months in Lewisburg, Philip and David Eberhardt, convicted with him for pouring blood into Baltimore draft files, clashed repeatedly with prison authorities.

In a statement they managed to get to their allies outside the walls, Berrigan and Eberhardt cited examples of alleged harassment and charged that "political prisoners at Lewisburg are persecuted beyond the routine dehumanization given to the other inmates."

An examination of the two men, on July 20, 1970, by Dr. Robert Coles, a Harvard research psychiatrist, found both to be showing psychological scars from their treatment—Eberhardt more than Berrigan. Coles entered the case reluctantly at the urgent request of more than twenty-five Boston doctors who were disturbed by published reports they had read of how Eberhardt and Berrigan were faring. Though he protested the arrangement, Coles was required to conduct the examination with a prison official looking on—initially Associate Warden Robert L. Hendricks and later the prison doctor.

He found Eberhardt to be a "severely anxious young man, who is constantly afraid he will be assaulted by any one of several inmates at Lewisburg who have importuned him, threatened him and told him that eventually they will 'get him.' "

Coles said Eberhardt was experiencing a "homosexual panic," which he emphasized "can be a thoroughly normal response on the part of a normal married man, such as Mr. Eberhardt is, to the obvious sexual threats facing him."

Contending there was "great urgency" to Eberhardt's situation, Coles warned that if he continued "in a maximum security situation at Lewisburg penitentiary, if his psychological condition continues to deteriorate, as it has in the past three months . . . then the possibility of a severe and seriously impairing psychotic break must be greatly considered."

The conclusions of Coles, whose highly praised psychiatric research had taken him to prisons before, were supported by other evidence, such as a letter Boyd Douglas had smuggled out from Philip Berrigan to Bucknell Professor Richard Drinnon. In a postscript to the letter, Eberhardt commented on life behind the walls: " . . . what people and what violence." He explained he was referring to the inmates' "wild sex mores."

While Coles' evaluation of Berrigan was nowhere near as alarming, the assessment contrasted sharply with the characteristics usually associated with the muscular priest—blustery self-confidence, outgoing warmth frequently demonstrated in all-embracing, strong hugs and the air of one with faith that he can make a difference.

Coles found Berrigan was "struggling hard against an incipient depression. His tendency to deny his difficulties, to protest his confidence and his ability to weather any storm, however difficult. On the other hand, gradually, week by week, he has become increasingly doubtful, increasingly fearful, increasingly embittered, and the content of his concerns and thoughts, by his own admission, has been increasingly directed at 'the way men are broken down under maximum confinement.' "

Berrigan was "particularly insulted and humiliated" when prison authorities searched the chapel after he had said mass, Coles said, and he was hurt that his niece was not able to see him before leaving for Europe for two years.

"The constant scrutiny that he has experienced—and it is scrutiny of a special kind, because it takes place in a maximum security situation, which is already highly charged with built-in routine security—has begun to have its effect on the man's mind," Coles said.

Berrigan revealed his concern over security measures to others as well.

In a letter to Drinnon, soon after arriving at Lewisburg, Berrigan wrote: "Naturally, I'm paranoic about mail, since there's been so much jazz with it. And I know they've been playing footsy with mine for months—years."

Berrigan's concern over his mail being tampered with and his drive to keep in touch with the antiwar campaign outside the prison helped form a close bond between him and Douglas, who carried communications back and forth for the priest.

Sister McAlister's letters to the imprisoned priest were a

running diary on the triumphs and defeats of the radical protesters, the health of his family, particularly his ailing mother, Frieda, efforts to move him from the oppressive security of Lewisburg, and a discussion of tactics and philosophy for "the movement" punctuated by expression of concern and endearment.

"Never, since we began this," the nun told the priest in one letter, "have I let this much time go by without a word to you. I'm sorry but beg you to understand & know that you do."

In a gallows-humor exercise, Sister McAlister wrote Father Berrigan of one rap session where a draft board raid was being plotted. One participant, she said, "out of some logic of his own, had his mother, his girl friend, a black boy friend and girl friend's dog on an already very complex scene."

Berrigan, in turn, advised the raiders, through Sister McAlister, to "be wise as serpents. The Man is getting better dove traps."

Observing that "the hunters increase," Berrigan wrote: "So the first protection is a resolute reliance on the Lord and the second, a fine intelligent caution. So take care, huh Irish? Love and peace."

In another letter Sister McAlister reported that a mutual friend had approached Senator Eugene McCarthy about prison disciplinary actions taken against Berrigan. McCarthy, she wrote, "is also working on your situation."

The nun told Berrigan that his mother had fallen and broken her left thigh. "Rest & a couple of weeks bed rest will heal it up. She's had a full dose of it but no sign of discouragement. We Berrigans never show the white flag!"

In his prison interview with Berrigan, Coles was struck particularly by a comment the priest dropped as the psychiatrist was leaving. After telling the doctor that he had been feeling "fine" in recent weeks, Berrigan added, " 'All isn't going that well for me,' " Coles recalled.

"Such an admission from him, however, understated and innocuous as it may sound, actually is alarmingly prognostic," Coles concluded." Men like Father Berrigan do not dramatically collapse; they do indeed gradually lose the kind of well-being and initiative, and sense of authority about themselves and their values that they have always had. In sum, they lose their dignity."

What was occurring behind the massive wall around Lewisburg to erode Philip Berrigan's well-established dignity?

Berrigan and Eberhardt originally were scheduled to be sent to Allenwood after some days of processing at Lewisburg, but they remained at the main prison for—an official originally said—"various reasons."

In addition to the highly restrictive atmosphere of the walled prison, remaining there meant Philip could not satisfy his need for outdoor physical exercise that he inherited from his father. He had spent eight weeks at Allenwood in 1968 before being released while the Baltimore Four conviction was appealed and in a letter had described with total delight the joy of cleaning several years deposit of cow manure from an idle barn. The change in plans also cut off the two men from other war resisters at the farm.

In July, prison authorities cited Berrigan and Eberhardt for minor violations of institution rules. When they refused to accept punishment, the two were sent to solitary—"segregation quarters," in prison parlance. They fasted in protest and were placed in the prison hospital. The episode lasted eighteen days.

In the midst of the clash with Lewisburg authorities, Berrigan and Eberhardt passed a protest statement through Boyd Douglas to their allies outside the prison. Philip charged in the statement that the prison administration had committed eleven acts of harassment against him. These included placing him under suspicion of organizing a penal strike "for no reason"; encouraging informers among the inmates "to report suspicious words, actions and associations" on the part of the priest; issuing a memorandum to the guards to watch him "as a dangerous organizer"; searching the chapel sacristy where he vested for mass; searching his quarters ostensibly for evidence of his involvement in the strike, but actually to seize his writing that was then used to charge him with circulating contraband information in and out of prison.

The protest statement, smuggled to Berrigan's allies, had its desired effect. On July 16, the prison administration had to contend with a rally of Catholic radicals and Bucknell University sympathizers who gathered just outside the wall to demonstrate against the treatment of Berrigan and Eberhardt.

" . . . political prisoners at Lewisburg are persecuted beyond the routine dehumanization given to the other inmates," Berrigan said in the statement. "The rightist policies of the staff are proverbial, and they profoundly fear anyone standing for justice and peace. God, flag, law, order, privilege—mask a policy of falsehood to the men, petty persecution, and at worst, brutality of an impressive type. Meanwhile, official propaganda boasts of rehabilitation—of tolerance, humaneness and creative innovation."

Philip discussed a subsequent prison strike in a letter smuggled to Sister McAlister, indicating by his criticism of the protest that he played no role in organizing it. "We had an industry strike here Tuesday and Wednesday," he said. "There were elements of gallantry in the thing, but no brains and no organization."

He also expressed disdain about leading prison protests in a letter smuggled to Professor Drinnon, in which he told of seeing the "head hack" at Lewisburg concerning a transfer to Allenwood.

" . . . he asked me very pointedly if I was addicted to prison reform, i.e., did I intend to agitate here? Demurely I said no! not my bag. Not where the power is—though I didn't tell him that. In a word, their main concern is whether one intends to screw up their bailiwick."

The director of the Bureau of Prisons, Norman A. Carlson, a crew-cut PhD, and one of the "new breed" of progressive prison administrators, rejected allegations that Philip Berrigan was being harassed.

"We have looked into Father Berrigan's situation at Lewisburg and are convinced that he has not been harassed," he wrote Senator Charles Goodell of New York. Goodell had urged Carlson to transfer Father Berrigan to a minimum security facility.

"Generally, the Allenwood Camp receives prisoners who have sentences of two years or less, or who are within about two years of a firm release date," Carlson wrote. "Father Berrigan had a sentence of six years, and will not be eligible for parole consideration until September, 1971. In addition, Father Berrigan was in fugitive status just prior to his most recent confinement at Lewisburg."

The senator's staff, suspicious of Carlson's explanation of why Philip Berrigan was being kept at Lewisburg, checked at a lower level in the Bureau of Prisons and found there was much more discretion to the decision than Carlson had indicated.

Goodell wrote Carlson again. "Increased security would seem most appropriate for individuals of a violent nature who might pose a further threat to society," he said.

Carlson did not reply, but shortly thereafter, on August 3, Eberhardt was moved to the Lewisburg farm camp, and Berrigan was transferred to Danbury August 25, two weeks after his brother was captured.

The transfer reunited the two brothers, but it separated Philip Berrigan from a fellow Lewisburg inmate with whom he had established a close, trusting relationship, Boyd Frederick Douglas, Jr.

CHAPTER FOUR

Minister with Portfolio

For Boyd Frederick Douglas, Jr. life had never been very easy. But for a federal prisoner he worked out an extraordinary arrangement.

In late 1969, after almost two years as an inmate at the Lewisburg, Pennsylvania, federal prison, he applied for permission to attend nearby Bucknell University under a special study-release program, a rare privilege that would require approval of the U.S. Bureau of Prisons in Washington.

When his application was approved by prison authorities in late January, Dennis Baumwoll, a Bucknell professor who directed the program, was pleased even though his advice had not been sought prior to Douglas' selection. Baumwoll regarded Douglas' selection as "a great symbolic breakthrough." The professor later recalled, "We had had three prisoners at Bucknell in previous years and all had been Establishment types—two lawyers and the head of an import-export firm. All had had substantial education. But here was Boyd Douglas, a real felon with little education. That's what the study-release program ought to be all about. And when the prison sprung Douglas on me—I knew nothing about him before that—I was glad because I was about ready to start hassling them about the kind of prisoners they had been approving for the program."

Baumwoll interviewed Douglas at the prison and the convict, using a favorite expression, assured him "I'm good people. There's cons out here and then there's good people. And I'm good people."

Douglas told Baumwoll that in the prison he had become good friends with one of its most famous inmates, Teamsters Union President, James R. Hoffa. "Douglas seemed very proud of

81

knowing Hoffa," Baumwoll said, "and he would go around saying Jimmy and me this and Jimmy and me that. He once said, 'A lot of cons go around kissing Jimmy's ass and trying to get in good with him because he's a big name. But Jimmy's one of my people—he's good people.' It was not until much later that I found out from other prisoners I trusted that Douglas barely knew Hoffa."

When Douglas began attending classes in February, 1970, of the prison's 1,400 convicts he was the only one enrolled at Bucknell. He appeared lonely and apprehensive in the beginning. Baumwoll arranged to get him a part-time job as a cataloguer at the Bucknell library. There Douglas at first felt that some of the women employees were whispering behind his back about "the con from the wall" who was in their midst.

Douglas had been a student only a few weeks, however, when he began making friends among campus liberals. Two of them were librarians who took an interest in him, Patricia Rom, twenty-seven, a brunette, and Zoia Horn, fifty-two, a strikingly handsome woman who looked at least ten years younger. Both discerned in Douglas an urgent need to feel important and both encouraged him in his studies and in the writing he said he planned to do on prison problems.

One of the first persons to see in Douglas a chance to improve the communications between the campus and the prison was Richard Drinnon, forty-five, perhaps Bucknell's most radical professor. Broad-shouldered and bearded with long, wavy salt and pepper hair, Drinnon was a historian and a vehement antiwar critic. He had made headlines and irritated much of the Lewisburg community by walking out on a Bucknell ceremony at which Vice President Hubert H. Humphrey was receiving an honorary degree. Reflecting disgust with the Johnson Administration's Vietnam policies, Drinnon had shouted at the Vice President: "You're a disgrace."

Although Douglas had shown no social concern in conversations with Baumwoll, the convict told Drinnon he felt deeply about the need for penal reform. "Boyd said he knew he could trust me," the history professor later said. "He said Baumwoll was okay but was too close to the prison administration and he needed someone he could trust. He wanted me to understand that he was very anti-establishment. He indicated he was bitter against the Federal Bureau of Prisons because of medical experiments in prison that had left him badly scarred. I asked him how I knew I could trust him since I had been keeping in contact with some of the war resisters at the prison and he might be a spy for the prison. He lowered his trousers and showed me deep scars on his legs. Then he showed me some news clippings about a civil suit against the Bureau of Prisons that he settled out of court. And he said if the prison knew he was saying such things and was showing the clippings he would be in trouble. I didn't know how far I could trust him, but he was in a position to help me communicate with some of the prisoners."

Drinnon encouraged Douglas' interest in penal problems and it seemed to buoy his spirits and give him self-confidence. Although Drinnon was not convinced that Douglas had any genuine interest in social problems, he introduced him to another liberal professor, Gene Chenoweth, chairman of the political science department, who had been criticizing American policies in Vietnam since 1962.

Chenoweth, at thirty-seven only seven years older than Douglas, taught a class at the prison and welcomed the opportunity to meet the convict. He was so impressed by Douglas' talk of the need for prison reform that he set aside an office for him in the political science department, which Douglas used for his studies.

As the professor later said, he became "sort of Boyd's counsellor." Douglas stopped seeing Professor Baumwoll altogether. "Boyd expressed a deep interest in the peace movement and in peace movement people," Chenoweth said, "and I felt it was a genuine interest. It seemed to be the first time that he had found people in any numbers who would accept him and talk to him as though he were just another human being— people who asked him about things other than why he was in prison. People who accepted him at face value."

Most people at Bucknell who knew Douglas accepted him at face value. He volunteered little personal information about himself, asked many more questions than he answered, and seemed to resent it when questioners persisted. But his Bucknell acquaintances seemed to agree with Chenoweth's feeling: "If you're too cynical or suspicious about a guy who's in prison, you're not likely to help him very much."

Douglas joined in campus discussions of civil rights and the need for stopping the war in Vietnam and for demonstrating opposition to the war. And in a letter he smuggled from Father Berrigan to Sister McAlister, the priest warmly praised him:

> The local minister with portfolio has emerged as the best thing hereabouts since polio vaccine. His ministrations have been no less than providential—and given the setting here, very nearly heroic. Later on, I consider he'll be a burr in the saddle for many of our people.

In the same letter, Father Berrigan suggested that other convicts might be recruited for the movement, but expressed concern about the problem of informants:

> As he might have told you, there are guys here with comparable potential. Somehow, one must break through Little Brother's net of informers, spy glass and omnipresence to get them looking beyond themselves. To feed a regular influx of ingenious and reliable ex-cons into the ranks would make a resounding blow for public integrity. Some would have a bit of bad education to shuck off, but they would help with some of the bad education of our people. And they do know the law and order people like we'll never know them.

War resistance was hardly a popular subject at Bucknell when Douglas became the liaison man between the campus and the Catholic Resistance. Except for a handful of faculty members and a small group of students, few Bucknellians had bothered to become involved to any extent in the peace movement.

Traditionally, Bucknell was conservative—white, Protestant, middle and upper classes, virtually untouched by the liberal influence that characterized other eastern colleges and universities. Founded by a small group of Baptists in 1846, Bucknell's original charter provided that students would be admitted and teachers elected without regard to religious preference. But the Protestant cast had been set and it remained pretty much that way despite the fact Bucknell became independent and privately endowed. The university's three thousand students in 1970 came largely from white, suburban families from Pennsylvania and other Middle Atlantic states. The student body was so homogeneous that in September, 1970, at the beginning of the university's 125th year, the *Bucknellian* would editorially call for "a radical reordering" of student population. Noting that 81 percent of the class of 1974 came from Middle Atlantic states and 9 percent from New England, the campus newspaper said: "Eight black freshmen enrolled this year in a class of 800, and one would have to look hard to find any Chicanos, Puerto Ricans or other minority groups. Yet we glide blissfully on; all fine at Camp Bucknell."

Bucknell took pride in its patriotism and historical contributions to war efforts dating back to the Civil War. Like many universities, Bucknell took part during World War II in the Navy College Training Program and had Marine and Navy detachments on campus. During the Korean and Vietnam wars, it had active ROTC units.

Douglas ridiculed the ROTC to his newfound friends as an evil instrument of an unjust war. He emphasized to antiwar activists that he knew first-hand of the war's injustice because he had seen it while serving with the Army in Vietnam. He seemed unusually anxious to convince his friends of his commitment to the antiwar movement.

He had first become involved with antiwar activists late in April. Drinnon called him in and told him that Philip Berrigan, who had been captured several days earlier in New York, was being sent to Lewisburg prison. "Give him my greetings when he arrives," Drinnon said. "And check on his condition and see if he needs anything."

Douglas met Father Berrigan in the prison yard at the end of April and told the priest of his Bucknell studies and of the message from Drinnon. He emphasized, as he had to Drinnon, that he was bitter against the government because he had been badly scarred by the medical experiments.

Father Berrigan trusted Douglas from the start. When Douglas asked if he could do anything for him, the priest said he would like him to carry out a message for a friend. In the mess hall the next morning, the priest slipped two letters to him, one for Drinnon and one for Sister McAlister, and asked him to give both to the professor.

Before giving the letters to Drinnon later that day, Douglas opened the envelopes and read the contents. The one to the nun intrigued him—it was of a highly personal nature. He re-sealed the envelopes and gave them to Drinnon. The letter to Drinnon said:

Great making contact with you again—However indirectly. Thanks for sending our friend to us. He's already been of considerable help. If any of us are left here, it will be imperative to remain in close contact with him.

Two things strike me at the moment. First, it appears I'm slated for Allenwood. Therefore, if any profs from the campus continue to have access there, they can be very helpful. Could you work on this, if it is at all a possibility. In a word, communications out of there may exist, but they need to continue on a sustained basis. Secondly, could you get the enclosed to Sister McAlister, 137 W. 85th St., NYC 10024? You might remember her briefly from the NYC rap that you and Mary attended. She is a very good friend of Dave and myself, deep in movement affairs and absolutely reliable. We hope you and Mary can get to know her better. She keeps in close contact with friends scattered near and far and works closely with our defense committee. Moreover, after the semester ends—she teaches college—she will be entirely free for the summer to work full time.

Don't expect to be here after Wed., but our friend will keep you informed. Know that your values make thanks from us an extravagance. But thanks anyway. And love to Mary and yourself. Peace!

Fraternally, P.B.

Despite his hopes of being transferred to Allenwood, a minimum security farm eighteen miles away, Berrigan was kept confined to the Lewisburg prison. The Bureau of Prisons explained that because he had been a fugitive and had been sentenced to more than two years, he did not qualify as a minimum security prisoner.

Immediately after getting Berrigan's message, Drinnon passed along the letter for Elizabeth McAlister and included a note of his own. On May 7 she replied in a letter:

> Many, many thanks for the communique—good to hear from both you and him. The enclosed are for his nibs if they can be gotten to him. Tomorrow I'll send you some copies of Dan's latest communique and if one can be gotten to Phil—great. Sr. Jogues and I would be anxious to meet with you and Mary whenever the opportunity comes up . . .

Douglas thus became a regular conduit for Berrigan messages. In another note to Drinnon the priest wrote of Douglas: "No question about it, he has been a vast help to us, in every imaginable way. Once sprung, he could be a very valuable man."

A priest in prison not only was smuggling out messages to various friends, but was staying in contact with his fugitive brother—all through the cooperative efforts of a convict, a college professor and a nun. "Am anxious to get the enclosed to my brother through Liz," Philip Berrigan wrote to Professor Drinnon.

> Both of us can only inadequately express our gratitude for the service from Boyd and you. It is hope-giving, by way of understatement. Situation unchanged here. We're feeling out of the scene—I'm convinced something political can be begun here—if only modest at first. There are too many good men here to ignore, or to ignore their futures. Will let this go with Boyd. Hello to Mary, and love to you both. You are teaching us about friendship. Shalom!

Later, the following message, signed, "Gratefully, Daniel Berrigan," was mailed to Drinnon:

> My brother Philip indicated that you would be able to get the enclosed note to him. I should be so grateful if you could. I add my thanks to his own, for this and other kindnesses.

Please disregard the postmark on this letter; it is much safer in my situation if no one speaks of my whereabouts.

It was Philip Berrigan's first message from his brother since being arrested and he savored it as Daniel obviously had his letter. Daniel wrote:

Dear Bruv, An ache of recognition getting yrs. What a joy, what a score! I have been getting good vibes from various quarters, including Jerry, but of course, there's nothing like a word from headquarters; and that's what yez supplies! I think we probably make a good team as one can slap together in a hurry in such mad March days.

Daniel went on to write that he was:

heartened to see that what we hoped for at Cville is occurring and is mainly in younger hands, smart tough youngsters who are not afraid to try new things in the same spirit. Had a good account of the family visit. Jerry seemed to think you had reservations about my staying around until invaded; I hope the present ramblings go somewhat toward relieving your mind. They will rattle sabres in both our ears; and you mainly will have to hear them loudest, and take the actual small animal turds they throw about, for awhile. I don't let my mind dwell on their threats to me . . .

Drinnon had become a key link in the communications network Douglas operated for Philip Berrigan. Sister Elizabeth McAlister, who referred to the priest in one note as "our silver friend," wrote Drinnon a letter that showed the professor also was privy to some of the antiwar strategy of the Catholic Resistance. "Enclosed is a letter for Phil Berrigan," she wrote. "A run down on recent developments in the groups, i.e., more information than was possible to code." In another note to Drinnon, she wrote, "Incredibly strong search on for Dan. He'll soon be numbered among the 10-12 most wanted men." She added, facetiously, "And he should be considered dangerous!"

Word of Drinnon's part in the network got around the Catholic Resistance quickly. Anne Walsh, a former nun and a member of the New York Eight, wrote the following "Dear Dick" letter, referring to an antiwar action by the code name "Shit City":

> Liz McAlister said you might get this into Phil. If you speak to him give him my love and tell him we're real busy cleaning up Shit City near bridge to Baltimore—he'll know. Saw you at Allenwood but I was peddling records and books (for the Defense Committee). Don't know if you remember me—I met you and Mary at the church here in New York. Thanks for this service. Please send letter back if you can't get it in and I'll send it to Jerry Berrigan.

Presumably she thought the priest's brother Jerry could carry the letter in on a visit to Father Berrigan.

In a letter of reply Drinnon wrote that he would try to get her message through and added:

> Can imagine that you have been REAL busy. I wish you would turn to other Shit Cities once you finish cleaning up the one that presently engages your attention. Buddha knows, there is a great sufficiency of such stretching from sea to shining sea.

Drinnon, meanwhile, received a letter from Sister McAlister enclosing a message for Father Berrigan, a reply to the priest's earlier letter. The professor turned it over to Douglas, who Drinnon thought seemed unusually eager to act as courier. Once outside Drinnon's office, Douglas opened the letter. He was fascinated—a love affair between a nun and a priest. He carefully resealed the letter and carried it with him when he returned to the prison.

After giving the letter to Father Berrigan, Douglas discussed with him the possibility of setting up mail drops so that letters would not have to be routed through Drinnon. They agreed it was a good idea, and the priest gave him a telephone number in New York where he could call Sister McAlister and discuss it with her. She also liked the idea and gave Douglas the name and address of Sister Judith Savard in New York as a mail drop where she could receive letters. She told Douglas to send her letters from Father Berrigan in a sealed envelope inside another envelope addressed to Sister Savard.

When Sister McAlister next visited Father Berrigan on May 22, pretending to be the priest's cousin, she met Douglas at Bucknell. He told her of the medical experiments and rolled up a shirt sleeve to reveal an ugly scar. He always wore long sleeves to hide the scars, but frequently rolled them up to impress upon people the severity of his reaction to the experiments. Sister McAlister later recalled that she felt sorry for him and had not blamed him for being bitter. During their meeting, they agreed he would use the code name "Pete" when he telephoned her or she telephoned him. He told her he would find the location of several pay telephones in Lewisburg and at Bucknell where she could call him by pre-arrangement.

Shortly after Sister McAlister's visit, Father Berrigan gave Douglas another letter for her. Once outside the prison, he carefully unsealed the envelope. "These are Friday notes, May 22nd, the Year of our Lord, 1970," it began. "Concocted the above preamble to offset roving eye of Pete's shakedown artists, in case any of them have that kind of perception . . ."

Suddenly, there it was: "Your visit leaves me speechless, at least on paper, though not in heart . . . I watched your lips get red as we talked and knew once again the life surging in you . . . ."

The letter—written on May 22-23-24—rambled on at great length, mixing personal passages in with general comments about mail drops and antiwar activities. The personal passages, some of them quite explicit, captivated Douglas. He headed for the Bucknell library where he copied the letters on a Xerox machine. He resealed the letter and mailed it in another envelope to Sister Savard. He put the copy in a briefcase he used for his studies. Before returning to prison that evening, he locked the briefcase and left it in his office in the political science department.

As Father Berrigan's link to the outside world, Douglas was more and more involving himself in the activities of the antiwar priest. One day he rushed into Professor Chenoweth's office, his eyes burning with excitement. "Hey, I hear you're coming out to the Jaycee program at the prison tonight," he said. "I'll see you there. I've got someone I want you to meet."

The Lewisburg prison chapter of the U.S. Junior Chamber of Commerce, one of many Jaycee chapters at prisons across the country, was holding an annual meeting to which Jaycees from outside the prison and other guests were invited. Although Douglas was not a Jaycee, he as well as some other non-member prisoners enjoyed the privilege of attending the meeting.

At the session in the prison cafeteria that night Douglas introduced Chenoweth to a tall, silver-haired prisoner who smiled broadly and gripped the professor's hand as though he were meeting a long lost friend. But the broadest smile of all broke across Douglas' face.

"For one of the few times in his life I guess Boyd had a big deal," Chenoweth later recalled. "He was introducing me to 'good people'—to his friend, Phil Berrigan."

Although Douglas had exaggerated about his relationship with Jimmy Hoffa, there was no question but that he had become friends with Philip Berrigan. Nothing else was heard about "Jimmy and me." It was always "Phil and me." Douglas began reporting periodically to Professor Drinnon and other antiwar activists on the priest's frustrating existence in prison, his continued advocacy of resistance to the war but a feeling of helplessness at being unable to take an active part in the resistance actions. "Phil and me would like to get some action going," Douglas would say.

Neither Drinnon nor his wife Mary, also an activist, could understand why a convict was permitted to associate freely with peace movement radicals, some of them likely subjects for police and FBI surveillance. Drinnon had known Berrigan since October, 1969, and had been involved in protest movements for at least a decade. He participated in the 1961 Freedom Rides in the South and in 1964 he was arrested during a sit-in in San Francisco protesting employment bias. As a participant in antiwar demonstrations, he considered himself a likely candidate for surveillance. "And there was Phil going to Lewisburg after all the publicity about his capture and about Catonsville," Drinnon said later, "and then his being as visible in prison as an elephant walking around, but somehow Boyd Douglas, with his access to the outside, always managing to spend a lot of time around him—and right under the eyes of prison officials. It made you wonder how Douglas got away with it."

For an imprisoned felon, Douglas did seem to have unusual freedom—later he even rented an apartment in Lewisburg—and an inordinate interest in the Resistance. But his Bucknell friends reasoned that the Bureau of Prisons was lenient with him to compensate for the ugly scars the medical experiments had caused. And Douglas explained his antiwar feelings by saying that he had been sickened by what he had seen in Vietnam and that he had been sent to prison for an antiwar act in California— conspiring to bomb trucks carrying napalm. Also, he said, he had been influenced greatly by Philip Berrigan, a man he held in high esteem.

There was no indication that anyone at the prison or Bucknell ever officially questioned Douglas' extraordinary freedom.

When he first began attending Bucknell, he almost always traveled the two miles between the prison and the university in the prison mail truck. Soon he bought a bicycle and used it most of the time. Later, he often would get rides in cars with friends he made at the university. He left the prison about 7 A.M. and returned by 6 P.M., always being careful to get back on time.

Usually wearing dark sunglasses, regardless of whether it was sunny or overcast, Douglas became a familiar figure on the hilly Bucknell grounds. He would walk among the stately elms and century-old oaks that dot the campus, or between the academic buildings on College Hill, overlooking the Susquehanna River, flashing the V-sign for peace and calling out to coeds, "Peace, baby." It was a far cry from the stark prison surroundings he returned to in the evenings and he savored the open spaces and his new-found identity.

Although some Bucknell acquaintances considered his personality rather unpleasant—they said he was officious and boastful—he ingratiated himself with his enthusiasm for the movement and his relationship with Philip Berrigan. When word of the convict's role as a courier for the priest got out—and he saw to it that it did—he became even more popular with students who had read of the exploits of the Berrigan brothers.

One of Douglas' friends was Thomas H. Love, a skinny youth with a sparse, straggly beard. In 1969, Love had burned his draft card and refused induction into the military service. For some reason Love, son of an Air Force career officer, had never been arrested, although FBI agents had questioned him about his obvious law violation for which hundreds of others had been prosecuted. Love ran a one-man program to facilitate the visits of relatives and friends to inmates at the prison. He had never attended Bucknell, but had an older brother who had been a student there.

Douglas rented the downstairs apartment of an old, two-story, white frame house at 204 South Sixth Street, several blocks from the Bucknell campus. He let Love live there free. The rent was $100, which seemed rather extravagant for a convict who could use the apartment only during daytime hours. But Douglas always seemed to have an abundant supply of money. He came to use the apartment, sparsely furnished with mattresses on the floor serving as beds, as a meeting place for Sister McAlister, the Scoblicks, Fathers Wenderoth and McLaughlin and other members of the Catholic Resistance.

The antiwar movement had brought Douglas prestige and attention that he had never known before and the movement now became almost an obsession with him. Always alert for anyone who might be interested in it, he made friends with a geology student who rented the apartment upstairs from his at 204 South Sixth Street—Robert Raymond, twenty.

Raymond and his roommate, Peter Doscher, also twenty, a major in American history, thought Douglas romanticized too much in talking about the movement. But, like other students at Bucknell, they were impressed by his aggressiveness and enthusiasm and—most of all—by his relationship with Philip Berrigan.

At the end of the spring semester, Raymond and Doscher returned to their New Jersey homes for the summer. Before leaving, Raymond sublet his apartment to his girl friend, Jane Hoover, twenty, a blonde, and two of her friends, Betsy (Mary Elizabeth) Sandel, twenty, a red-head, and Joyce Frederick, twenty, a brunette. All three were juniors at Bucknell.

Douglas had earned a reputation for having an eye for the girls and he was to have an eye for all the new tenants, beginning with Jane. Soft-spoken and somewhat shy, she was willowy with sad brown eyes and long, straight, dark-blond hair. She had little interest in the movement until she met Douglas.

Jane later recalled: "One of the first things Boyd told me was that he was smuggling messages for Philip Berrigan and that he was dealing with the Catholic peace underground which had contact with Daniel Berrigan. I really didn't know much about the Berrigans at first—their name was vaguely familiar. Boyd showed me a letter—I don't remember what it said—but it was typed on both sides and it was signed 'Dan.' It was sort of like Boyd was trying to impress me—and I guess he did."

On June 2, the day Douglas met Jane Hoover, a guard shaking down Father Berrigan's cell found a letter the priest had written to Sister McAlister concealed in a *Newsweek* magazine. After Douglas returned to the prison that evening, Father Berrigan met him in the mess hall and told him about the discovery, but said not to worry, that he had only mentioned him in the letter by the code name "Pete."

Associate Warden Robert L. Hendricks confronted Father Berrigan and Douglas separately about the matter. Hendricks mentioned to the priest that he thought he knew the identity of "Pete," but Father Berrigan decided he was bluffing. Douglas later told the priest that he had admitted nothing, and that Hendricks was ignorant of their letter-smuggling operation.

The letter tipped off prison authorities, however, that Father Berrigan was managing to maintain contact with the antiwar movement through smuggled letters; that he had a close relationship with Sister McAlister; that his relatives were in contact with his fugitive brother Daniel; and, perhaps most alarming to the authorities, that he was considering organizing convicts for the antiwar movement.

"Two interviews today—one with a Virginian with excessive sentence for income tax evasion," Father Berrigan had started the letter that was found in his cell, "another with a New Yorker, here for stolen cars, apparently responding to rehabilitative process.

"The above buncha guff for the beady eye of the fuzz. Will try to hunt down Pete later to see if he has news, or has brought in news. Sunday, an inmate hit us with the rumor that Pete was a courier of contraband, and that they were looking to bust him. Naturally, caution resulted. So now, on irregular channels, the flow is mostly one way—he is confident of getting things out, but has gotten nothing in for over a week."

In a reference to the wife of his brother Jerry, Father Berrigan had noted: "Carol writes that they have contact with the blood line [Dan Berrigan] . . . maybe we'll hear directly one of these days—though if he would feel tight about writing, I'd rather he wouldn't."

The passage that shocked Hendricks and caused great concern among attorneys in the Justice Department's Criminal division was one that suggested organizing "some of the young guys here—who more and more, sit in on the raps—car thieves, bank robbers, old and experienced cons, for all of their young ages. They are creative, personable, funny, violent, racist. But what an injection they'll add to our movement. We hope, before we leave here, to have them started on an investigation of life— one which will put their obvious talents at our disposal. It is a longshot, but not unlikely."

Father Berrigan heard nothing further about this letter from prison authorities after his conference with Hendricks. And Douglas agreed to continue smuggling letters between the priest and Sister McAlister.

Although Sister McAlister was on the priest's list of approved correspondents, he and the nun felt that they could write of their love and antiwar activities only in letters that would not go through normal channels and be subjected to inspection by prison authorities. Meanwhile, their close allies in the Resistance knew little or nothing about the contents of their letters. In fact, Eqbal Ahmad later said he knew nothing about the letters or Douglas. "Boyd Douglas was a very personal link between Phil and Liz" he said, "and you don't tell that part of your private life to everyone. Liz didn't tell me anything about Phil and what he was doing or thinking in prison."

Douglas, meanwhile, had so impressed Jane Hoover that she agreed to transcribe a letter from Sister McAlister to Father Berrigan. The letter was handwritten on yellow legal-pad paper, and Douglas told Jane he needed it copied on loose-leaf notebook paper so he could carry it into prison in the notebook he used for his Bucknell classes. He explained he was too busy to copy it himself, an explanation that Jane accepted at face value, and said the copy was necessary so that if the guards shook his notebook looking for contraband the letter would not fall out.

By now Jane had read some of Father Berrigan's writing and "had come to respect him a great deal." She was glad to help get word from the outside to him.

Douglas' courier role had increased in importance to the priest and the nun because prison officials had revoked Sister McAlister's visiting privileges after learning that she had been falsely representing herself as the priest's cousin to assure herself a place on his approved visitors' list. As Father Wenderoth later explained: "There was a deep psychological need for Phil and Liz to communicate with each other. When you love each other that much, it's hard not to communicate. Their personal relationship was a real hang-up and quite a handicap at times."

It became Jane Hoover's regular chore to transcribe the letters to Berrigan because Douglas always claimed to be too busy. He assured her that she would not get into trouble and that he frequently carried messages for other prisoners.

Unknown to Jane, Father Berrigan and Sister McAlister, Douglas was also Xeroxing copies of every letter at the Bucknell library. And he was receiving the letters from the nun now without their going through Professor Drinnon. He arranged to have them sent to him in care of Jane. Later he would use Betsy Sandel and Patricia Rom, the Bucknell librarian, as mail drops for Sister McAlister's letters.

Although in all of the letters there were expressions of affection as well as cryptic references to antiwar "projects," including draft board raids, Jane later said she saw nothing in them that she considered especially startling. She said that even though she was dating Douglas at the time, he repelled her by "trying to make something dirty out of the personal passages."

Jane was not particularly surprised when Douglas dwelled on the intimate expressions in the letters, however. She and other friends of Douglas—male and female, including her former boy friend, Robert Raymond—thought he had a hang-up on sex. Professor Chenoweth called it "some kind of woman problem."

Patricia Rom thought Douglas "had an incredible illusion that he was attractive to all women."

Douglas was forever making passes at women he met and he bragged to young men on campus that he had had many sexual conquests. He relished talking about how it was during R & R (rest and recreation) in Tokyo while on a break from Vietnam duty. He once told Robert Raymond: "I get laid by any movement chick I want, but I really dig Jane." And he told Raymond and his roommate, Peter Doscher, "If you ever do any cocaine, do it with someone of the opposite sex around."

Homosexuality in prison was a problem that seemed to cause Douglas great anguish. He frequently discussed the subject with Bucknell students and once showed Sister McAlister a nine-page paper he said he had written on the subject. Actually, it had been written by David Eberhardt, who voiced his own fears of male rape on several occasions.

Douglas, dark and stocky, was, as Sister McAlister described him, "ruggedly handsome." He also was well dressed and had an expensive wardrobe. He wore stylish sweaters and flare-bottom trousers on campus.

"But he looked 'straight' no matter what he wore or did and he didn't understand that people in the movement didn't care about clothes," said Doscher.

Raymond recalled: "We asked him why he didn't get rid of all that greasy gook and quit combing his hair straight back and let it grow over his ears and he said, 'Not yet.' It was as if he had to get the prison thing over with first."

Douglas, a big spender with expensive tastes, was generous and often bought liquor for his friends. "He kept us supplied with booze," said Betsy Sandel. He drank Cutty Sark scotch and Löwenbräu beer imported from Germany. He smoked cigarettes imported from Greece, as well as State Express 555 cigarettes (95 cents a box) from Piccadilly, London. He had a stereo and a large collection of records, including many of protest songs.

Douglas explained he came by his money through settlement of the damage suit against the Bureau of Prisons. He told some friends he got $15,000 and told others it was $23,000. His expensive clothes, he said, came from his "rather wealthy brother from Philadelphia."

He subscribed to the *Village Voice* and to *Ramparts*, a radical magazine which began as an ultra-leftwing Catholic publication. While his Bucknell friends thought there was little depth to his understanding of the Vietnam war issues, he admired his efforts to become acquainted with radical literature. Joyce Frederick said, "Boyd had the underground line down so well and he sounded super serious about it. I wasn't active and he'd talk to me and pressure me to get involved. He would make you feel guilty for not being active. He would say 'There's no movement at Bucknell, just a bunch of satisfied kids. He would talk about your being comfortable and going to college and being wrapped up in a warm house while the world was going to hell. I left the room one time in tears when he kept going on like that."

In June, Douglas began arranging meetings of the Catholic war resisters and Bucknell students and faculty members. One was held Saturday, June 13. "Boyd told me some radical Catholics of the Berrigan stripe were coming up on the weekend and they needed a place to talk," according to Chenoweth. "I told him okay, we could have a picnic at my place."

Before the afternoon picnic, several members of the Resistance met in the apartment Douglas shared with Tom Love to watch the filming of part of a television documentary on draft resistance. Another visitor—and the star of the filming—was David Miller, one of the first persons convicted of violating the 1965 federal law prohibiting destruction of draft cards. Miller, like Love, had burned his. A friend of Daniel Berrigan from the priest's days at LeMoyne, Miller recently had been paroled.

After the filming, Douglas urged persons driving in different cars to take different and circuitous routes to Chenoweth's house, implying that they might be followed because of the nature of the upcoming discussions. Among those present at the filming were the Reverend Philip Linden and Sister Susan Cordes, members of the East Coast Conspiracy to Save Lives, which had already publicly taken responsibility for the Philadelphia draft board raids and destruction of General Electric records in Washington. Tony Scoblick and Mary Cain of the Boston Eight also attended.

Four days after the picnic two of the participants, Tony Scoblick and Mary Cain, together with Sister Elizabeth

McAlister, Joseph Wenderoth, Thomas Davidson (a twenty-five-year-old conscientious objector and one-time Eagle Scout), and several others destroyed records in three selective service offices in Delaware. The group, which had carefully planned the night-time raids well in advance, passed up a fourth draft board office at the last minute after discovering an armed guard on duty.

The next day two of the raiders, Barry Wingard and Frank LaProesti, both college students, were arrested when they returned to the scene of the crime. Except for that, the raiders had escaped undetected. The two students refused to cooperate with the FBI and no other arrests were made.

In several letters Douglas smuggled into Lewisburg prison, Sister McAlister reported the success of the raids, describing with some glee how two of the raiders had entered one of the offices during the day and managed to remove part of the ceiling in the men's room where they hid until the raid began. She also wrote that the group had argued over whether they should try to raid the office that was guarded. Davidson, a muscular, heavy-set youth with a quarrelsome manner, had argued in favor of raiding the office, she wrote, but the others had decided against it on grounds of possible violence.

Several days after the raid, Fathers Wenderoth and McLaughlin traveled to Lewisburg to talk things over with the man who kept Philip Berrigan apprised of the Catholic Resistance's continuing antiwar activities. Boyd Douglas had told Jane Hoover he wanted her to meet "two priests involved in the movement." They showed up at 204 South Sixth Street wearing sport shirts, which surprised Jane even though she knew that priests in the movement did not always wear clerical collars.

On July 6, Douglas arranged another meeting with Wenderoth and McLaughlin, this one in Jane Hoover's apartment, and he invited two other students—Betsy Sandel and Alice Erickson, twenty, a junior—he said he especially wanted the priests to meet. Alice, who later said, "Boyd was always trying to get me involved," missed the meeting because of a trip to Philadelphia. With the priests was William Au, a seminarian from Baltimore and a member of the Boston Eight. Tom Love, Pat Rom and David G. Sholl, twenty-one, a junior majoring in art, also attended the session.

Jane Hoover later said—and others agreed—that "we talked about economics and about how big business exploits workers in this country and how much you're exploited if you're a little person." Someone mentioned that Perkins Pancake House in Lewisburg was a good example. Jane, Betsy and Alice Erickson all worked there four hours a day for eighty-five cents an hour, plus "lousy tips" of $1.50 to $2 a day. After the discussion, Betsy went to work that night at Perkins.

They also discussed generally whether one should become involved in civil disobedience to protest the war. And one of the students—Sholl—commented that resisters who broke the law led a paranoid existence he would rather avoid. Sholl later recalled:

"I had met Boyd during the spring while playing in a jazz group in a benefit performance at the prison. Later I began seeing him off and on campus. During the student strike at Bucknell after the shootings at Kent State, he started talking politics with me and I expressed a lot of negative feelings about this country. He seemed to take an interest in that.

"All the time I thought there were some inconsistencies in what he was telling me. He would tell me different times he would be getting out of prison. He first said June, but then he didn't get out. And later when he said he was going to get out, he didn't. And he seemed to have too many privileges for a prisoner. I wondered what he was all about.

"We had a couple of long talks in the summer and during one he invited me to come to one of the meetings. It was all very secret. He named a few priests and nuns, mostly from Baltimore. He hinted around that it was big action. I told him yes, I'd like to see what they were doing, that I would go to the meeting. He kept talking about action and commitment and how committed he was.

"I went to this meeting and Joe Wenderoth and Neil McLaughlin asked if I wanted to get involved in civil disobedience. I told them that being an artist could be a political life-style, too, but that I figured what they were talking about involved a paranoid existence where you're not going to be settled or comfortable very often. They were secretive. I thought they were self-righteous, but very committed. I respected them."

By early July, Boyd Douglas had begun pressing Jane Hoover not only to get more involved in the Catholic Resistance, but to get more involved with him. "I really admired him and I thought he had a lot of courage," she said, "but I didn't know—I was confused. He wanted to get married and insisted I agree to it, but I put him off."

Raised in Sunbury, about ten miles south of Lewisburg, the daughter of a Penn Central Railroad employee, Jane was reserved and known as "super straight" in high school. In her senior year, she won a good citizenship award from the Daughters of the American Revolution. At college she became part of the "new culture," but she had little interest in the politics of protest and civil disobedience until she met Douglas.

He frequently chastized her for not being more serious about the movement. Once, when she was reading *Women in Love*, he told her she should be reading something worthwhile, such as Bobby Seale's *Seize the Time*. In the beginning, he also complained that Bucknell students were hung up on dope. "At first he was really down on dope, like condescending, looking down on you," Peter Doscher recalled. "But then he started smoking some pot and one time he took some back to prison with him—I rolled them and put them in his cigarette package for him."

Jane, in addition to feeling Douglas was pressing too hard on the marriage proposal, found herself increasingly unsettled by the cloak-and-dagger image he projected. "One morning early in July, about 7:30, I drove to the prison and picked up Boyd in a car I had borrowed," she said. "We were a couple of miles from the prison, almost downtown, when a prison guard pulled us over and said, 'Who is this young lady, Douglas?' The guard was intimidating, but Boyd had insisted I cooperate with him. I told the guard I was a student taking Boyd to classes. He made me show my license. I didn't think a prison guard had the right to do that and I thought the way Boyd was acting he was being a little bit too much cops-and-robbers."

Douglas, using pseudonyms of "Frank," "Gary," and "Peter," also spent a lot of time on secretive long-distance calls on pay telephones. Usually he told friends he was contacting different members of the Catholic Resistance. He used two different credit card numbers and gave one of the numbers to several Bucknell students and told them it was the number registered in the name of actor Paul Newman.

Most everywhere he went, Douglas carried a locked briefcase which he intimated contained sensitive information on the Resistance. "If anybody ever comes in here on a bust for drugs or anything," he once told Robert Raymond and Peter Doscher, "get rid of the briefcase." They said he kept it locked except when he was working on papers and documents in it.

If Douglas generated excitement with his secretive manner, it wore thin on people who spent very much time with him. "Boyd used to make remarks once in a while, just to be cool," Jane said. "He would say, 'Some day the FBI might come knocking on your door. This isn't child's play we're in, you know.' But he always told me that only prison regulations were involved in smuggling the letters and he was the only one taking a risk, that I should not worry. He was romanticizing a lot, I thought, trying to excite me."

Such talk by Douglas, together with his proposal of marriage, had done nothing to enhance Jane's commitment either to the Resistance or to him. And she told him she was confused and didn't feel like making any decisions. He pleaded with her, finally telling her that he had cancer caused by the medical experiments. "He said he would die in six to twelve months and he wanted me to marry him and go to some place like Nevada or Puerto Rico after he got out," Jane said. "If I would just give him six to twelve months of happiness, he said, he would be satisfied."

He told Jane she was the only girl he had really loved other than a girl named Nancy in Rochester he knew as a teen-ager. "And she had blond hair, too," Douglas said, looking at Jane's hair.

When Jane still pleaded for more time to think, he suggested that she go to see Sister Elizabeth McAlister at the Sacred Heart of Mary convent in New York. "Boyd kept telling me what a fantastic person Liz was and how she could talk to girls," Jane said, "and I did want to meet her." Douglas arranged the meeting, apparently feeling the nun would help him with his romance. After all, had he not helped her stay in contact with the man she loved?

Douglas offered to pay Jane's plane fare to New York, but instead of flying, she got a ride with a friend and first went by Glen Ridge, New Jersey, to see her old boy friend, Robert Raymond. Raymond, who later was to complain that Douglas had "moved in on Jane as soon as I left Lewisburg and took advantage of my being gone," accompanied her to the convent. It was a Saturday, July 11, and two students from Marymount College, where Sister Elizabeth taught art, also were there. Much of the discussion centered around the war and protests, but once Jane got Sister Elizabeth alone, she sought her advice on Douglas' efforts to push her farther than she cared to go. Sister Elizabeth advised her to follow her own conscience.

Raymond drove her back to Lewisburg the following Monday and she saw Douglas briefly in the apartment in the afternoon, but he had to return to prison and they had time to say little more than hello and goodbye. She told him she still wanted a chance to think before discussing his proposal.

Chatting briefly with Raymond, Douglas expressed confidence Jane would marry him. "He said he knew that Jane and I had been real close," Raymond recalled, "but he was telling me that she would never go back on her word, that she would marry him. He said there was something he knew about he couldn't tell me. Later I found out he was talking about telling Jane he had cancer."

Two days after returning from New York Jane told Douglas, "I just can't go through with it. It's not right." She later recalled, "He was very upset and cried and carried on. He said he wouldn't take it as a final answer." The following day, July 16, was Jane's twenty-first birthday and Douglas gave her a necklace with a silver peace symbol which Sisters Elizabeth and Jogues had found for him after shopping for hours in New York. He also gave her a wall plaque emblazoned with a peace message: "War is Not Healthy for Children and Other Living Things."

The same day members of the Resistance staged a demonstration outside the Lewisburg prison to protest what they considered to be unfair treatment of Philip Berrigan and David Eberhardt, who had been moved to the prison hospital after beginning their fast.

Fathers Wenderoth and McLaughlin and their ex-priest

colleague, Tony Scoblick, accompanied by his bride of three weeks, ex-nun Mary Cain, showed up outside the prison walls with a message Daniel Berrigan had recorded, especially for the occasion, while hiding out from the FBI. They played the tape over an amplifier while scores of demonstrators cheered and FBI agents looked on grim-faced. Several students took pictures of agents taking pictures of students and other demonstrators. It all added up to more taunting of the FBI, which J. Edgar Hoover already had put under increasing pressure to find the fugitive priest.

Daniel Berrigan's voice blared out, declaring that "in the case of my brother or David or Bobby Seale we are no longer speaking of political prisoners in any legitimate sense. These men are simply hostages of war.

"Perhaps a few facts are in order here," he continued. "Philip and David have been kept for some three months in high security prison at Lewisburg. They have been told simply there will be no disposition of their case, no transfer to Lewisburg farm or Allenwood, until I have surrendered or been captured. Also, their sentence of six years, in Philip's case, and three years in David's, for destruction of draft files stands unchanged because of a period of ten days they refused to surrender to illegitimate power. Meantime, the sentence of Tom Lewis, who turned himself in, was immediately reduced by half. So in simple mathematics Philip and David are paying three years of their lives for ten days at large, a ratio of about one hundred days in prison for each day they withstood. This I submit is a ratio of punishment to crime which recalls the wartime activities and judgments of occupying Nazis or Fascists against war hostages. It recalls also the South African or Angolan government in its dealings with captured guerrillas. It recalls the Ky government disposing of Buddhists and students. It recalls finally our own government and its recent activity against Panthers . . . .

"These are ominous signs of things to come. They are signs for all who can read. To be underground, to be in jail, are going to be more and more the fate of good men in America. Just as these same things more and more have become the common fate of good men throughout the world. In view of all this I face the fate of my brother and his friends with a certain tranquility of spirit.

We have never been able simply to stand about wriggling our hands in distress over the latest outrage of Johnson or Nixon or their myrmidons. Therefore in face of the Lewisburg outrages I am not seeking to arouse sympathy or compassion for my brother or for myself. Because we have chosen our fate, we have not been condemned to it.

"Our task is by no means crushed, it is only unfinished. Those in prison and those in the underground are required to act in unison together with their friends, to continue to join in conspiracy, to join in common jeopardy, to join in illegal non-violent actions, to hotten up whatever scene, to hotten up the scenes we live in. In such a way we will undoubtedly bring more and more revenge upon ourselves whether in the form of longer prison sentences, harassment of our families, solitary confinement in prison, or a hotter chase by the FBI bloodhounds. But none of these, I submit, are to the point as Philip and I have long ago agreed. What we seek, acting deliberately and coolly and politically, is to peel the mask of legitimacy from the face of blind and inhuman and violent power. What we seek at the same time is to open the eyes of more and more of our friends, to bring a larger community of resistance into being . . . ."

The message droned on in a despairing tone ("We must expect bloodshed, agony, prison, exile, separation from those we love, underground, death itself."), winding up with a plaintive cry: "All prisoners are at the mercy of mad politics. All political prisoners are hostages of war. Stop the war! Stop the war against man! Stop the war against decency and justice and hope! Shalom to you all!"

Soon after the playing of the Berrigan tape, the demonstration broke up, but some demonstrators lingered in Lewisburg to discuss antiwar activities. Some of them milled around the Academic Quad at Bucknell where Douglas sat on the grass, his head bowed, explaining to his friends that he probably was under FBI surveillance. Sullen most of the day, he several times complained that Bucknell students were "just a bunch of children playing around with drugs," one of his common gripes when he seemed depressed.

That the Lewisburg-Bucknell scene was under unusually heavy FBI surveillance that day there could be little doubt. For in addition to Wenderoth, McLaughlin and the Scoblicks, several other known members or sympathizers of the Resistance attended, including Sister Beverly Bell, forty-three, former director of the St. Martin de Porres Center in Baltimore, a ghetto school where Mary Cain Scoblick was one of the first teachers; Paul Mayer, thirty-eight, a married ex-priest who had been a Benedictine monk for eighteen years after he fled Nazi Germany as a Jewish refugee; and two former nuns, Anne Walsh, twenty-seven, of Boston, a member of the New York Eight, and Marjorie Shuman, forty-six, vice-president of the Martin de Porres Center, and a sister of Notre Dame de Namur for twenty-two years.

Although Douglas seemed to be pleased by the number of Resisters present, Jane's rejection of his marriage proposal had left him in a bad frame of mind. In measured tones of disgust he told Tony Scoblick, "Phil Berrigan's right—marriage *is* going to be the ruin of the Revolution." Scoblick, who resented the comment, later said, "I knew what Mary and I had been through in getting married—the hostility of my father to the idea, the failure to get dispensation, the fact we could not be married in a Catholic church—and I knew Phil knew about this, and it was too sensitive a matter for Phil to have said such a thing."

Inside Lewisburg, Father Berrigan emerged from solitary with an uneasy feeling that a fellow convict might be partially responsible for what he considered the "heat" that prison authorities had turned on him and Eberhardt. He even became suspicious of his trusted courier. Several times he told Douglas to keep away from him. He wondered if Douglas was trying to use him because of his prominence in the Resistance, if he might be expecting something in return for his many favors. On the other hand, he had seen Douglas do favors for inmates who could not possibly have reciprocated. Moreover, Douglas was vociferous in his opposition to the war.

Douglas, repeatedly proclaiming his loyalty, continued to bring Father Berrigan messages of phone calls from his friends, bits of news on the Resistance—and letters from Sister McAlister. The priest thought Douglas had "a kind of un-sophisticated openness" about him "which would pass as naïveté" and began to feel bad about distrusting him. The suspicions were soon forgotten and the bond between the men was resumed.

Outside the prison, Douglas continued working with the Resistance, showing an unusual knack for remaining at the center of the Resistance's communications web. He arranged a meeting in Lewisburg at which several Resistance members, including John Theodore Glick, twenty, a draft resister from Lancaster, Pennsylvania, discussed proposals for antiwar protests. Glick was a member of the East Coast Conspiracy to Save Lives. Upon learning that he and others would hold a later strategy session in Rochester, New York, Douglas gave his roommate, Tom Love, the round-trip bus fare so he could keep abreast of developments. Love returned with information that a raid on a Rochester draft board was being planned.

After Daniel Berrigan's capture on August 11, Douglas told Jane Hoover that "somebody in the movement" should take the priest's place in the underground. "He said maybe he ought to do it," Jane recalled. "He said he could just walk away one morning after leaving prison to go to Bucknell and then he could surface every now and then and release statements and keep the publicity coming in while keeping away from the FBI. He said he thought he ought to volunteer to be the one to do it and said he was going to check with Liz McAlister and see what she thought. He went down to the laundromat a block from our house and placed a call from the pay phone. Afterwards, he said Liz had advised him to forget about it."

Despite the fact his romance with Jane seemed to be going sour, Douglas planned to continue to use her to transcribe Elizabeth McAlister's letters, as he made clear in a letter to Professor Drinnon, who had been spending part of the summer in Westerly, Rhode Island, working on a book. On August 18 Douglas, addressing the professor by his first name as he did everyone he met, wrote him the following letter:

DEAR DICK:

Thought I would let you know what's going around here and also what I have been doing over the Summer.

Yesterday the Pen went on strike and all the guys stayed together. Atlanta, Leavenworth & Petersburg are presently on strike throughout the Federal Penal System. Don't know how long it will last. They are pretty up-tight out there now.

Dan is in Danbury and Phil will be going there in the near future. A good PR move for the Bureau. However, Phil will be going to Allenwood in about three months from Danbury. Some movement people had a meeting with Hendricks and the new warden last Friday for five hours. Phil and the other people really went at them on the human level. The warden asked Phil what he thought of going to Danbury. "I don't need to hold my brother's hand and he doesn't need to hold mine, we both know what we have to do in this life and I trust we are both doing it." Right on. At the present time I have a good system worked out for communications and it cost me a little cash to set it up. I am trying to get something set up at Danbury, but that may be a problem as there isn't too many good people there. Mostly an addict center and they send all the guys that testify for the government there.

Jane Hoover has been handling some very important letters for me. She is intelligent and can keep her mouth shut. It would be a personal favor to me if you would let her attend your class. She is a senior this year and wants very much to be in your History 217P. Also, since I would see her in the morning three times a week, she can deliver communications to me.

Will be anxious to see you. My values have changed a great deal and I feel the system must be changed and the only way I can help is by non-violent civil disobedience. I will be putting my freedom on the line again in the coming year. However, this time it will be for something that I hope will bring a change. I will be with some great people that feel the same way. Something more involved than SS Boards, but they are only boot camps at present anyway.

Please excuse the typing. Liz was down last week and stayed at Zoia's place. Plus another good person. She made several people start thinking.

Have some people coming down on the 29th.

Take care.

Peace
BOYD

Despite Douglas' reference to putting his freedom on the line "in the coming year," he had been enlisting support at Bucknell for his application for an early parole—long before the coming year. Professor Chenoweth, who had high hopes for Douglas' rehabilitation and educational future, arranged a $300 grant for him to work on a project in the university library and also supported his parole application. Chenoweth wrote a letter to Olymp Dainoff, chief of classification and parole at the prison, informing him of the grant and adding, "Mr. Douglas has been conscientious in his studies . . . and he seems determined to make the best of his opportunities to pursue his college education. He appears to be making good progress in adjusting to study routines and classwork requirements."

Douglas impressed other faculty members as well, and one of them, John C. Pyper, assistant to the dean, Colleges of Arts and Sciences, endorsed his efforts to secure an early parole. In a letter to the Lewisburg prison warden, Pyper reported that Douglas had worked diligently and performed well in two courses—introductory psychology and American Government. Pyper termed Douglas' academic record "outstanding," said the convict had been "a model citizen at all times," and added, "If anything can be done to facilitate his early release, it is our opinion that his educational experience would be enhanced immeasurably if he were a regular member of the academic community. We feel that he would gain a great deal by being an integral part of the campus environment."

On its face, Douglas' academic record actually was not so outstanding. He was a C student. But considering the fact he was a high-school drop-out who had not been to school in twelve years, it was an impressive beginning. Moreover, Bucknell professors and administrators were anxious to see the study-release program succeed, which helped explain the enthusiasm of their endorsement of Douglas.

Pyper also sent a carbon copy of his letter and a copy of Chenoweth's letter to Senator Richard S. Schweiker of Pennsylvania. And Douglas himself penned a plaintive note to the senator: "I have been denied parole so many times in the past, that I feel it would be useless for me to write the U.S. Parole

Board. However, I can't see what more evidence they need of my intentions. The Bucknell program speaks for itself. Your help will be appreciated."

Douglas' half-brother, Jack D. Weckman, of Ambler, Pennsylvania, a man of modest means who at the time owned a small printing shop, also wrote Schweiker a letter asking that he support the appeal for parole:

> Boyd has been through a great deal over the past few years. I won't go into detail on this matter as it is something he wishes to forget. He has, if he wishes, a position in my business as a partner. Also, he may live at my home for as long as he wishes. The United States Board of Parole has this information. Boyd would like to continue at Bucknell under better conditions. He is due for full term release in December of this year. It would seem to me, and I would think to anyone else at this time, that further confinement would serve "no purpose."

Schweiker wrote letters of reply to Pyper, Douglas and Weckman saying he was pleased to hear of Douglas' satisfactory work at the college. But he wrote Douglas that he had "no jurisdiction," adding, "I wish to commend your efforts and hope that things work out satisfactorily for you."

Although he had failed to get Schweiker to intervene and was denied a parole, Douglas assured his Bucknell friends that the senator was working on the matter and that he probably would get the parole in the fall. Also, Douglas said, his "rather wealthy" half-brother was a heavy contributor to Schweiker and was using his influence with the senator on the parole matter.

CHAPTER FIVE

The "Kidnap" Letters

With both Berrigans behind bars—Philip at Lewisburg and Daniel at Danbury—some of their friends in the Resistance began searching for a means of dramatic protest and civil disobedience to assure the two priests that the Resistance was alive and well and able to function. Elizabeth McAlister, in a letter to Philip Berrigan, discussed possible courses of action and the fact that some people thought the movement could not "go on" without one or both brothers.

Elizabeth McAlister wrote her letter on August 18, the day after she, Sister Jogues Egan, Paul Mayer and William Davidon, forty-two, a physics professor at Haverford College, Pennsylvania, met with Eqbal Ahmad at the summer home of his in-laws, the Abraham Diamonds, in Weston, Connecticut, where they discussed possible antiwar tactics.

The Diamonds were traveling in Europe at the time and Ahmad and his wife Julie were using the house. Ahmad had known Daniel Berrigan for some time, of course, and so had Davidon, an activist who was a member of the national steering committee of RESIST.

Ahmad said later that he had telephoned the two nuns in New York and invited them up for the weekend, telling them to bring their swimming suits because of the sweltering heat. "And I'll cook you a fabulous meal," promised Ahmad, a superb cook. Davidon, his pacifist wife Ann, a playwright, and their two daughters were invited over, too, because they happened to be passing through town and telephoned to say hello.

Ahmad said that other than telling Sisters Elizabeth and Jogues that "we would relax and talk things over" there was no stated purpose of the meeting. In any event, there was little time

111

for serious discussion until the Ahmads and their guests had consumed a dinner of hot chicken curry and rice, with cold vin rosé the nuns had brought from New York.

About 8 P.M. , after Davidon had put his daughters to bed and the four women had washed the dishes and cleaned up the kitchen, the group assembled on the screened porch. Relaxed now, and sipping cognac, they first discussed the capture of Daniel Berrigan six days earlier, wondering aloud how FBI agents had gotten on his track. Ahmad discounted the possibility an informant had tipped them off and said with some heat: "If he had not broken discipline, he would not have been captured." Daniel Berrigan had been warned to stay away from known friends, Ahmad said, and should not have visited Towne and Stringfellow.

The real problem, they finally agreed, was that after four months of taunting the FBI and keeping the Catholic Resistance in the limelight, the priest had become overconfident. Whatever the reason for his capture, the important thing now, they decided, was to find means of keeping the Resistance going.

As the participants later recalled the ensuing discussion, it began with talk of the possibility of a "non-violent" jail break for one or both of the Berrigans. Daniel was at Danbury, only thirty miles from Weston, and Phil already had been alerted that he was going to be moved there shortly from the prison at Lewisburg. But the idea of trying to free either of them was quickly dismissed as ridiculous.

Then the after-dinner conversation turned to the war and what resistance actions could be effective. The first proposal, Ahmad later said, was to enlist a massive number of people to each buy $200 in stocks at the same time, hopefully choking the communications of Wall Street. He recalled that a second idea was to arrange for 200,000 persons to call Washington simultaneously, clogging the switchboards. The group also discussed staging May Day demonstrations.

Ahmad himself brought up the possibility of a "citizen's arrest" of a government official, a tactic he had discussed previously both privately and publicly. He was so enamored of the idea, in fact, that he had spent a great deal of time talking about it after reading an account in the *Village Voice* of a speech on the subject by David McReynolds, a long-time pacifist and head of the War Resistance League. The subject also had come up at the public antiwar rally on April 21, 1970, at New York's St. Gregory the Great Church. The rally was held a few hours after FBI agents had captured Philip Berrigan and David Eberhardt in the church rectory.

Ahmad recalled that the "citizen's arrest" discussion centered around the feasibility of arresting a Government official without making a public announcement at the same time. The idea was to carry him to a meeting of antiwar intellectuals and question him for a day or two about war policies, and then issue a statement that he had been arrested for "the crime of war" and would be released only if the Government would cease B-52 bombing raids in North Vietnam.

"Some serious objections were raised to this kind of thinking," Ahmad said later. "What would you do if there was resistance? Would this contain an element of a threat of violence? I argued that philosophically that was not important, that you release the Government official unharmed, preferably in front of a press conference. It would dramatize the fact that we cared more for human life than the government did. We knew the government would not stop the bombing because it was more keen to perpetuate murder than to secure the life of one of its officials."

Sister Jogues remembered being shocked by the suggestion and thinking that her usually pragmatic Pakistani friend must have been joking or fantasizing. Although Ann Davidon rejected the idea immediately as contrary to her pacifist convictions, her husband Bill thought it should at least be discussed.

Finally, as Ahmad recalled, it was agreed that such a "citizen's arrest" was too risky, that it could not be carried out non-violently because high government officials would have bodyguards. "But then I said," Ahmad added, " 'Yes, very risky unless you go for someone like Henry Kissinger. He's a bachelor with girl friends and wouldn't want a lot of bodyguards around. And as a professor he would not want police around his academic friends. We would invite him over to dinner with some antiwar intellectuals. Then, instead of serving him dessert, we would serve him with a notice of arrest.' " (Ahmad had met Kissinger at a seminar on Vietnam and their remarks, along with comments by other members of the seminar, were published in a book, *No More Vietnams*.)

Ahmad and the others who participated in the hours-long discussion that night in Weston, Connecticut, said no plans were ever made and they finally dropped the talk of a citizen's arrest and went on to other things. Elizabeth McAlister put it quite another way in her letter to Philip Berrigan, however. And later the participants in the discussion would say that she intended to buoy the priest's spirits and assure him that the movement was functioning and therefore stretched the truth not only on the subject of the citizen's arrest, but on other aspects of the discussion. Whatever the explanation, her letter did emphasize her desire to reassure him, which should have surprised none of their close friends. For this was more than just a communication between Sister Elizabeth McAlister and the Reverend Philip Berrigan on matters of antiwar activities. It was a letter between Liz and Phil on matters of love and affection. An urgent message not to despair, to say that the movement could function well despite the fact that both Berrigans were behind bars. That big things were going on outside "the wall," so big that the Catholic Resistance could arrange to free both Phil and Dan—non-violently, of course, and if that was what Phil wanted. Heady stuff, of course, and the other participants in the discussion later said they thought of it as bordering on fantasizing. But her letter—and his letter in reply, buttressed by an FBI informant—were to form the basis for J. Edgar Hoover's accusation about a kidnap-bombing plot.

As Sister McAlister's letter reflected, imprisonment had not dampened the relationship between the priest and the nun. To use one of his expressions, it may have even "hottened" it. They had first met in 1966 when he already had a long record as an activist and she still wore ankle-length habits and led a cloistered life. At first, it was hero worship from a distance. But his smiling, gregarious, free-wheeling style so impressed her that she soon became active in the antiwar movement. As soon as her order made traditional garb optional, she changed from long, drab habits to short, bright dresses. And she became more outgoing like Phil. At first she had considered him to be rather arrogant, a trait other friends continued to see in him. But as their

relationship deepened, arrogance seemed to be of little con-
sequence. In fact, if the letter was any gauge, she was developing
the same trait.

As usual, she opened her letter with a phony beginning as
though it were a college essay, just in case a prison guard might
discover it in Boyd Douglas' notebook when he smuggled it into
the prison. The letter, headed, "The Lot of Political Prisoners in
the Federal Penal System," began:

> Before engaging a question like federal penal system policy
> toward political prisoners, one must provide a context for its
> operations, both national and local. Otherwise, like a few
> behaviorist penologists, one deals with penal reality as an
> isolated phenomenon, subject in no sense to deeper causes. In
> this limited view, the inmate becomes one victimized by a
> backward penal system.

Without indenting for a paragraph, she dropped the façade
and began writing for the eyes of Philip Berrigan, reflecting on
the fact that he was being transferred to Danbury where they had
no Boyd Douglas to smuggle such letters: "Time considerations
being what they are, guess this will be the last effort along these
lines and may even come too late—who knows." She wrote about
having enjoyed a visit with him at the prison: "The best part was
seeing you and the old fighting spirit and to know first hand that
beyond physical confinement, they had no control over you." She
went on to mention a proposal of an escape attempt that "half
jokingly" she had whispered to him during the visit:

> En route to Danbury might be too soon at this point to do
> anything. Either while there or a later passage is subject to
> discussion. We can also arrange it "non-violently." I say this
> not to exert pressure one way or another . . . . One problem I
> have with that (i.e. either you or D. coming out) is that it says
> the movement can't go on without one of you or both. And I'm
> arrogant enough to think I believe that your being where you
> are is enough to make the rest of us get off our tails to prove
> that it can.

Now her letter reached the crux of the accusation that J. Edgar

Hoover was to level against the Berrigans and the East Coast Conspiracy to Save Lives:

. . . this is in utter confidence & should not be committed to paper & I would want you not even to say a word of it to Dan until we have a fuller grasp of it. I say it to you for two reasons. The first obviously is to get your thinking on it, the second to give you some confidence that people are thinking seriously of escalating resistance. Eq called us up to Conn. last night along with Bill Davidon who, in case people have not told you, has become one of our better people. Parenthetically someone with a knowledge of the scene, a keen sense for tactic & detail & little fear of risk for himself. He's the most central fig. in the Phila. scene & went into the Boards in Georgetown with those kids. Eq outlined a plan for an action which would say— escalated seriousness—& we discussed pros and cons for several hours. It needs much more thought & careful selection of personnel. To kidnap—in our terminology make a citizen's arrest of—someone like Henry Kissinger. Him because of his influence as policy maker and yet sans cabinet status, he would therefore not be as much protected as one of the bigger wigs; he is a bachelor which would mean if he were so guarded, he would be anxious to have unguarded moments where he could carry on his private affairs—literally & figuratively. To issue a set of demands, e.g. cessation of use of B52s over N. Vietnam, Laos, Cambodia, & release of political prisoners. Hold him for about a week during which time big wigs of the liberal ilk would be brought to him—also kidnapped if necessary (which, for the most part it would be)—& hold a trial or grand jury affair out of which an indictment would be brought. There is no pretense of these demands being met & he would be released after this time with a word that we're non-violent as opposed to you who would let a man be killed—one of your own—so that you can go on killing. The liberals would also be released as would a film of the whole proceedings in which, hopefully, he would be far more honest than he is on his own territory. The impact of such a thing would be phenomenal.

Reasons for wanting to do it: it will ultimately be done by someone here & end in fiasco or violence & killing. Eq wants to do it & do it well before anyone else does it badly & I believe he has the know how to direct such an escapade. The major problem as I see it, is the severe consequences for something that is largely "drama" with little lasting effect. Second problem I envision is position of something like this in a movement context, i.e. what next. Some thought would have to be given to that. It seems at least possible to have 2 fairly distinct groups. On the one hand the felons who have scant chance but a chance of remaining anonymous & the big wigs who will prove the "public" aspect of the action who are preserved by their own position as "captives" also. The concept of a film of the trial to be released to TV etc. is phenomenal. Then, his aspect of the war will be at least impeded by his absence & the involvement of all close to him in an investigate [sic] of his whereabouts. Think about it & maybe when I see you in Danbury I can get your thoughts as well as fill you in on where the plan lies.

Sister McAlister signed off, "Right on!" As usual, however, she did not sign her name. She put the letter and a note for Douglas in a separate envelope for him, sealed it and placed it in another envelope addressed to Patricia Rom, the young librarian at Bucknell. Pat Rom passed the unopened envelope on to Douglas.

In a note to Douglas, the nun wrote:

The enclosed is dynamite & I mean it. The proposal (#3) is something no one and I mean no one should know about. I want his nibs to for the reasons indicated & you must of necessity. So it's something I'm entrusting to you. I want him to get this letter if at all possible, if not at least the contents of it.

Douglas, showing an increasing interest in Jane Hoover's redheaded roommate, Betsy Sandel, asked Betsy to transcribe the letter. If she was hesitant, she also was flattered. Moreover, she found it exciting to be around a man like Douglas with all his contacts in the Catholic Rèsistance. In contrast to Jane's shy, soft-spoken ways, Betsy was effervescent and outspoken. She smiled almost constantly and seemed always about to burst into laughter, which she frequently did. Her conversation was liberally sprinkled with "Oh, wow!" and "No, shit!" and other exclamations that had become common on college campuses.

Betsy, whose parents were librarians, came from Hummelstown, a small town near Harrisburg. Like Jane, she had little interest in the Resistance until she met Douglas. A religion major at Bucknell, she planned to teach.

Douglas assured Betsy, as he had Jane, that he was the only one risking punishment in dealing with the contraband letters. She never questioned Douglas' explanation of the need to transcribe the letter, and Douglas carried the copy to Philip Berrigan.

Father Berrigan replied almost immediately. At the top of the first page of his August 22 letter, the priest printed in large letters: THE USE AND EFFECTIVENESS OF GROUP THERAPY IN THE FEDERAL PENAL SYSTEM. Then in his own hand, he began the opening paragraph: "An emphasis on relationship seems to have sponsored a growing tendency on the part of the penal administrators to have inmates in more personal contact with one another and with staff members."

He wrote a long and rambling reply, interspersing expressions of personal endearment ("the best part of the afternoon was seeing your glowing person") with comments on what Sister Elizabeth had written about an escape attempt and the possibility of making a "citizen's arrest." Berrigan interpreted her reference to an escape attempt to also encompass the possibility of their marriage and weighed the advisability of talking it over with Daniel.

Philip Berrigan referred to the suggestion of an escape attempt as #2 and the suggestion of a "citizen's arrest" as #3, as Elizabeth McAlister had done in her letter. He also used initials or various code names for different persons: "brew" for his brother Daniel; "E" or "Eq" for Eqbal Ahmad; "Little Shane" for Neil McLaughlin; "Big Joe German" for Joseph Wenderoth; "the chargé" for Boyd Douglas; and "K" or "Brain Child" or "our angel" for Henry Kissinger. A rather superficial code, but nonetheless a code, and he used it in this lengthy section of the letter:

I don't know precisely how to answer #2. I presume you

refer to a switch back here after a sojourn with the brew. Unless the new place offers unusual potential, would be partial to that. As I see it, there's no overriding reason why we should be together longer than a couple of months. Our approaches to the movement are quite different. Dan is a superior propagandist and does it incomparably well. But I have different views about priorities, as you know. Then in #2, you make reference to us "coming out." As I might have told you before, I would come out only if the movement is much more than it is now—I mean generally, not our crowd—or if it became clear that the feds would stick firm with the 6 yr. bit, which would mean another 34 mos. From their viewpoint, that would be absurd and I'd take my chances on resisting it. You know, if there's no reduction in the offing, there's a good chance that national legislation will be passed in the Fall which opts for release of 1st offenders with 1/3 of sentence served. We'll beat them one way or another.

I don't know what effect Dan's position and mine has had on our people. I would like to think it had none, which is to say, your arrogance love, is well founded. Will you permit me a little compliment, Sister? The big difference rests largely with your coming in. Will you permit me another observation? My affinity for you was not wholly personal—I would have been a fool to ignore what you had to offer to revolution. Re spirit—you insisted on your own freedom, you had incomparable generosity and you loved the Book of Jesus. It was all there, and one merely had to give it time. And when this odyssey is over, I will learn from you—that's why I want six months to do the bends, and get my head together in an atmosphere where I can get several kinds of education—not just philosophical or ideological. But the Communal thing and the Eucharist, and the kind of silence that we've had before, and which has taught me so much.

It occurs to me also that you might refer (in #2) to a confab with Dan about widening the inner circle. To be frank, I've thought a bit about this since a move to Danbury came on the horizon. And decided against it, that is telling him alone. It strikes me that we should announce this new development of sacrament together, or not at all. In any event, you can clear up my confusion about #2 when you come to Danbury. I hear that visiting is much more human there, more frequent, etc.

Now we come to #3. Just between you and me, I have never been overmuch impressed w/Eq. He's dear friend, very helpful in the last months, lovely guy, good ideologue, but still to produce. I think the role of man from Missouri is the safest one with him. (I have this terrible suspicion regarding academics.) With few exceptions, the b-stards will let others go to the gallows without a *serious* murmur. They did it in Germany and they're doing it here. And E is from that strain. You see love, the belief isn't there—Stringfellow at least believes in something. But these are mere reservations—I'd be delighted to be wrong.

About the plan—the first time opens the door to murder— the Tupamaros are finding that out in Uruguay—I hope you're following them (last 2 issues of the Guardian). When I refer to murder it is not to prohibit it absolutely (violence against non-violence bag) it is merely to observe that one has set the precedent, and that later on, when govm't resistance to this sort of thing stiffens, men will be killed. More to the point, the project as you outlined it is brilliant, but grandiose. I've found, with bitter experience, that when people opt for too much, they're either stupid or egotistical (another red light about friend E). Which is to say that grabbing the gentleman will take a force of perhaps 10 of your best people—guarding him, getting communications out, perhaps moving him 2 or 3 times within the week. Now, in addition, to grab a prosecution of liberals would take dozens more, making the network too wide. But even if that were possible, how can it be guaranteed that they would indict him in any sort of real fashion? Then too, the common view is that K is the architect of honorable withdrawal from S.E. Asia, and even some of the liberals believe that. How to get the truth out, i.e., that the economy needs war, and it might as well be there as elsewhere, and that we intend to stay. That might mean a Korean type answer, but then we'd have to hot it up elsewhere. Or go into the dilemma of more serious recession, rising unemployment at home. This is what should be gotten from K, but can the liberals do it?

Nonetheless, I like the plan and am just trying to weave elements of modesty into it. Why not coordinate it with the one against capitol utilities—you should talk more thoroughly with the chargé about this, or with Little Shane or Big Joe

German. To disrupt them, and then grab the Brain Child—
This would be escalation enough.

This comes off the top of my head. Why not grab the Brain
Child, treat him decently, but tell him nothing of his fate—or
tell him his fate hinges on release of pol. people or cessation of
air strikes in Laos. Then have batteries of movement people—
Brain Child blindfolded—engage him on policy. After he had
been taught (the consideration of his safety will make him
more and more human in his answers) get it filmed and
recorded. One thing should be implanted in that pea brain—
that respectable murderers like himself are no longer in-
violable. (This should be done just before release.) And that if
he doesn't work to humanize policy, the likes of him will be
killed by less scrupulous people. Finally, that political
prisoners are the best guarantee of his sweet skin's safety and
that he better get them out of jail.

Taken along these lines, you have both a material and
personal confrontation with the warmakers. The trick to pull
off is to hit them very, very hard without giving them violence
to react to, or justify themselves with.

He can be kept blindfolded, and participants can wear
stocking masks & disguise their voices. It can be done and
brilliantly.

I would sic Eq on it immediately, but tie it in with the *D.C.*
fiasco, and keep his imagination under ropes. If the in-
vestment in our best people is excessive, and if they're
caught—there'd be a massive manhunt—it would mean life.
And this is a factor to be considered.

Grabbing our angel would involve 2 or 3 mos. discreet work.
I would imagine that he would have devices in his car to call
for police assistance at the slightest danger. The thing to do is
find out where he goes for weekends, or where he shacks up—
if he shacks up.

I don't think E can build his own team on this—he'll
probably need help. But a rein of both ideas and modesty
should be kept on him. Furthermore, I don't think he'd be the
easiest guy to work with. Mind you, the criticism comes with
love for the guy, with gratitude for the past months, and with a
recognition of his intelligence and talent. Davidon is good—a
few wrinkles there—but perhaps these have already been
ironed out.

Berrigan, signed off, "Be Well—everything good from me . . . and from the Lord," and gave the letter to Boyd Douglas. Without telling the priest, Douglas wrote a cover note to Sister McAlister telling her that he thought he could obtain a gun that could not be traced if it were needed for the kidnap proposal. He mailed the letter and note to a nun in New York for forwarding to Sister McAlister on August 22—two days after he had delivered the letter from her to Father Berrigan.

The Phil-Liz letters spurred Douglas to boast to Betsy Sandel: "Something big is coming up. Ripping off draft boards is just the beginning." Although Betsy had transcribed Sister McAlister's letter into Douglas' notebook, she had regarded the kidnapping suggestion only as a "citizen's arrest" and even that just as a possible tactic for discussion. She later would contend that she never considered the proposal seriously.

Meanwhile, several members of the Catholic Resistance who had discussed antiwar activities with Douglas in Lewisburg and later with Tom Love in Rochester ran into a trap trying to raid a draft board in Rochester. Douglas had paid Love's bus fare to go to Rochester and learn of plans for the raid, and Love had briefed him prior to the raid. Eight persons were arrested on September 6 in the case, which became known as the "Flower City Conspiracy." Among them were John Theodore Glick, Frank Callahan and Joan Nicholson, who had attended a session in Lewisburg on August 10 with Douglas and several of his Bucknell friends.

The Rochester arrests seemed only to enhance Douglas' enthusiasm for the Resistance, however, and he continued to talk of "bigger action" to come and to impress movement members with his criticism of the penal system for its treatment of persons charged with war resistance crimes. Anticipating his release from prison soon, Douglas arranged for the *Bucknellian*, the Bucknell University student newspaper, to publish two anonymous essays critical of the system. The articles, attributed to "A Revolutionary," included an editor's note that they were written by a former federal prisoner.

The first essay, published September 18, included this paragraph:

To conclude, therefore, federal policy towards prisoners has implicit discrimination written into it—men in prison are criminals, unfit to live with "normal" people. This discrimination becomes more pronounced against those who voice opposition to national policy and purpose. And it becomes particularly pronounced against those who have publicly acted (illegally) in opposition to native immoralities like racism and especially warmaking.

The second essay, published September 25, contended that "the penal atmosphere into which a political prisoner steps is coercive to a high degree." "Pragmatically," the essay continued, "the power structure and the society cannot allow any other fate for its serious critics . . . . When it becomes serious to the point of becoming threatening, it is simply crushed—by police action, by the bench, and in prisons."

Douglas spread the word around Bucknell and among members of the Catholic Resistance that he had written the essays. As some of his acquaintances said, however, the essays obviously were the work of a more sophisticated and better educated person for Douglas' grammar was "atrocious." Actually, the essays were written by the prolific priest, Philip Berrigan, who also found time to help Douglas with his school work.

In October Douglas, who had told Betsy Sandel, just as he had told Jane Hoover, that he was dying of cancer, mentioned to Betsy that he was being taken for medical tests at the National Institutes of Health in Bethesda, Maryland. "Later he told me the tests were negative and he felt great," she said. "He said a drug he was taking was arresting the cancer. He joked that they had handcuffed him when taking him to Bethesda even though he had freedom of movement in Lewisburg."

Although Douglas was now wooing Betsy, he also had turned his attention to Jane Hoover's other roommate—Joyce Frederick. Just before the second essay on the penal system was published, Joyce received a letter from him which mentioned a banquet he wanted her to attend at the prison, referred to a survey of prisons he had said he would make following his release, and included a strange reference to the FBI that she later said she never understood and he never attempted to explain. He wrote:

DEAR JOYCE,

I just finished typing my next article for the Bucknellian.

Joyce, I am really sorry if at times I seem distant to you, but I have been that way since someone close to me testified for the F.B.I.

You know what I am about and I am totally committed to the movement. There is a possibility that I will return to prison and at the least, I will be under government surveillance as long as I live. That also means anyone near me. Anyone who talks about change in the system, faces the possibility of losing his freedom. But that doesn't paralyze me because I don't see my individual life as being so important. I have given my life to the struggle. If I lose my freedom or life in the struggle, well, then, that's the way it will have to be. I want no mysticism in regards to me.

As for you working with the movement, no problem. However, I get warm vibrations from you and I feel we can tune in on the same wave length. You are a very strong and human woman. Possible we can work together.

I know most of the people in the Midwest and East. They are very real people and they trust me. That is why I am always sensitive to certain elements.

The chaplain has my request for you to attend the banquet. He may or may not approve same. Let me know if you get an invitation.

My rather wealthy brother from Philly is paying for a weeks vacation after I am released. Plus a new car. I have been on his conscious [sic] for some time as I did what he was afraid to do. I would like for you to go with me. My only time to relax as the prison survey will start in January, and more involved things.

My function in the movement is organization after people are definitly [sic] committed to some type of civil disobedience. That means after February, my official supervision ends, I will be on the road constantly. From California to New York City.

I want our relationship to be real for both of us. There can

be no half-way point, and you have to support what I am
about. Need I say more? No strings though.

Peace & Love,
BOYD

On the back of the letter Douglas typed a P.S.:

Dr. Rosemary Ruether is coming in Friday evening for a
lecture at 8:30 P.M. She is a friend of Liz and has been on TV
many times. She is very strong on prison reform. I invited her
down and Hammerlee [James Hammerlee, Bucknell's director
of Office of Student Programs] is tickled to death. Talk on The
End of the World & The Birth of the Messiah. See you at 5:00
P.M. for chow.

Mrs. Rosemary Ruether, a theologian at Washington's
Howard University, was one of several lecturers from the antiwar
movement Douglas arranged to speak at Bucknell. She had been
a friend of Sister Elizabeth McAlister since July when Mrs.
Ruether helped the nun publicize a written statement about
political prisoners that Douglas had smuggled out from Philip
Berrigan and David Eberhardt. Elizabeth McAlister also spoke
on the colloquy program. So did the Reverend Philip Linden of
the East Coast Conspiracy to Save Lives, whose topic was: "Civil
Disobedience: Humanism in an Inhumane Society."

Mrs. Ruether had never heard of Douglas when he telephoned
her at her house and invited her to speak at Bucknell. Later she
jotted down this recollection:

Boyd Douglas indicated close contacts with the Catholic
radicals. He probably mentioned his friendship with Phil. He
also indicated a deep interest in prison reform, and said that a
conference was being planned on the "counter-culture." He
wanted me to give one of the talks. I told him that I would give
a talk entitled, "The End of the World and the Birth of the
Messiah" and he asked me how to spell "Messiah" being
unfamiliar with that word. I said "you must then not be an ex-
priest" and he laughed and said he wasn't. At that time he
probably gave me the impression that he was in prison for

some kind of draft action. Mr. Douglas behaved in a very furtive manner, over the phone and later in person. He explained this on the grounds that he was in great jeopardy with the prison officials because he was playing a double role as a prisoner and yet one who was intimate with the Catholic Resistance.

Douglas arranged for Mrs. Ruether to spend the night in Betsy Sandel's dormitory room on campus. At the beginning of the school year in September, Betsy had moved from the apartment in Lewisburg to the New Dorm, a modern girls' dormitory. "I believe it was in the hall of this dorm that I first actually met Boyd," Mrs. Ruether recalled.

He came up silently behind me, and in some way it was indicated that this was "he." He had a smiling, furtive manner, but it became apparent that in Liz's company this manner was taken as a joke. When I mentioned the strangely furtive manner of his phone contact with me to Liz in his company, she laughed and said, "Oh Boyd, you didn't." It appeared that Boyd was patronized as a star convict "convert" whose little hang-overs from bad days must be "understood."

After the colloquy program, Mrs. Ruether, Elizabeth McAlister and Philip Linden and two students went to the Bison, a barn-like cafeteria and student hang-out on campus, for a discussion of antiwar activities. "We talked of 'actions' and strategy," Mrs. Ruether noted. "It was a very deep and intensive conversation, and such escalated actions as shutting down factories producing chemical weapons and other such things were discussed in a very cursory manner, but Liz was consistent in rejecting such actions as soon as they got into any area of bombing that might threaten human life."

Douglas, who missed the discussions only because he had had to return to prison earlier in the evening, later invited William Kunstler, the famous attorney for radicals, to speak on a colloquy program. Kunstler accepted, but ran into a conflicting engagement. One of his colleagues at New York's Center for

Constitutional Rights, the Reverend William Cunningham, a Jesuit and an attorney for the Berrigans, lectured on the program as Kunstler's substitute. During Cunningham's Bucknell visit he was a guest at Professor Chenoweth's house and so was Douglas, who, whenever possible in arranging invitations, invariably included himself.

If Douglas had lost some of his importance to the Catholic Resistance since the transfer of Philip Berrigan to Danbury, he had lost none of his fervor. In fact, he sometimes became so absorbed in antiwar and prison reform activities that he seemed to be obsessed, as though he felt his total energies were now needed because he no longer could serve as a courier for Philip Berrigan. Zoia Horn, the Bucknell librarian, said, "Boyd seemed to have a desperate need to feel important. He bragged about having a knowledge of explosives and said this could come in handy for antiwar activities. I said, 'Aw come on, Boyd,' but he talked quite seriously about it."

Douglas also mailed a letter to Mrs. Rosemary Ruether, thanking her for participating in the colloquy program and enclosing several pieces of written material that he said were important to have published if she could arrange it. He described the material as "very confidential at this time" and added, "Please write me and let me know what your thoughts are on this type of material. You may show it to whomever you feel can keep it in confidence at this time. I plan to be coming to D. C. in January. You may write to me at the below address. Just enclose a second envelope marked 'Boyd.' You stayed in Betsy's room when you was here and we are pretty tight . . . ." He signed off, "In Peace and Love," and included Betsy Sandel's address at the bottom of the page.

The enclosed papers included the two articles on prison reform, actually written by Father Berrigan and already published by the *Bucknellian*, and the piece on homosexuality in prison, for which Douglas also claimed authorship but which had been written by David Eberhardt. Douglas also tucked in the packet a crudely written piece on life in prison. Mrs. Ruether thought the two articles which had been published were "very good." Having met Douglas, she concluded that he had had a great deal of help if he had written the articles, but that he might have been the sole author of the piece on prison life. She assessed it as "without insight and with unnecessary use of vulgar language." It told of the drudgery of prison life: "Work, work, work, yes sir! no sir! What a fucking laugh. They must be nuts."

Douglas fretted over receiving no reply from Mrs. Ruether and finally, on November 26, he wrote her a short "Dear Rosemary" letter: "I haven't heard if you received that literature as yet? I realize it needed some editing. Since I sent that material to you, I have retyped the articles. There is more to come if you feel that there is something we can do with this material. Possibly a small pamphlet devoted to this type of material from the underground of prison?"

The following day, however, more important things occupied Douglas' mind. He heard the news that J. Edgar Hoover had just accused the Berrigans of being leaders of a kidnap-bombing plot. If the news gave him a feeling of self-importance, it also appeared to worry him.

CHAPTER SIX

Paranoia or a Reason for Distrust?

Betsy Sandel was attending a conference on "Liberation Movements in Theological Perspective" at the Chicago Theological Seminary when she read of Hoover's accusation in a newspaper. By now she was Douglas' steady girl friend and he had given her $40—about half her plane fare to Chicago—as a Thanksgiving gift.

"I called him right after reading about it in the paper," she recalled, "and he was so uptight he said he didn't want to discuss it. I was really concerned and I asked him about the letter I had transcribed. He said, 'Oh, don't worry about that. It was flushed down the shitter.' He said 'You know and I know about it, but don't worry. It's confidential.' "

Douglas appeared quite worried, however. He had been telling everyone the date for his release was now firm—December 16. Since he had been leading a rather casual life for a prisoner anyway, he had not seemed overly anxious about his release. But now, with the release date less than three weeks away, he suddenly could hardly suppress his anxiety about it. He became unusually nervous. Always fairly moderate in his drinking habits, most of the time when he did indulge he chewed Certs before going back to prison. But now he began drinking excessively and Certs could hardly conceal the alcohol on his breath. He also started returning to prison in the evenings an hour or even longer past his deadline to be back.

On the day of Hoover's testimony, Joyce Frederick and another senior, Elizabeth Edwards, were trying to study in their apartment when he came in half-drunk. "He kept trying to pour scotch down us, trying to get us drunk," Joyce recalled. "We finally made him leave so we could work. He made me nervous. If he did something you didn't like, you always made allowances because he was in prison. But he could get on your nerves. Unless he had alcohol he was very flat, no joking or anything, just a super serious, very flat party line on the movement. Of course, when he got drunk and started playing around I didn't like that either. He was obnoxious."

Robert Raymond, who had begun dating Jane Hoover again, described Douglas as "really upset" by news of the FBI director's accusation. "After hearing about it," Raymond said, "I told Boyd, 'It's so ridiculous, who would believe this?' And he said, 'It's true enough. It's not just superficial. Only six people know about this—I wonder how Hoover found out.' "

And when Betsy returned from Chicago, Douglas told her, "About this kidnapping thing, it's true you know. They must have tapped Phil's prison cell." Douglas seemed anxious to persuade Betsy that she had knowledge that the kidnapping allegation was factual, even though she had regarded it only as a "citizen's arrest" and a possible tactic that, as far as she knew, had been discussed only in the letter from Elizabeth McAlister to Philip Berrigan that she had transcribed. She had never seen the reply that Douglas had smuggled from the prison.

While Betsy was attending classes one day, Douglas went to her second-floor room in the New Dorm at Bucknell and used her telephone to call Sister McAlister and try to get her reaction to Hoover's allegation. He reached her at the convent in New York, but she was uneasy and hesitant about discussing the matter, especially on the telephone.

"Have you seen Phil or Dan yet?" Douglas asked her.

"No," she replied.

She said, "I just don't know what to say." But Douglas persisted. "Have you heard anything?"

"No," she said, "the whole thing is a kind of anomaly I'm afraid."

"Yeah, well if it [Hoover's statement] hadn't been so specific, it wouldn't have bothered me so much," Douglas said, sighing. "I can't figure it out where they could have gotten it from."

"I know," she said, "that's the mind-blowing thing about it."

"Yeah, yeah," said Douglas, now breathing heavily. "I know. I've just been expecting any day for them to come and pounce."

He laughed as though nervous about the possibility the FBI might arrest him.

But Sister McAlister said nothing and Douglas, apparently sensing her uneasiness, changed the subject. "Do you plan on going to see Phil soon?" he asked.

"Yes," she said, "but I'm not exactly sure when."

Douglas finally told her, "Just be cool, I know Joe [Wenderoth] told me that," and then he added with a laugh, "I was ready to pack and leave."

"What good would that do?" she asked.

"None, but you know what I heard," he said, still laughing. "I listened to Walter Cronkite that night and have read it in the papers. I just couldn't figure it out. Wow! Have they questioned you, Liz?"

Her uneasiness mounting, she shuddered, "I, I don't know anything." She said she had to go, and hung up.

Douglas turned off the tape recorder that he had attached to Betsy's phone and hung up.

Mrs. Rosemary Ruether, meanwhile, wrote Douglas a non-committal letter about the material he had sent her and enclosed in the letter a notice of a demonstration the Catholic Resistance planned for Washington to protest Hoover's accusations as false and repressive.

Douglas began making plans to attend the Washington demonstration, which would start two days after his release from prison. Betsy Sandel agreed to go with him. On December 3, he bought a 1971 Javelin sports car from a car dealer in Sunbury, ten miles from Lewisburg. He wrote a $3,940 check for the car.

On December 8, he wrote Mrs. Ruether that he had received her letter and was relieved to know she had received the written material he had sent her. He was being paroled on December 16, he told her, and he and Betsy would be going to the Washington demonstration.

Two nights later Douglas took Betsy to see *The Serpent*, a play about the mythical origin of man and presented by the Bucknell Players. But he seemed preoccupied and left midway in the play, about 9 P.M., saying he would be back after a telephone call. He went to Betsy's room in the New Dorm, attached his tape recorder to her telephone, and called Father Wenderoth.

Douglas had been planning a "coming out" party on December 18 and was encouraging the antiwar activists he knew to attend. But Father Wenderoth told him that he was not sure he should come. "One thing we're worried about is the conspiracy," the priest said, "seeing it doesn't get any further beyond the eleven of us [the East Coast Conspiracy to Save Lives] and we're trying the best we can to be the spokesmen and take the responsibility for it. The way we look at the thing is being a pure concoction on Hoover's part."

Douglas interrupted at this point, laughing again and returning to the subject of his party: "Yeah, yeah, well, jeez, well, we really, you know, I was planning on some of you coming up here, you know."

"I know," said Wenderoth, explaining that he still did not see how he could attend the party.

Douglas made another telephone call that night, too, but the Resistance people knew nothing about that one. And he never returned to *The Serpent*. The next day he told Betsy that he had gone back to the auditorium, but decided to return to the prison when he found the building's door locked and he could not get in. Betsy accepted the explanation without question.

But Father Wenderoth and several other members of the Catholic Resistance had begun to wonder about him. They knew he made an extraordinary number of telephone calls and they did not always know who was on the other end of the line. Could it be someone other than Resistance people? What did they really know about Douglas anyway, except what he had told them? Was he really so dedicated to the Resistance?

Paranoia was nothing new to Resistance people. And they often felt ashamed about harboring suspicions about other people in the movement. On the other hand they knew the FBI was constantly trying to infiltrate their ranks and consciously following a policy of promoting paranoia. The questions persisted. Had prison authorities perhaps caught Douglas with one of the Phil-Liz letters and turned him into an informant? Had he possibly been a plant for the FBI from the beginning? And what about his roommate, Tom Love? Why had he never been prosecuted for refusing induction? Could there be two or three or even more informants?

If such nagging questions began to bother the Resistance people, the questions had not entered the minds of most of Douglas' Bucknell friends. Professor Chenoweth, for example, wrote a letter on December 11, 1970, to Eugene Curtis, U.S. probation officer in Lewisburg, informing him that Douglas hoped to participate in a university-sponsored study program of prisons after his release on probation the following week.

Chenoweth wrote that Douglas wanted permission to travel to New York, Philadelphia, Baltimore, Washington, Boston and Lorton, Virginia for the survey. Chenoweth wrote:

> While I have not had Boyd in class myself, I have followed his work at Bucknell very closely and believe that he has done very well here. Boyd has paid the cost of his own tuition at Bucknell for a total of three semesters now, and a summer school session. In addition he has worked in the University Library and for the University Buildings and Grounds Department to help pay his way. Last summer, we in the Department of Political Science awarded Boyd a small grant to undertake some work directly related to our departmental curriculum. To my knowledge, and in my experience with Boyd during the past year, he has earned the respect of faculty members and administrators on campus. Also, to my knowledge he has been very careful to observe the rules of the Federal Penitentiary in connection with his study-release program.

Patricia Rom, the Bucknell librarian, permitted Douglas to use her apartment at 60 South Second Street, near the university campus for his coming out party. Douglas sent out hand-printed invitation cards emblazoned with the peace symbol and a motto: "Persevere for Peace and Love." The cards, signed "Boyd," said: " You are invited to my party, Friday, December 18, 1970, at 8 P.M. at Pat's."

Although Joseph Wenderoth had declined to attend the party, he did agree to meet Douglas on December 17, the day after Douglas was released, in the cocktail lounge at Baltimore's Friendship Airport. The priest, suspicious, but concerned that he was being unfair to Douglas, told him again that members of the Resistance were taking the position that Hoover had concocted the whole conspiracy allegation. Douglas repeatedly expressed bewilderment over how Hoover had learned that there had been discussions of kidnapping and bombing. Father Wenderoth, trying to conceal his suspicions, suggested that the source was electronic surveillance of Father Philip Berrigan at Danbury. He told Douglas there had been a rumor of a bug in the priest's cell about two weeks before Hoover's statement.

Douglas again urged Father Wenderoth to attend his party, but the priest declined. A disappointed Douglas drove back to Bucknell.

Also invited to the party were Sister McAlister, Father McLaughlin, the Scoblicks, and several other members of the Resistance. But none of them attended. They, too, had become too uneasy about him.

Douglas poured down one scotch after another at the party and sat off to the side sulking most of the evening. He got sloppy drunk and Pat Rom had to fight off his advances. Finally, he was helped to his car and someone drove him to the apartment of Zoia Horn, who was out of town. He spent the night there.

The next day Douglas and Betsy Sandel drove to Washington to participate in the protest against J. Edgar Hoover. She later recalled that while Douglas had been anxious to get to the vigil at the Justice Department, once there he acted nervous and said he was afraid of being photographed by FBI agents.

After the demonstration, the two of them went to a buffet party in the evening at the home of Mrs. Ruether. Douglas seemed to be depressed during the party, apparently because some of the radicals there avoided him.

Betsy also was becoming a little uneasy about Douglas and sought his assurance that he had not misled her. She told him she had heard "some contradictory stories going around" about why he was in prison. "He had told me about the napalm truck thing in California," she recalled, "but I had heard somewhere that he had been in prison for passing bad checks. I told him, 'If you get to the point that you're a compulsive liar nobody will believe you.' He just sloughed it off."

Douglas visited his half-brother in Ambler following the trip to Washington, but arranged to spend Christmas Day with Betsy and her parents at their home in Hummelstown. "He was wearing a Stetson hat he called a Stetson one hundred, indicating that's what it cost," Betsy said, "and he had a gold cigarette case. He said his father had given him the hat for Christmas. Seeing how I looked and knowing how I felt about material things like that, he said, 'Isn't this ridiculous?' "

Douglas told Betsy he was counting on her going with him to his half-brother's house in Ambler for New Year's Eve. "I had told him before that I would go," she said, "but now I was uncertain of him. I told him I wouldn't be going and maybe we shouldn't be seeing so much of each other. He had been spending a lot of time going out making telephone calls from pay phones and I was angry about that, too."

Erupting emotionally, as he had done when Jane Hoover rejected his marriage proposal, Douglas broke down and cried. He told Betsy that she was the only girl he had really loved other than a girl named Nancy in Rochester he knew as a teen-ager. "And she had red hair, too," he said, looking at Betsy's long red hair.

Douglas finally left, telling Betsy he would call her at 12:01 A.M. New Year's Eve. He said he was going to Ambler.

For the next several days he tried to telephone Sister McAlister at the convent in New York. But she had grown so suspicious of him that she told other nuns at the convent to tell him she was not in.

Fathers Wenderoth and McLaughlin, meanwhile, had written Douglas a letter saying they were sorry they had not seen him in Washington when he was there for the demonstration. They referred to the FBI's "violent and low tactic" in making the kidnap-bombing accusation and added, "There is no greater revolutionary force than oppression.

"You know a plot mentioned by Hoover could never seriously be considered by any of the people that would be a way to further our message of non-violent change," they wrote. "Yet even as an idea it would have to be rejected as impossible since it had no guarantee that injury or loss of human rights of people would be prevented."

In another letter to Douglas, Father Wenderoth said, "The whole Hoover incident has done more to strengthen the hundreds of people who are involved in their conspiracy of conscience against the war and violence." He wrote that the incident was helping get "widespread publicity in order to show what we are about."

Douglas continued telephoning the convent several times a day, leaving messages that it was important for Sister McAlister to call him. She finally decided to return one of the calls to see what he wanted, but upon telephoning his half-brother's home in Ambler, she was told Douglas had left for New York.

On New Year's Eve, Douglas checked into the Sheraton Motor Inn in New York with a young girl named Estelle he had met through a convict at Lewisburg. He wasted no time calling the convent and when a nun answered the phone, he said, "Hello, Jogues?"

"No, she's not here."

"Is Elizabeth in?"

"No, she's not in either. May I take a message?"

"Yes . . . tell her Gary called and tell Elizabeth I'm getting a little upset to say the least because you know I came up here specifically to see her you know and no one has called or anything."

"She called you yesterday," the nun replied, going on to explain that the call had been made to Ambler and he had already left.

Douglas hinted that he would like to be invited to a New Year's Eve party "if Liz and Jogues are going to one," then casually added that he would appreciate an early return call "because I'm going to a little party myself, I have a friend with me you know." With that, Douglas switched off his tape recorder and hung up.

Betsy, who knew nothing about Estelle, got a call from Douglas about 6 P.M. "He told me that Joe and Neil had advised him to call early because the long-distance lines would be tied up around midnight," she later recalled. "He said he was calling from some cheap hotel in New York where he had registered under an assumed name. He said he needed some cash because he had had $200 stolen from him. I wired him $70."

Sister McAlister did not return Douglas' call until New Year's Day. Estelle answered the telephone and told her that Boyd had gone to get tickets to the theater. She left word for him to call her back.

He returned the call shortly, again recording the conversation. Sister McAlister nervously answered the phone. Trying to appear casual at first, she asked, "Did you see the snow?"

"Yes, it's nice out."

"Beautiful and it looks like it's still coming."

"You evidently have been pretty busy lately. Can't seem to ever . . . "

She interrupted sharply, "So have you, buddy!"

"Well, you know," he stammered, clearing his throat. "How's Phil and Dan?"

"Just fine, just fine. I think they're exhausted at this point."

"What do you mean, exhausted?"

"Well you know, they had a lot of visitors during Christmas holidays."

"Well, Phil knows I'm out now, right?"

"Oh, yes."

"Well, I wouldn't want to talk too much here. Would you want to get together or what?"

"I think that's important."

They agreed to meet at ten o'clock the next morning at the coffee shop in the Sheraton Motor Inn. Douglas was still smarting from her earlier refusal to return his calls, but now he had the upper hand. She was as interested in seeing him as he was in seeing her. So when she asked about the location of the Sheraton Motor Inn, he laughed sarcastically and said, "There is only one, Liz, you know, look it up in the phone book."

At the coffee shop the next morning she got right to the point. She later recalled, "I indicated right away that some of us were really concerned that he was an FBI informant. He said people were really being paranoid and I said people have reason to be. He said, 'Do they distrust me?' And I said yes, they felt he had been talking to the government. He said, 'Time will tell.' He said he thought it happened at Danbury, that Dan and Phil's conversations in prison probably had been bugged. He blamed Phil, and said he had a big mouth."

Douglas also told her he wanted to remain active in the

movement and she replied that there was plenty of work to do. It was an uneasy session for both of them. Philip Berrigan had trusted Douglas implicitly, and she could not be absolutely certain he was an informant. She finally left and Douglas said he would be back in touch.

Three days later, Douglas wrote the following note to Fathers Wenderoth and McLaughlin:

DEAR JOE AND NEIL,

Liz was very frank with me and I want to be the same with you.

I have no idea as to what is going on. However, I want you to know that there are other people around here that know what you people are about or was before Hoover's statement. Namely, Tom Love, Jane, Betsy. Liz seems to think that I am the leak and she is really wrong . . . . However, I have no idea if the Feds have been watching me around here. At least not right now. Thats all I have to say on the matter. I do want to say this . . . you people had better be really sure before any rumors go out concerning me. That is one thing I am very serious about . . . .

Take care and peace,
BOYD

If the two priests and other members of the Resistance had known Douglas' real background, they would have been more suspicious of him in the beginning.

The only child of an itinerant pipeline worker, Douglas was born on September 10, 1940, in Creston, Iowa. His parents separated when he was a baby. His mother, Marjorie Hopkins Weckman Douglas, took with her a son by a previous marriage, Jack Weckman, then two years old, but left Boyd with his father, who raised him, taking him around the country on construction jobs. Mrs. Douglas was living with her son Jack and a daughter in a trailer at Falls City, Nebraska, when she apparently drowned on February 5, 1948. Earlier in the day she had complained of feeling ill and spent an hour at a doctor's office. Later her car was found near the icy Missouri River, with footprints in the snow leading to the riverbank. Her body was never found.

Boyd's father regarded him as a problem child, one who lied and was always in trouble at the many schools he attended. The father, who eventually remarried, thought of his only son as "nothing but trouble and heartaches" for him and his second wife, Vivian. From 1947 to 1952 Boyd Douglas attended sixteen different schools in eleven different states—Iowa, Illinois, West Virginia, Oklahoma, Minnesota, Alabama, Texas, Michigan, Wisconsin, Indiana and Pennsylvania.

On September 15, 1952, Douglas was enrolled in Boys Town, Nebraska, an institution for wayward boys and youths from broken homes. There he stayed until June 16, 1956, graduating from the eighth grade and earning a reputation as a bully and petty thief. He entered the ninth grade at Indian Lake High School in Lewistown, Ohio, in the fall of 1956 and remained there until dropping out in his junior year in 1958 after repeatedly getting into trouble. The principal of the high school, Dwight Spencer, recalled that Douglas quit school after being caught stealing $40 from a teacher. He also was put on probation in 1958 after being convicted of passing a bad check.

After another scrape with the law, he enlisted in the Army on November 17, 1959. His uncle, Jack Douglas, of Creston, Iowa, later recalled, "The way I understand it, Boyd had the choice of going to jail or into service. There was something about a ring stolen from a store."

Douglas' background did not adversely affect his Army career, but his continuing criminal behavior was to wreck it. He went through basic training at Fort Leonard Wood, Missouri, trained at the Provost Marshal School at Fort Gordon, Georgia, and qualified as an expert with a pistol and sharpshooter with a rifle. He was promoted to private first class, and on October 17, 1960, was transferred to Korea. Transferred back to Fort Gordon, he was listed by the Army as a deserter in April, 1962. Army records showed him back on the rolls on April 26, but on May 22 he again was listed as a deserter.

He was not apprehended until December 17, 1962, and by then he was in even deeper trouble, charged with impersonating a U.S. Army captain and also with obtaining between $50,000 and $60,000 through fraudulent checks. On January 21, 1963, Douglas pleaded guilty to both charges and was sentenced to six years. He was given an undesirable discharge and imprisoned at the federal reformatory at El Reno, Oklahoma. A month later he was transferred to the prison at Lewisburg.

While at Lewisburg in 1964 Douglas volunteered for a National Institutes of Health experiment to study genetic and other properties of human proteins. The study called for several injections of an emulsion into the muscles of human guinea pigs. Douglas reacted severely to the injections and huge abscesses developed on his arms and legs. He required extensive treatment, including twenty-three surgical procedures over a three-year period at the National Institutes of Health in Bethesda, Maryland.

Left with deep scars on the arms and legs and a continuing need for medical attention, he sued the government for $2 million, charging negligence and medical malpractice. The suit alleged that he would suffer pain indefinitely and "will in the probable future suffer loss of use of both his arms and legs."

He was paroled in April, 1966, from the National Institutes of Health, but quickly developed more abscesses and had to be returned as a patient for additional treatment. While there this time he violated parole and pulled a consummate con job, but one he must have known eventually would be traced to him. He counterfeited, forged and cashed four checks totaling $17,465 at the National Institutes of Health branch of the Bank of Bethesda. The checks, all cashed within a week, were made payable to Boyd F. Douglas, Jr. The first, for $895, was cashed on July 15. It bore the forged signature of Mrs. Ralph Smith and was drawn on the Bank of America, Santa Maria, California. The others, bearing the forged signature of Robert Dunlap, Dunlap Construction Company, were drawn on the Bank of America, San Francisco, in the amounts of $970, $7,400 and $8,200, and were cashed on July 18, July 20 and July 22.

By the time the checks had bounced, Douglas had fled the National Institutes of Health. On October 3, he surfaced again, opening an account in the First Wisconsin National Bank in Milwaukee with a $1,750 check payable to B.F. Douglas and drawn on the Bank of America at San Diego, California. Written on the account of Strand Construction Company, it bore a forged signature, "Carl Strand." Four days later Douglas returned to the bank and sought to withdraw the deposit in cash. A bank auditor, already informed by the Bank of America that there was no Strand Construction Company account, sought to question Douglas and he drew a 9-millimeter Beretta automatic pistol. Pointing it at the auditor and waving it at several startled bank patrons, he backed away, then fled the bank, chased by Thomas J. Tully, a secret service agent who had been in the bank on other business.

Douglas ignored a warning shot fired by Tully and headed for a 1964 Cadillac in the parking lot three blocks from the bank. He jumped into the car, but backed into another vehicle and was stranded when Tully, FBI Agent Robert E. Schoenecker, and a couple of sheriff's deputies who had joined the chase, closed in on him. He finally surrendered meekly, leaving the pistol on the car seat. FBI agents found $2,500 in cash on him.

Imprisoned in the county jail at Waukesha, Wisconsin, he slashed his wrists, but suffered only superficial wounds. A federal grand jury in Milwaukee indicted him on charges of assaulting an FBI agent (Schoenecker) who was performing his duties, and interstate transportation of a forged check. And a federal grand jury in Maryland indicted him on four charges of interstate transportation of forged checks.

Accompanied by a court-appointed attorney, Douglas appeared before U.S. District Judge Robert E. Tehan in Milwaukee on December 15, 1966, and pleaded guilty to all six charges. At a pre-sentence hearing three weeks later Judge Tehan asked him if he had anything to say before sentencing and Douglas replied:

"When I was in the hospital in the National Institutes of Health and when I was given parole from the hospital and they sent me home, and I got to Chicago and overnight I had reoccurrence of the same ailment and which I had to be shipped back to the National Institutes of Health for surgery again, and at this time is when I forged the checks and the hospital bank itself underneath my own name and this is when I took off on this spree, and since that time—I'd like to add, as far as the gun was concerned, I did not have the gun in my possession with intent to hurt anybody, but to hurt myself if I was apprehended. And also, your Honor, I have been in the county jail out here since Christmas Eve with the ailment that I have at the present, which was initiated by this experiment. I was given shots in both arms and both legs, and I have an abscess or the doctors here anyway said they don't know what it is, but I know that it is because I have had fifteen of them, which is in my leg at the present time."

Judge Tehan, noting that deputy U.S. marshals were standing by to take Douglas to the U.S. medical center at Springfield for treatment, sentenced him to five years on each charge, with the sentences to run concurrently. Three weeks later Douglas wrote the judge a letter appealing for a lighter sentence. Judge Tehan treated the letter as a motion for reduction of sentence, but denied the motion. Douglas then faced not only a five-year sentence on the new convictions, but the remainder of the six-year sentence he had received in 1963. His 1966 parole from that sentence was revoked because of the new convictions and because of other parole violations.

Douglas made another attempt at suicide on August 25, 1967, at the medical center, again slashing his wrists, but officials felt it amounted to little more than a protest of his plight and an attempt to get attention.

Through an attorney in Washington, Douglas continued to press his damage suit against the government. The Department of Justice had moved to have the U.S. district court in Baltimore dismiss the suit in 1966 on grounds he lacked standing because he was a fugitive from justice. The court had denied the motion, however, and now Douglas was complaining bitterly that he was maimed for life and should be compensated. His attorney, realizing that physicians at the National Institutes of Health had concluded that Douglas was "a sociopath and a pathological liar," deemed it prudent to settle the $2,000,000 claim out of court. It was settled in 1968, after Douglas had been returned to the Lewisburg prison, and was advised the government suspected some of the abscesses were self-induced. Out of $15,000, he netted only $10,688, with the balance going for attorney fees and other legal expenses.

Not only did Douglas' friends in the Catholic Resistance know nothing of his criminal background, they did not know he had never been in Vietnam, had never been charged with conspiring to bomb trucks carrying napalm and had no record of any involvement in antiwar activities.

After Douglas' release from prison, it finally began to dawn on several of his friends that he seemed to have an extraordinary interest in Hoover's accusations and in rumors that a grand jury had been convened in connection with the FBI investigation. The grand jury probe had not yet been reported in the press. Robert Raymond and Peter Doscher found it extremely unusual when Douglas told them that since they had been around some of the members of the Catholic Resistance they probably would be subpoenaed to testify before a secret grand jury. And he advised them, "If you're subpoenaed, testify, don't perjure yourself."

Douglas himself testified before a federal grand jury in Harrisburg on January 7. The Justice Department's Internal Security Division, which had taken over the investigation, kept the matter as quiet as possible. Before testifying, however, Douglas had told his roommate Tom Love that he had been subpoenaed and Love telephoned Sister Elizabeth and told her. Although there still was no public notice of the grand jury investigation, word of it spread quickly throughout the Resistance.

There was little doubt in anyone's mind now that Douglas was an FBI informant. After he testified he telephoned Betsy Sandel and told her he had answered some of the jury's questions and had pleaded the Fifth Amendment on others. He said he could say nothing further about it because he had been put under an oath of secrecy.

At 8:15 A.M. on the day Douglas testified, FBI agents working in pairs simultaneously served grand jury subpoenas on Joseph M. Joynt, a government employee in Washington, and on his sister, Mrs. Patricia Chanel, at her home in Silver Spring, Maryland, a Washington suburb. Both were ordered to appear the next morning before the federal grand jury in Harrisburg.

FBI agents normally don't serve subpoenas, a routine task usually left to a single deputy U.S. marshal who merely serves the summons and leaves. And normally, witnesses do not get such short notice to appear before a federal grand jury, especially one sitting in another city. But this was no routine case. It involved an FBI investigation of an alleged plot to kidnap a top government official and to blow up federal utilities in Washington. Moreover, it involved J. Edgar Hoover's prestige for he had emphasized privately and publicly that the conspiracy

THE FBI AND THE BERRIGANS

THE FBI AND THE BERRIGANS

existed and that it was directed by the Berrigan brothers and the East Coast Conspiracy to Save Lives.

Joynt, a slim, sandy-haired elevator mechanic at the Defense Department's Forrestal Building, a Catholic and a father of six, was shocked by the talk and manner of the two agents who served the subpoena on him. "They told me that my sister Pat was in a lot of trouble," recalled Joynt, "and later she told me that the agents who served her told her I was in a lot of trouble. They told me they knew I was the engineer who took Joe Wenderoth and Phil Berrigan into the tunnel. I told them 'bullshit.' They told me that I would be considered hostile if I brought an attorney with me to the grand jury hearing and there wouldn't be anything they could do for me."

Joynt's sister, Mrs. Chanel, a divorcee and devout Catholic who went to mass daily, had sometimes made her home a gathering place for Catholic activists in the Washington area. Her brother had never been active in the antiwar movement, but he had been at her house when some of the activists were present. In fact, he had been there at a party in March, 1970, which Philip Berrigan and Joseph Wenderoth attended. Both he and his sister insisted, however, that they knew nothing of a kidnap or bombing conspiracy. She later said that the agents who handed her a subpoena told her that her brother was "going to hang by his thumbs." Mrs. Chanel, a mother of three with a history of mental illness that was known to the FBI, was shaken by the comment and called her brother for reassurance.

Joynt, despite the warning that he would be considered hostile if he obtained an attorney, contacted William Kunstler and the Reverend William Cunningham in New York to represent himself and his sister. Kunstler and Cunningham represented them only temporarily, explaining that there might be a conflict of interest because they represented some of the persons under investigation. At the attorneys' request, U.S. District Judge R. Dixon Herman postponed the appearance of Joynt and his sister before the grand jury until the following Tuesday, January 12, to give them time to obtain other counsel.

On Monday, January 11, FBI agents working in pairs descended on the Bucknell community, beginning about 8:15 A.M. Betsy Sandel was in her room on the second floor of the New

Dorm when she was awakened by a telephone call. A man's voice said, "This is Mr. Smith and I have a message for you. I'm at the desk downstairs." Betsy later recalled, "I told him I wasn't dressed and he said, 'I'll give you a few minutes to get dressed.' I dressed and went down and there were two men there. They asked if we could go somewhere and talk and we went into the lounge. Then one of them laughed—sort of a hollow ha ha—and said, 'My name is Smith, one of the many Smiths in the FBI.' "

The agents handed her a subpeona to appear before the grand jury the next morning and also gave her a routine written statement of her constitutional rights to counsel, to remain silent and to not incriminate herself. "Then they asked me to sign a waiver of the rights and talk to them," Betsy said, "but I refused."

The same morning, within a period of two hours, agents served subpoenas on Jane Hoover, who also lived on the second floor of the New Dorm, and on Bucknell librarians Patricia Rom and Zoia Horn at their Lewisburg apartments. All were ordered to appear before the grand jury the next morning. Jane Hoover signed the waiver card, answered several questions the agents asked, and identified several members of the Catholic Resistance in photographs the agents had. Both librarians refused to be interviewed or to sign the waiver.

Explaining later why she had cooperated with the agents when others hadn't Jane said, "I didn't think I had done anything wrong or knew about anything particularly wrong. If I had thought anything in the letters Boyd had me transcribe was dangerous, I wouldn't have transcribed them. I didn't think anyone would go ape-shit about what was in the letters. They were personal letters and I thought if they were intercepted I might be warned about it, but that's all. Boyd said it was only prison regulations involved and any danger was only to him."

After the agents who had served her with a subpoena left, Betsy Sandel telephoned Arthur Burger, member of a Harrisburg law firm. Burger advised she should take the Fifth Amendment before the grand jury unless she were granted immunity from prosecution. About one-thirty in the morning, Betsy later recounted, "Boyd called me. He didn't know I had contacted an attorney. He said, 'I have a feeling that Kunstler or

somebody from his office will be at the courthouse when you go
to testify and probably will try to talk you into not testifying. But
you know how the movement lawyers are.' Then he laughed. But
he warned me not to listen to the movement lawyers and he said
the prosecutor [Guy L. Goodwin, an Internal Security Division
attorney from Washington] 'is effeminate, but he's tough and
sharp and he'll lead you so don't perjure yourself.' "

Sisters Judith Savard and Grace Marie Russell, both of New
York, also were subpoenaed to appear before the grand jury on
January 12. The two nuns had received letters for Elizabeth
McAlister from Philip Berrigan by way of Boyd Douglas. But
they had passed on the sealed messages without looking at them.
Each testified briefly, then left the jury room.

Betsy Sandel, Jane Hoover, Patricia Rom, Zoia Horn, Joseph
Joynt and Mrs. Pat Chanel all showed up at the sterile looking,
glass and brick federal building in Harrisburg accompanied by
attorneys. They refused to testify on Fifth Amendment grounds
of self-incrimination and Guy Goodwin prepared to seek court
orders granting immunity so they could be compelled to testify or
face a charge of contempt of court.

At 9 A.M. that day the telephone rang in the convent on West
85th Street in New York. Sister Jogues Egan answered and a
man's voice said, "My name is Quinn, can you hear me? Can you
hear me?" After repeated clicking sounds, the connection was
broken.

Sister Jogues recalled, "I waited a few minutes to see if he
would call back. When he didn't, I knew it must be just another
one of the FBI's little tricks so I went upstairs and prepared my
soul for what was coming. In a little while two agents named
Riley and Devine showed up. Devine said, 'We'd like to talk to
you,' and I said that I wasn't interested in answering questions.
They tried to show me some pictures to identify, but I wouldn't
look at them. They then produced a subpoena for me to go to the
federal grand jury in Harrisburg the next morning. And they still
tried to get me to talk, but I told them I would save it for the
grand jury. They asked why I wouldn't talk and I said I think you
people have too many little tricks and they said, 'Don't you have
tricks? Don't Father Phil and Father Dan have tricks?' Then

Riley asked what I meant about tricks and I told him that one thing was the call from 'Quinn,' that I knew it was either him or the other agent. I told them I figured they were Irish Catholics and Riley said, 'we're proud of being good Irish Catholics.' I told them to go home and read the gospel instead of harassing innocent people."

Later that day the grand jury in Harrisburg acted on the case in dramatic fashion without waiting for further testimony. But the word of its action came from the Department of Justice in Washington, not from Harrisburg.

CHAPTER SEVEN

On a Scale of Ten, a Twelve

The Justice Department's public information staff in Washington began calling correspondents and news desks of the major newspapers after 4 P.M. on January 12 to alert them that an important announcement was imminent. The wire associations—Associated Press, United Press International and the British Reuters News Service—all kept correspondents on duty in the fifth-floor press room at Justice. But most newspapers and magazines, television and radio stations that tried to keep track of Justice would depend on calling in twice a day—or being called when a development of major proportions was about to break.

There was a difference in the calls that day, however—a note of special urgency that piqued reporters' curiosity. Robert L. Stevenson, a member of the staff who prided himself on being "a public information officer, not a publicist," confided to reporters he called: "On a scale of one to ten—with ten the newsiest—this one would be twelve."

Within an hour, the calls had attracted between fifteen and twenty reporters who were passed through the department's tight security precautions that Deputy Attorney General Richard G. Kleindienst had instituted in 1970 after a wave of bomb threats. The reporters gathered in the dilapidated press room directly across the muraled hall from Attorney General Mitchell's suite of offices. (Later that year, the department was to spend $3,300 moving the press into more modern quarters, located 300 feet further down the hallway—out of sight of the flow of visitors in and out of Mitchell's office.)

Reporters killed time by glancing at the journalistic graffiti their wire service colleagues had tacked to the bulletin board.

There was a letter from a fledgling Justice Department correspondent to J. Edgar Hoover, following up a chance encounter they had in the hallway by asking for an interview appointment—a syrupy proposal that drew a guffaw or a shake of the head by most who read it. The FBI director rarely submitted to interviews and then only by newsmen he was assured were not members of what he called "jackals of the press"; there were photographs of the FBI director, clipped from the bureau's own *Law Enforcement Bulletin*, which usually ran two or three of the director in each issue; and there were the latest Martha Mitchell quotations.

As the wait stretched past two hours, the reporters began to grumble and speculate about the nature of the impending announcement. One suggested that Hoover would resign or be kicked upstairs to a newly created honorary position with little real power. But most of the newsmen dismissed the idea. That possibility had been dubbed the "Hershey solution," after Lewis Hershey, the outspoken selective service director whom President Nixon had eased upstairs. Mitchell, the waiting reporters figured, would seek to minimize, not play up such a development. Besides, despite the unprecedented criticism of Hoover from press and politicians, the reporters thought there was virtually no chance that a "law and order" administration would dump him.

The suggestion that it had something to do with Black Panthers seemed more likely to some of the waiting reporters, but no one could think of a specific investigation that had ripened to the announcement stage. Not one newsman voiced the idea that the government might be dropping the other shoe on Hoover's accusation that the Berrigans headed a group of militant Catholics planning to kidnap a high government official and blow up underground utility lines serving Washington.

Thus, when the Justic Department's public information director, John W. Hushen, appeared carrying stacks of a four-page press release and an eleven-page indictment, even the wire service reporters, accustomed to scanning complicated legal papers before grabbing their phones to dictate a bulletin, did a doubletake. The news release stated:

Six persons were indicted today on charges of plotting to blow up the heating systems of Federal buildings in the Nation's capital and also to kidnap Presidential Advisor Henry Kissinger, Attorney General John N. Mitchell announced.

One of those named in the indictment was Reverend Philip Berrigan, forty-seven, presently serving a prison sentence at the Federal Correctional Institution at Danbury, Conn., for his participation in the destruction of Selective Service records in Catonsville, Md., in 1968.

The release added that FBI agents had arrested the five other defendants, "including a Catholic nun, two other priests and a former priest. The seven-count indictment was returned by a federal grand jury in Harrisburg, Pa., following an extensive investigation by FBI agents."

Contrary to the usual practice when a news release cited arrests and investigation by the FBI, there was no mention of Director J. Edgar Hoover. Nor did the official department statement make reference to his Senate testimony nearly seven weeks earlier outlining such a plot and alleging it was the work of the East Coast Conspiracy to Save Lives.

The Justice Department's failure to include Hoover's name in the news release infuriated the FBI director. He told several subordinates that Attorney General Mitchell was trying to steal publicity from him, and he made a blue-ink notation to that effect on one of the records of the case. Although Hoover and Mitchell had a close working relationship, a longtime FBI official involved in the Berrigan case investigation said, "Actually, Mr. Hoover didn't like any superior, I don't care who it was. On the surface he got along with Mitchell, but he didn't like to think anyone was over him. Deep down, he never believed anyone was."

Hoover said the East Coast Conspiracy was headed by Daniel and Philip Berrigan. Almost a year before, the conspiracy had publicly identified its eleven members—neither Berrigan was among them—and claimed responsibility for destroying draft files in Philadelphia and disrupting General Electric offices in Washington.

Daniel Berrigan's name first appeared in the twenty-first paragraph of the twenty-seven-paragraph press release, leading off a list of seven persons named as co-conspirators, but not indicted. The only one of the thirteen persons cited in the indictment who was a self-proclaimed member of the East Coast Conspiracy to Save Lives was the Reverend Joseph R. Wenderoth. Neither the release nor the indictment mentioned the organization that Hoover had focused so much attention on.

In addition to Philip Berrigan and Wenderoth, the defendants were Sister Elizabeth McAlister, the Reverend Neil R. McLaughlin, Anthony Scoblick and Eqbal Ahmad.

Listed with Daniel Berrigan as co-conspirators were Sister Jogues Egan, Sister Beverly Bell and Marjorie A. Shuman, an ex-nun, and Paul Mayer, a former Benedictine monk, all of whom attended the July demonstration outside the gates of Lewisburg Penitentiary protesting the treatment of Philip Berrigan; William Davidon, the Haverford College physics professor who was among those present at the Diamond home in Weston, Connecticut, when the possibility of a citizen's arrest was discussed; and Thomas Davidson, twenty-five, a conscientious objector and one-time Eagle Scout who lived in Washington and worked with such peace groups as Clergy and Laymen Concerned about Vietnam and Fellowship of Reconciliation.

The indictment charged the defendants with conspiring with the un-indicted co-conspirators "and with others whose names are not known to the Grand Jury" to obtain maps and diagrams of the tunnels beneath Washington, D.C., that contain heating systems for government buildings and then to explore the tunnels to pinpoint the locations of the heating pipes.

The conspirators were to obtain dynamite and other explosive devices which they would set off on Washington's Birthday in 1971 at five locations in the underground tunnels to knock out the sytems heating federal buildings, the indictment alleged.

On the next day (the indictment did not specify which Washington's Birthday the plotters were supposed to have had in mind, the traditional February 22 or February 15 to which Congress moved it in 1971), the conspirators would "seize, kidnap, abduct and carry away Presidential advisor Henry Kissinger, and issue a statement that his safety depends upon the satisfaction of certain demands to be made by the defendants and un-indicted co-conspirators."

Although the indictment did not list the demands, press accounts recalled that Hoover had testified the "plotters would demand an end to United States bombing operations in Southeast Asia and the release of all political prisoners at ransom."

As for possible punishment, the indictment said the defendants' acts violated Section 1201(C) of Title 18, United States Code, conspiracy to kidnap, a point that would later assume major importance, and the general conspiracy law—Section 371 of Title 18. Conviction on the kidnap conspiracy count could be punished by a maximum of life imprisonment. The general conspiracy violation carried maximum punishment of five years in prison.

Sister Elizabeth and Philip Berrigan were also charged with three counts each of attempting to smuggle communications in and out of Lewisburg Penitentiary. Conviction on a single count could be punished by ten years' imprisonment.

The indictment listed twenty-two overt acts the defendants and co-conspirators allegedly committed to carry out the conspiracy, beginning with an April 1, 1970, entry into the underground tunnels by Philip Berrigan and Wenderoth. The acts included telephone calls and trips some defendants made to Lewisburg, a meeting by five of them there the day of the demonstration outside the prison, Sister Beverly Bell's move to Washington, the Connecticut meeting August 17, a letter from Sister Elizabeth to the imprisoned Philip Berrigan and a reply containing "instructions," and Wenderoth's allegedly discussing the tunnel system with an engineer for the General Services Administration, the government's housekeeping agency.

All the defendants were mentioned in at least one overt act, as were all of the co-conspirators, except for Daniel Berrigan and Thomas Davidson.

That same day reporters covering the federal building in Harrisburg could not obtain a copy of the indictment, which the grand jury sealed before handing up. This was to give the FBI time to round up the defendants before the charges were made public. But the arrangement also insured the action would receive immediate national attention, moving as an "urgent" bulletin by the wire associations from Washington.

In picking up the defendants, the FBI used the kind of show-of-force precautions usually reserved for highly dangerous suspects. Sister Elizabeth, accompanied by her superior, Sister Jogues, had gone to Newark that Tuesday afternoon to meet with the Jesuit lawyer William Cunningham. Sister Jogues had been subpoenaed by the Harrisburg grand jury to appear the following day and wanted Cunningham's counsel. Three FBI agents approached the two nuns and Cunningham as they were walking across a parking lot outside a law office where they had been meeting.

"Sister Liz, you are under arrest on an indictment handed down by a federal grand jury in Harrisburg, Pennsylvania," said the agent she had come to know as Riley. "I presume this is your attorney," he said, gesturing toward Cunningham.

"What are the charges?" Cunningham asked.

Another agent replied: "There are about twenty of them . . . ."

Sister Jogues remembered that Sister Elizabeth's mouth kept dropping open as the agent went on, explaining that he had no copy of the indictment with him. "She was stunned," the nun said.

Sister Jogues was to react similarly several hours later when just before midnight she learned that the indictment named her as a co-conspirator. She had been subpoenaed that morning to testify before that same grand jury. She said that the concept of a grand jury summoning a person it alleged to have participated in a plot under investigation "outraged" her, a reaction she later coupled with other legal reasons in refusing to testify.

The agents arresting Elizabeth remarked that she had traveled a great deal that day.

"Yes, and I've had company all the way, huh?" the nun asked. At 6 A.M. that day, she had left Manhattan for Philadelphia, then to Tarrytown, back to New York and across the Hudson to Newark.

Five cars carrying some fifteen agents made up the convoy assigned to bring Sister Elizabeth to the Newark FBI office. During the short ride, she remembered that one agent radioed in: " 'We've got the package'—meaning me—'and we're coming in.' " She recalled that an agent continually called her "Sister Liz."

"I finally said: 'Please, my name is Elizabeth. My friends call me Liz.' "

Nine agents crowded into the elevator that took her up to the office, she said. "When we got off, one of the agents asked for a nurse. He explained that she was to do a search of me and said that if they couldn't find one, they would have to do it themselves. I said: 'You will not.' " But the matter was not pressed, and the nun was not searched.

Elizabeth recalled that the agents had difficulty accepting the fact that her coat had only one pocket. One asked: "The coat has one pocket—no sewed-up seams, no hidden compartments?"

While agents asked whether she was ready "to answer questions . . . to make a statement"—she declined—others were calling their homes.

" 'We got her,' " she remembered one saying. " ' I'll be late for dinner.' It was a constant procession."

Elizabeth spent the night in the Bergen County Jail and was released the following day on $50,000 bail. She told newsmen she was "stunned" by the indictment. "We have all stood for nonviolence, and such acts as those described to me would be violent," she said. Marymount College where Sister Elizabeth taught art history suspended the nun two days after the indictment, until final disposition of the charges, but she was kept on the payroll.

Several days later, in the familiar surroundings of the five-story, brownstone convent where she, Sister Jogues and six other nuns lived, Sister Elizabeth elaborated on her reaction. Alternating between sipping coffee and chain-smoking, the nun, clad in yellow mini skirt, beckoned one of the authors of this book to sit beside her on the couch. She turned up the volume on the table radio, explaining that would prevent their conversation from being monitored electronically.

"They have put us in the big league," she said, her hand shaking and sloshing coffee in the saucer. "They have taken simple people and put them in the big league. We're not in the big league. To do what the government charged would be absolutely contradictory to everything all of us stand for."

The reaction of Catholic hierarchy to the sensational charges was a study in contrasts. Sister Elizabeth said that Terence Cardinal Cooke of New York had sent a message to Sister Jogues through his secretary saying that he was praying for her. Elizabeth covered her mouth as if to stifle a snicker when she related the message.

When a newsman attempted to interview Cardinal Cooke soon after the indictment, his secretary, Monsignor Eugene V. Clark, indicated the prelate did not want to be drawn into the inner-church controversy over the Berrigans. He said: "The Cardinal would rather not be interviewed on this matter since he doesn't quite know which end is up. He feels that no matter what he said, it would end up applying to the Berrigans."

In Baltimore, however, Lawrence Cardinal Shehan went to city jail the night of the indictment to visit his two subordinates, Wenderoth and McLaughlin, and ex-priest Scoblick. When some in the Catholic community reacted critically, Cardinal Shehan issued a statement that began with a quotation from the Gospel According to Saint Matthew. The text portrayed Christ at the last judgment commending the righteous for their humane acts.

"I was in prison and you visited me. Come. I was in prison and you visited me not. Depart. As long as you did it to one of these, my least brethren, you did it to me."

Said the Cardinal: "My visit to the two Baltimore priests in jail has its full explanation in the above quotation of scripture."

After his visit, Cardinal Shehan requested that the three defendants be released. But U.S. Magistrate Clarence E. Goetz refused and set bail at $50,000 each. The defendants were taken to Harrisburg. In a statement issued through their lawyer, they accused the government of trying "to crush the antiwar movement." They said that "to attribute kidnapping and bombing to priests who have neither the philosophy nor the resources to support such activity" revealed "the desperation of men who have decided to stop at nothing" to destroy the peace movement.

Despite the vigorous opposition of the Justice Department, United States District Judge R. Dixon Herman halved their bail and released them to the custody of Cardinal Shehan under the added condition that they not travel outside of Maryland and Pennsylvania. The bail money—$7,500 or 10 percent of the total bond—came not from the church but from private donations collected by ten priests, headed by Father Joseph M. Connolly, the white pastor of St. Catherine of Siena Church in the midst of a sprawling black Baltimore ghetto.

Connolly said $2,000 of the funds came from laymen, nearly all the rest from Catholic clergy. "Even an Episcopal priest gave $500. Any time you get sixty-nine honky-ass priests to put up $5,000, you've got something," Connolly said.

Ten days after his visit to the jail, Cardinal Shehan had received 145 letters commenting on his support of the defendants—106 praising him and 39 registering opposition. However, telephone calls—his aides handled more than 100—ran two-to-one opposed.

"As individuals who long for and work toward brotherhood and peace," wrote a non-Catholic couple in Wilmington, Delaware, "we recognize how meaningful is the position you have taken."

A nun wrote: "You are an example of Christ's concern for all men."

But a family, identifying its members as "disgusted Catholics," wrote that they would give no more money to the church unless their funds would be used to buy "one-way tickets for you and every radical un-American priest in this archdiocese to Red China and Korea."

And a woman who indicated she strongly opposed changes in liturgy directed by Vatican II, especially celebrating mass in English, said in a letter: "How dare you! You who should be fired yourself for past offenses! You devil! . . . You're the follower of the Devil."

The fervor with which the government fought releasing the three Baltimore defendants, who were required to report to Cardinal Shehan every other day, provided an inkling of what lay ahead. Guy L. Goodwin, the Internal Security Division lawyer who supervised the investigation from the start, stressed in the bail hearing that convictions could result in life imprisonment for the men. He said that the target day for the alleged plot—Washington's Birthday—had not yet occurred, thus implying that if the defendants remained free Kissinger and the heating pipes would be in danger.

Eleven witnesses, including five pastors of Baltimore parishes who knew the defendants, swore to their veracity and urged that they be released on bail.

E. Clinton Bamberger, Jr., dean of the Catholic University Law School in Washington, testified of Father Wenderoth: "I would believe everything he told me."

Goodwin popped up, and, as if he could not believe Bamberger would make such a statement, asked: "Would you believe him if he signed a leaflet saying he raided General Electric files and draft files at three Philadelphia locations in February, 1970?"

Bamberger, noting that Goodwin had not distinguished between signing a statement of responsibility for such illegal acts and actually performing them, asked to see the leaflet, but Goodwin refused.

Only the arrest of Ahmad had a humorous side to it. Two FBI agents came to Ahmad's second-floor offices at the Adlai Stevenson Institute of International Affairs in Chicago around 7 P.M. on January 12. Other agents waited in four cars outside the Robie House, one of Frank Lloyd Wright's earliest buildings, which served as the institute's headquarters.

Connie Ferrin, who worked in the office next to Ahmad's, was first aware her colleague had visitors when he shouted to her.

"I've been arrested. Will you please call my wife? Will you please call Julie?"

"What are you arrested for?" Connie asked.

"What have I been arrested for?" Ahmad asked the agents.

"Conspiracy," explained one of the FBI men.

"Conspiracy to do what?" Connie asked.

"Conspiracy to do what?" Ahmad asked his captors.

"Conspiracy to kidnap a high government official," an agent replied.

"Connie, conspiracy to kidnap a government official."

Ahmad later recalled that he did not learn about the tunnel charge "until they brought me newspapers in jail the next day and I read the stories."

After a hearing, his bail was cut from $75,000 to $60,000 and he was released the afternoon of January 13. A member of the University of Chicago faculty put up $2,000 of the $6,000 cash required, and the remainder came from other scholars at the institute.

At Danbury, the Berrigans issued a statement on January 13 denying the allegations through the attorney who defended them at the Catonsville trial, William M. Kunstler. The priests, who had responded to Hoover's Senate testimony by challenging him "either to prosecute us or publicly retract the charges he has made," said in their joint statement:

> Thirty-eight years ago, the Nazi party burnt the Reichstag in order to stampede the German people into supporting a policy of repression at home and militarism abroad. Yesterday the government of the United States, for much the same purposes, created a grotesque conspiracy. . . .
>
> The objective is a simple but deadly one—to destroy the American peace movement by creating caricatures of those who oppose the war in Southeast Asia. Knowing that most Americans are against the war, the government has embarked on a most tragic and outrageous course—to stigmatize millions of morally dedicated opponents of our military involvement in Indochina as violent and deranged people. These indictments are a stark cover-up for our past and future mad adventures abroad and our inability to solve the pressing problems of our people at home.
>
> If the Germans had not been panicked by the Reichstag charges, perhaps the world might have been spared the nightmare of genocide and war. If the American people will only recognize the true nature of the motivation behind the charges against us and our brothers and sisters in the peace movement, then it will be possible to halt our pellmell retreat from reason. We call on all our fellow citizens—whatever their political or religious beliefs—to repudiate the use of

fabricated accusations and state trials to facilitate the implementation of foreign and domestic policies that may, if unchecked now, make peace, freedom, truth and love anachronisms of another day.

Kunstler said the Berrigans regarded the charges as "a colossal blunder into which the government was stampeded after J. Edgar Hoover, director of the Federal Bureau of Investigation concocted them to justify an appropriation for an additional thousand agents."

The co-conspirators were equally strong in their denials and denunciations. Mayer characterized the indictment as an attempt to "stifle the voices of dissent."

Davidon, reached in Culebra, Puerto Rico, where he was working with the Quaker Action Group, a pacifist organization, said the indictment represented Hoover's "wild determination to discredit those who have been struggling by non-violent means to produce fundamental changes in our society."

Sister Beverly Bell, whose co-conspirator role was outlined in two overt acts—having "met in Lewisburg" with three of the defendants and another unindicted co-conspirator on July 16, 1970, and having moved to Washington August 20, 1970—discussed those actions in an interview with Morton Mintz of the Washington *Post* on January 17.

Sister Beverly, whose appearance and demeanor could have won her the role of a nun in a Barry Fitzgerald movie, said that to view her visit to Lewisburg in any way as conspiratorial was "incredible." She said she drove there from Baltimore to attend a rally at the gates of the penitentiary protesting the treatment of Philip Berrigan. She said she entered no building during her ninety-minute visit there, and that she returned to Baltimore after the rally.

As for the move to Washington, she said this was to pursue graduate studies which she had not done for ten years, an unusually long period in her order, Sisters of Notre Dame de Namur. Sister Rosalie Murphy, her provincial superior, backed her statement, noting that the nun was one of 190 in the province who drew new orders in late July or early August, 1970.

"The whole thing is preposterous," said Sister Rosalie.

Representative William R. Anderson, who had led the criticism of Hoover for his November 27 testimony, issued a statement the night of the indictment saying he was "delighted that the matter has finally been removed from the trial-by-headline arena. At last the matter is in proper judicial channels."

But twelve days later, the Tennessee Congressman, so soft-spoken and reserved that the strength of his statements often took listeners by surprise, became embroiled with another Administration official, Vice President Spiro T. Agnew, in a dispute over the case.

Anderson, addressing the board of the National Council of Churches in Louisville on January 24, spoke warmly of the imprisoned Berrigans—"their dedication to peace, to the poor, to the hungry and naked. Let us know them as dedicated, decent, intellectual men serving God and country in a federal penitentiary."

He said that although as a Congressman he could not "condone illegal acts because to do so might incite a lawless society, I must applaud Fathers Philip and Daniel Berrigan for the extraordinary care they exercised to be certain no person would be injured in body or prestige by their draft record acts. Their sacrifice in prison, like Jesus and his apostle Paul before them, is causing an awakening of national conscience, including mine, and I am sure, yours."

Anderson urged the churchmen to take steps to "dampen any violent potential" of demonstrations on behalf of the Berrigans. He said demonstrations were being promoted and were "inevitable." (However, no major demonstrations ever developed.)

The next day, Agnew, reacting to a newspaper report of Anderson's speech, issued a five-paragraph statement accusing the Congressman of calling for "nationwide demonstrations against the indictment" and of characterizing "the defendants as heroes."

"If our system of jurisprudence is to survive, I deem it imperative that Americans reject this emotional, self-serving claptrap," the Vice President said. "Demonstrations, while constitutionally guaranteed when lawful and peaceful, are not necessarily the best fact-finding bodies. Impugning the motives of that Grand Jury and the investigative agencies which brought the matter to their attention—in other words, popping off for political advantage prior to trial—is nearly as reprehensible as finding the defendants guilty before they have been tried and convicted. What it amounts to is a vote of no confidence in our judicial institutions, and it ill becomes a member of the Congress."

In the same statement, Agnew borrowed a page from the FBI director he so fervently admired by stating that the federal grand jury in Harrisburg had "returned indictments against the Berrigan brothers and others in connection with a kidnap plot" and he referred to them as "defendants." The Vice President, who once taught at the Baltimore Law School, had either missed or ignored the point that Daniel Berrigan was charged with no crime and faced no trial, having been listed only as an unindicted co-conspirator.

Anderson immediately countercharged that Agnew "has used his high office to comment on a serious matter without having the facts before him." The Congressman denied ever encouraging any demonstrations, saying: "Demonstrations are simply not my cup of tea. Nor have I referred to the Berrigans as heroes, though history may ultimately so judge them."

The peppery exchange illustrated that contrary to Anderson's own expectation that the case had "been removed from the trial-by-headline arena," the political potential was more acute than ever.

Not all Administration figures, however, treated the matter as one that had placed the nation in such dire peril. Kissinger, who had been accompanied by secret service agents since September at FBI request, was widely quoted after the indictment as quipping that he had heard "three sex-starved nuns" concocted the plot. But Kissinger, who enjoyed the reputation of being the White House "swinger," claimed he had been misquoted and apologetically called Cardinal Cooke in New York who had made known his displeasure over the remark. He did josh that the bodyguards were tarnishing his reputation. And he said his staff had written President Nixon "stating that under no conditions am I to be ransomed."

Privately, Kissinger told friends he knew nothing about the plot and had asked no questions about it because he found the whole matter so distasteful. And he expressed respect for the depth of the Berrigans' commitment to peace.

The press reacted to the indictment with an extraordinary amount of skepticism. The St. Louis *Post-Dispatch* said in an editorial: "The federal conspiracy indictment against the Reverend Philip Berrigan and five other pacifists must be one of the flimsiest on record." The New York *Times* found the indictment to be "itself almost a conspiracy against sober reason."

The roughest treatment of all came from columnists who refused to take the charges seriously.

Clare Crawford, society columnist for the Washington *Daily News*, questioned: "Are the Brothers Berrigan putting the FBI on?" She reported that one theory making the rounds of the Washington cocktail party circuit was that the Berrigans devised "an outlandish plot" to regain a platform because they had "only their cellmates for an audience." According to the theory, the priests "will tell the world it's a spoof when they come to court."

Arthur Hoppe, the syndicated columnist for the San Francisco *Chronicle*, said the charges had inspired his friend, "Sherman the Scriptwriter," who had been trying for twenty years to sell Hollywood a sequel to that highly successful film about nuns and priests, *Going My Way*.

As Sherman saw it, the title would be *Trashing My Way* and the film would open "in the rectory of St. Bridgit's Church." Six nuns and priests would be sipping tea, with the sisters "knitting fuses."

Hoppe wrote that he finally "tossed the script back at Sherman. 'You've gone crackers, Sherman,' I said. 'Nobody but a certified nut would believe a kooky plot like this.'

"Sherman drew himself up to his full height. 'That,' he told me coldly, 'is no way to talk about J. Edgar Hoover.' "

But while the humor columnists rejoiced at the wealth of material they had been provided, the FBI, the rejuvenated Internal Security Division of the Justice Department and the federal grand jury at Harrisburg accelerated their deadly serious investigation.

CHAPTER EIGHT

The Fishing Expedition

The shock waves from the indictment were still rolling the next morning when Guy L. Goodwin, the government attorney, disclosed that the Harrisburg grand jury would continue its probe and possibly indict others. After being granted immunity, Betsy Sandel and Jane Hoover, the Bucknell coeds, each testified for about four hours. They told of transcribing Sister Elizabeth's letters to Philip Berrigan into Boyd Douglas' notebook—corroboration for the heart of the indictment that the grand jury had handed up the day before. The crucial information they provided, however, covered no new ground.

Guy Goodwin ran the show, asking all the questions. About two hours into the session, Jane recalled, one man on the jury interrupted.

"I can't hear her. Will you tell her to speak up?"

During Betsy's four hours—she testified for about thirty minutes on the day of the indictment and for about three and one half hours the next day—no juror broke the train of Goodwin's questioning. But at the end, the attorney asked if there were any questions.

Betsy recalled that, "a guy at the back, on the right, said: 'I'd like to have her answer all the questions again and speak up so I can hear her.' "

The experiences of Betsy and Jane before the grand jury were similar to those of scores of witnesses that year in at least eight other cities across the United States where Federal grand juries probed actions by radical elements of the antiwar movement. The sharp upturn in such grand jury activity came at a time when many serious students of American jurisprudence questioned whether the juries had been diverted from their

164

historical mission of protecting the innocent and serving as a buffer between the accuser and the accused. Critics contended the grand jury had been turned into a rubber stamp for the prosecutor and one that granted such investigative agencies as the FBI the authority to compel a person's appearance through a subpoena, an awesome power that Congress had refused to extend to the FBI.

The grand jury, rooted in English law, can be traced at least as far back as the reign of King Henry II in the twelfth century. Originally made up of twelve "good and lawful men" of each community, its job was to identify local offenders and charge them for trial by a traveling judge. As government prosecutors assumed the accusatory function, the grand jury took on its buffer role, conducting secret hearings to pass on the merits of serious charges before making them public. Thus by 1682, John Somers, lord chancellor of England, commented after a grand jury refused to indict Lord Shaftesbury on treason charges: "Grand juries are our only security inasmuch as our lives cannot be drawn into jeopardy by all the malicious crafts of the devil, unless such a number of our honest countrymen shall be satisfied in the truth of the accusations."

Brought to America by the colonists, the grand jury became one of the earliest official institutions to oppose British rule. In 1765, for example, a Boston grand jury refused to indict leaders of the Stamp Act riots. The Founding Fathers, mindful of the dangers of oppressive prosecution, provided for the grand jury in the Fifth Amendment to the Constitution: "No person shall be held to answer for a capital, or otherwise infamous crime, unless on a presentment or indictment of a Grand Jury. . . ."

Because grand juries were thought of as a screening mechanism to protect the innocent rather than as a means of securing evidence for use at trial, not all the rights accorded witnesses and defendants in a trial were extended in the grand jury room.

A series of Supreme Court decisions in the early 1900s limited the rights a citizen possesses behind the grand jury door. At that time, there was only minimum federal criminal law affecting individual citizens, and those most often summoned before grand juries were agents of corporations well staffed with skilled lawyers. The justices denied the witness the right to challenge the relevancy of questions being put to him, held that the grand jury need have no particular defendant in mind for a prospective indictment and ruled that a witness could not attack the constitutionality of a statute that was the basis of an investigation.

Witnesses were barred from having a lawyer with them inside the grand jury room. Hearsay evidence—that which a witness has heard someone else say and thus evidence that is dependent on the veracity of someone other than the witness—was upheld as grounds for indictment by the Supreme Court in 1956. The court noted that grand juries in pre-revolutionary England acted upon hearsay and rumor.

The increased complexity of law and society has deprived grand jurors of the familiarity with all elements of their community that formerly equipped them to judge on their own whether to indict. As a result, the jurors have become more and more the passive instrument of the forceful prosecutor.

Although Robert C. Mardian, assistant attorney general for Internal Security, contended that the surge of grand jury activity in 1971 constituted a rebirth of the "investigative grand jury," which he said "ran the tails off" government lawyers with questions, there was no sign this was so inside the grand jury rooms. There, witnesses would relate later, government attorneys dominated the proceedings, and the jury members seldom posed questions. The rare jury that did buck the will of the prosecutor was dubbed a "runaway" grand jury. To critics who wanted the United States to follow England's lead, which abolished grand juries in 1933, the grand jury was on the same oppressive course in the 1970s that overzealous congressional investigating committees had charted in the subversive-conscious 1950s.

After testifying before the grand jury, Betsy Sandel returned to the Bucknell campus, thoroughly shaken by the experience. Boyd Douglas called that night and said he could not understand why she was upset. He pointed out that she stood in no danger of prosecution because she had been granted immunity. Douglas told her he had pleaded the Fifth Amendment protection against self-incrimination on some questions Goodwin put to him, implying that he had not been granted immunity.

Later that week, Douglas wrote her on stationery from the Holiday Inn of Williamsport, Pennsylvania, about twenty-five miles north of Lewsiburg.

January 17, 1971

DEAR BETSY,

At this time I won't attempt to give my version of what happened. However, I believe a lot of people will be surprised when things really come out at the forthcoming trial. I would also like to talk with you sometime in the future and before the trial. That is if you wish to talk to me. I would imagine that everyone now realizes that the Government is taking people serious. This is no fabrication as you well know.

There is no need for us to be at one anothers throat. I can see no reason for Jane to want to talk with me. I did call her room and no answer. I will call her this week. However, you can tell her that if she only wants to say things that I wouldn't want to hear, I will just hang up. I won't explain things on a phone.

Well you have your life to live and I have mine. You are a wonderful woman and I am sorry things happened as they did. You will be out of college when the actual trial begins and since you already testified, you probably won't be needed at the trial.

I wish you the best of luck in life. I will call you again this week and if you wish to talk sometime in the future, I will drop by or meet you someplace.

Take care.   B

P.S. Someone will be there at 10:00 A.M. to pick the things up. I had already sent you a card as I knew this could happen.

Boyd had left at Betsy's apartment a mahogany end table and coffee table that he said a prisoner friend, Jim Clark, had made for him. The postal card he mentioned arrived with the letter, and a moving and van truck came to pick up the furniture as he said it would. In the card, he also asked Betsy to send smaller items, such as glasses, to the home of Jack Weckman, his half-brother.

A few days later, the Los Angeles *Times* disclosed that the government's case against Philip Berrigan and his five co-defendants depended heavily on information supplied by Boyd F. Douglas, Jr. The newspaper sketched Douglas' extensive criminal record, his violation of a previous parole and his bitter experience with the medical experiments for which he later sued the government.

In detailing Douglas' early release on December 16, 1970, the newspaper noted that he had received 253 days of "statutory good time"—eight days for each month of his sentence provided by law for prisoners who do not break rules—and another sixty-six days of meritorious good time for work inside the prison and participation in the Bucknell program. But this still was twenty-seven days short of the days needed to set him free December 16—the day he was released. Officials of the federal bureau of prisons said he had also earned these days with good time credits, but they declined to explain how.

As reporters attempted to round out the picture of Douglas, the bureau of prisons sealed his bulky records—at the direction of Attorney General Mitchell's office. Newsmen complained to the House Freedom of Information subcommittee, which began to make inquiries. The seal was lifted partially, but the twenty-seven extra good time days remained unexplained.

No one was more suprised to learn of Douglas' role as an FBI informer than his father, then living in Fargo, Oklahoma, but staying temporarily at a motel in Borger, Texas, where he was working on a construction job. The elder Douglas told a newsman: "That's sure unusual, Boyd being on the side of the law.

"He's been in trouble practically all his life. It just seemed like he always went from one thing to another. It started when he was about seven years old. Petty things, like stealing candy out of a store and stealing from his own home. I ain't been in contact with him since he went in the Army, except he's written some letters. He's lied to me all of his life and that's one of the main reasons I more or less forgot about him, because if he was gonna get out of prison and make a man of himself I'd help him."

Boyd's father returned to his son's "lying" several times during the interview. At one point, he volunteered: "He has told so many lies practically all his life that I can't believe nothing he tells me.''

After the newspaper story revealing Douglas' role as an informer, Betsy tried to call him at the home of his half-brother, Jack Weckman, in Ambler. He returned the call the following day, saying he could not divulge his whereabouts, that he had read the newspaper story and that he knew more about one of the reporters who wrote the story than the reporter knew about him—"and he better watch out.''

In a forty-minute conversation with Betsy, Douglas changed his story about testifying before the grand jury. He now claimed he had never appeared before the grand jury and predicted that the defense side would be getting all the attention for the next two months.

"Remember, the government will have the last word," he said. "They've got documents. They don't need me to corroborate anything. I'll see you at the trial—if not before," he told Betsy.

Much of the conversation was strained, Betsy recalled. "He insisted he had not duped me, but admitted he had duped Jane. He said he only had me do the one letter because Jane was not there to do it.''

"He said his arm wasn't twisted" to provide information to the FBI, Betsy remembered, "and I asked if he did it for patriotism. He indicated he thought that was right, and he said he didn't get any money (for the information). He didn't need it, he said, reminding me that I knew he had fifteen thousand dollars in the bank.''

Referring again to the news story sketching his criminal background, Douglas told Betsy: "I never claimed to be an angel.''

"He said he would keep in touch by phone," Betsy recalled, "and I said, 'ok, peace,' and hung up.''

By now, Betsy and Jane Hoover had undergone a total change of heart about their erstwhile suitor. The awareness of the extent to which Douglas had used and jeopardized them transformed the sympathy they once felt for the young convict into a desire to help in exposing him.

Betsy turned over to defense lawyers a notebook filled with names and telephone numbers that Douglas had left behind in his apartment. Both coeds cooperated fully with newsmen seeking to sift the facts about Douglas from the tales he had spun.

Subpoenaed witnesses who followed Betsy and Jane into the grand jury room gave Goodwin more trouble. Lawyers for four of them contended the government was fishing for evidence to support the indictment handed down the day before. The lawyers argued this was a reversal of the usual order of investigating first and indicting later. If this didn't persuade Judge Herman to quash their clients' subpoenas, they asked that he bar the grand jury's questions about persons already indicted or about activities outside the Middle District of Pennsylvania, the jurisdiction of the Harrisburg grand jury.

Herman, aware of the independenct traditionally accorded grand juries, refused to interfere. No sooner had the government cleared that hurdle than the balky witnesses—Joseph M. Joynt, the GSA elevator engineer and his sister, Mrs. Patricia Chanel, and Zoia Horn and Patricia Rom, the Bucknell librarians, joined by Sister Jogues Egan—declined to testify on grounds of possible self-incrimination.

Goodwin moved to immunize the prospective witnesses from prosecution so that they could be compelled to testify under threat of imprisonment for contempt, the tactic he had used to persuade the Bucknell students, Betsy and Jane, to talk. It did not work, however, with Sister Jogues, which presented the Justice Department with a tough problem.

By moving against her, the government would be venturing more boldly onto the hallowed ground surrounding the institutionalized church than when it had indicted Philip Berrigan. Berrigan was already a felon, serving time for his antiwar acts. Sister Jogues, while a critic of the war, had committed no acts of civil disobedience. She had been the president of two of her order's colleges as well as provincial superior and now was a visiting scholar at Columbia.

Indeed, she had vowed to herself never to do anything that could land her in jail because, she explained, "I have suffered from claustrophobia, for one thing, and I didn't know if I could survive jail."

The fifty-two-year-old nun wore fashionable, knee-high black boots and a stylish, silver-gray wig. When she walked into a crowded room, there was an air of maturity and command about her that drew immediate attention.

To compel this highly respected individual to testify Guy Goodwin elected to bring to bear all the muscle the government had. Her attorney, Jack Levine of Philadelphia, initially challenged the constitutionality of the "use" immunity she was granted—a type of limited immunity proposed by the Nixon Administration and enacted as part of the Organized Crime Control Act of 1970. Under use immunity, a witness' words could not be used to prosecute him, but he could be prosecuted for the transaction about which he testified as long as the evidence was developed from other sources—the testimony of other persons, for example. Until use immunity went on the law books, the only immunity in the federal prosecutor's tool kit was "transactional" immunity under which a witness could not be prosecuted for the matter on which he testified, no matter what the source of the evidence.

Levine argued that immunizing the nun could influence a grand juror's thinking about her and that her testimony, while not usable against her, might corroborate testimony by other witnesses and lead to her being indicted. He had justification for this concern. An Associated Press report from Washington had quoted unnamed Justice Department sources as stating the grand jury was continuing its investigation to develop evidence against the seven persons who had been named as co-conspirators.

The reasoning did not impress Judge Herman. "You are suggesting they are going to indict her," he told Levine. "They are not. I get your point, but I just don't believe it . . . .My belief is this order granting immunity is commensurate with protection under the Fifth Amendment."

Later that week, Federal Judge Constance Baker Motley, who had been named to the bench by President Lyndon B. Johnson, ruled in another case in New York that use immunity violated the Fifth Amendment. Describing the protection against self-incrimination as "the touchstone of our adversarial system,"

Judge Motley said it must be upheld with a liberal construction "if we are to keep faith with the patriots who fought for the inclusion of the Bill of Rights in the Constitution."

Subsequently, the Supreme Court settled the matter by upholding the constitutionality of use immunity.

The day after Judge Herman rejected the attack on use immunity, Goodwin took the defense by surprise and granted Sister Jogues the broader transactional immunity. It was apparently an effort to show the government was willing to go the extra mile before jailing a nun for contempt of court.

But she returned to the grand jury room and, outside of identifying herself, continued to refuse to answer the questions. After each of more than eighty questions Goodwin put to her, she stepped into the hallway to confer with Levine. Following federal rules, Levine had to remain in the corridor outside the grand jury room.

Usually, after less than a minute of whispered conversation, Sister Egan would reenter the grand jury room, the door opened by one of the two FBI agents standing stiffly at guard in the hallway. This was one more indication of the priority the government assigned the case. Outside most federal grand jury sessions, a single deputy marshal would be posted. And he often demonstrated his relaxed attitude by burying his head in the morning sports pages.

Most of the questions the nun repeated to Levine dealt with the bombing-kidnap conspiracy allegations and the defendants in that case. For example: "Do you know Sister Elizabeth McAlister?" "What conversations did you have with her in 1970?" (A detailed answer could have taken hours because Sister Elizabeth served as Sister Jogues' secretary.)

Some questions branched out into new areas—her knowledge of the Picatinny Arsenal (mentioned in the letters between Sister Elizabeth and Berrigan), her knowledge of draft board "actions" in Philadelphia and whether she had discussed with Philip Berrigan plans to blow up Pentagon computers.

It was an obviously reluctant Judge Herman presiding over the courtroom when Guy Goodwin urged that Sister Jogues be held in contempt.

"I have no desire to be in contempt," the nun told Judge Herman. "But I have a duty to obey my conscience and a court which, I respectfully submit, is higher than this court."

Herman, who had stressed earlier that he had "no choice" but to sign the contempt order, said: "I understand."

Levine asked the judge either to stay the contempt order or release Sister Jogues while he appealed the ruling. The lawyer contended his client's refusal to testify was a matter of conscience and that jailing her would not benefit the government.

Goodwin, who had branded Sister Jogues' reasons for refusing to testify as "frivolous," opposed temporarily freeing her because she was "clearly in contempt."

"I refuse the stay order and deny bond," Herman said. "You have the key to your jail cell. All you have to do is comply with the court order and you are immune from any prosecution."

Sister Jogues did not troop off to jail without a final blow at the government. In a statement distributed to newsmen listing her reasons for maintaining silence, she alleged, without citing the basis for her allegation, that the government had tapped the telephones of her order, the Sacred Heart of Mary, throughout the United States, and at its Rome headquarters.

Justice Department officials initially waved off questions about the allegation with a "no comment." But nearly three weeks later, during an interview on CBS Morning News, Attorney General Mitchell was asked whether wiretapping had been used in the Berrigan case.

"I can assure you that with respect to the allegations that were made by some of the parties that appeared before the grand jury with respect to wiretapping, that this is absolutely, completely untrue," Mitchell said.

Before being led from the courtroom by two deputy marshals, Sister Jogues embraced her obviously distraught attorney. Under her civil contempt sentence, she was to remain in the York County prison, twenty-five miles south of Harrisburg, until she purged herself of contempt by answering the grand jury's questions or for the seventeen months left in the jury's eighteen-month term.

But she remained behind bars for only four days because the

U.S. Third Circuit Court of Appeals in Philadelphia agreed to hear her appeal and, despite Goodwin's request for high bail, freed the nun on her own recognizance.

Guy Goodwin encountered nearly as much difficulty with a witness who agreed to answer all the grand jury's questions after he was immunized, Joseph M. Joynt, the General Services Administration elevator engineer at the Forrestal Building in Washington. In the first weeks after the original indictment, Joynt, a sandy-haired, lanky man who looked several years younger than his thirty-five years, became a prominent figure in the conspiracy web spun by the government.

Of the twenty-two overt acts that the indictment alleged had been committed to further the conspiracy, the first stated that Philip Berrigan and Joseph Wenderoth on or about April 1, 1970, "entered underground tunnels in Washington, D.C." The government let it be known, mainly through a summary of the case in *Time* magazine, that Joynt had keys to the underground tunnels in his capacity as a GSA employee and that the tunnels could be entered from the Forrestal Building.

The twentieth count read that on September 20, 1970, "Joseph Wenderoth discussed the Washington, D.C. tunnel system with a General Service Administration engineer."

Inside the grand jury room, Joynt, after being granted the broader transactional immunity, denied he played any such role. A distressed Goodwin asked Joynt if anyone had threatened him, and the witness added to the prosecutor's discomfort.

Yes, he said, the FBI had. He explained that an FBI agent had warned him that if he brought an attorney with him to Harrisburg for the grand jury session, the FBI would consider him a "hostile witness" and could do nothing for him. Unlike most other witnesses, Joynt did not constantly consult his attorney, A. Harry Levitan of Philadelphia. During his nearly two hours of testimony, Joynt emerged only once to speak with Levitan and he later told newsmen that he had answered all questions asked of him.

Joynt subsequently complained that Goodwon had Goodwin had used a "doctored" photograph of him during the grand jury proceeding. The picture had been enlarged from a shot of six or eight persons at a Christmas party, Joynt said, and a small Christmas tree could still be seen in the background.

"But they had put a uniform on me — with GSA on one side and J.M. Joynt on the other," Joynt said. "I got into a hassle with Goodwin about it. He never admitted or denied it was doctored, but said something like they had a picture of me I didn't even know about, leaving the implication that it was not doctored."

Two weeks later, FBI agents were back to see Joynt at his government job. They told him that Goodwin was "not satisfied" with his testimony, and that four or five persons had made comments tying him to the alleged trip to the underground utility tunnels by Philip Berrigan and Wenderoth.

"I told them, 'You've got four or five liars you'd better check out,' " Joynt said.

He quoted the agents as telling him that he had made himself "look guilty" by invoking the Fifth Amendment protection against self-incrimination when he appeared initially before the grand jury.

"I told them I had to do that in order to get immunity, that that's what the Constitution is all about," Joynt said.

Lawyers for several witnesses called by the Harrisburg grand jury said that they felt obliged to counsel their clients to seek immunity no matter how firmly the clients asserted they were totally innocent of any wrongdoing. With the government spinning a conspiracy web, the attorneys contended, a seemingly innocent act that could be shown to have furthered the conspiracy would be enough to snare a person.

When the pressure did not work with Joynt, the agents left, indicating they would return to his place of work to question him again. They did not, however. Months later, in a court action that escaped public attention, the government would concede it did not know the identity of the GSA engineer with whom Wenderoth allegedly discussed the tunnel system beneath federal buildings in Washington. The admission came in response to the defense's request for more particulars on the allegations from the prosecutors.

Joynt was a logical selection for pressure. A father of six children — the youngest, five, the oldest, sixteen — he was a self-described "hard-hat when it comes to the FBI. I think it's an important institution."

But the pressure the bureau brought to bear on him gave the career government employee second thoughts. "I think they're misusing their power this time," he said.

Joynt's only contact with the Catholic peace radicals had been through his older sister, Patricia, a blond divorcee, mother of three and a rigorously devout Catholic. Unlike Joe, the forty-one-year-old Pat was no hard-hat. She had participated in several peace demonstrations and had opened her mother's Silver Spring, Maryland, home to movement people. It was at a party Pat gave for the peace activists in the spring of 1970 that her brother, Joe, met Wenderoth and Philip Berrigan. But Joe recalled no discussion of the tunnel system with either priest and said he had no further contact with them.

Because Patricia Chanel identified so closely with movement people, some of whom were at the center of the conspiracy investigation, she seemed likely to provide crucial information. It soon became apparent to Goodwin, however, that the best way to Patricia was through her brother, Joe.

Patricia was hardly the kind of witness to lend credible support to the government's case. Her attorney, A. Harry Levitan, asked Judge Herman to break with precedent and let him accompany her inside the grand jury room. His reason, supported by statements from two psychiatrists, was that Mrs. Chanel was not mentally competent to testify unassisted. He pointed out she had experienced severe emotional stress, climaxed by a paranoid psychotic episode which led to her hospitalization at the Taunton, Massachusetts, State Mental Hospital in the summer of 1970. Judge Herman, stating that he could find no precedent for letting the attorney accompany the client inside the grand jury room, refused Levitan's request.

Behind the guarded door, where proceedings had been dominated by the persistent, frequently sarcastic Goodwin, Mrs. Chanel presented a change of pace. Though immunized from prosecution, she refused to answer sixty-eight questions. From time to time, she would emerge from the jury room and clasp her hands over her head in victory style. Wearing a blue skirt and blue turtleneck jersey, set off by a large wooden peace symbol dangling from a chain around her neck, Patricia Chanel took the jurors and Goodwin by surprise at one point. A few minutes before noon, with no sign of a letup in the questioning, she announced she was going to mass. When Goodwin indicated the jury was not through questioning her, she said: "I don't know about you, but I'm going to mass." She did, and the jurors broke for lunch.

On March 11, after a month's layoff by the grand jury, Mrs. Chanel was cited for contempt of court because of her continued refusal to answer the questions. Over Goodwin's objections, she was not jailed, pending the outcome of Sister Jogue's contempt appeal.

Two other witnesses, who appeared before the grand jury about the same time as Mrs. Chanel, answered the questions put to them after being given immunity. Zoia Horn, the head reference librarian at Bucknell, and Patricia Rom, her assistant, each spent about two hours before the jurors. Both later said they thought Goodwin was deeply disappointed by their testimony.

The indictment alleged that Fathers Wenderoth and McLaughlin went to Zoia Horn's white-walled, second-floor duplex in Lewisburg on September 5, 1970. In addition to the trim, high-strung hostess, they were said to have met there with Mary Drinnon, wife of the Bucknell professor, and Boyd F. Douglas, Jr. The indictment listed the gathering as one of the overt acts to further the conspiracy.

Patricia Rom, who looked more like a Bucknell coed than a twenty-seven-year-old librarian, had received the "kidnap" letter sent by Sister Elizabeth to Philip Berrigan. She said she had passed it on to Boyd Douglas without examining the contents.

A steady stream of accusations from lawyers for witnesses summoned by the grand jury that the government had embarked on a "fishing expedition" in hopes of justifying the indictment handed down two weeks earlier finally drew a response from the Justice Department prosecutor. Guy Goodwin assured Judge Herman that the investigation was aimed at returning new indictments, and the judge declined a defense request that he intervene in the grand jury proceeding to see if Goodwin's questions were really leading is such a direction.

Goodwin's courtroom statements were one thing, but head-shaking doubts registered privately by veteran prosecutors back at Justice Department headquarters in Washington were another.

"Of course it's unusual — very unusual — to continue a grand jury investigation after the indictment," said one career Justice Department lawyer two weeks after the indictment.

"The closest parallel was last year's investigation of Detroit gamblers. First we indicted a bunch of the numbers writers — the guys who fill in the papers — then the bigger guys." Some of the numbers writers, he explained, provided crucial information against the major figures. "There was a real question of whether we could do it, but we got by with it."

The Harrisburg case was no parallel, however, because the "bigger guys" were named in the original indictment.

"The question is, 'Why all the rush to indict?' " asked the Justice Department official. He stressed that he was convinced there was a prima facie case, but said he had doubts about the legal procedures followed by the government.

"If the reason for the fast indictment was to abort the plan [to kidnap Kissinger and blow up the heating systems], why couldn't we have proceeded by filing a complaint, arresting the people and then having a preliminary hearing? This would have stopped the plot, and the grand jury could have kept investigating until it was ready to indict."

There was another possible motivation for the rush to indict, the official suggested. "Maybe the purpose was to try to please the bureau. Internal Security [the near-dormant division which took over the case from the Criminal Division soon after Hoover's November 27 testimony] has long had the reputation of being a Patsy for the bureau." He said, however, he knew of no evidence that pressure had been brought on the Internal Security Division.

Despite the fact that Attorney General Mitchell had privately expressed anger over Hoover's testimony, he gave no public indication that there was any need to take Hoover off the hook. Four months after the FBI director's testimony, Mitchell told Robert Shogan of *Newsweek* magazine that he was "sure" Hoover would not have given the testimony if he knew it was to be made public. Mitchell said the release of the testimony "was the problem of the committee" — not that of Hoover.

Under questioning by Shogan, Mitchell conceded that Hoover had not told him this was the case. The attorney general said he assumed it was so. Apparently Mitchell or his staff had not discovered that an FBI man had carried copies of Hoover's testimony to the Senate subcommittee for immediate distribution to the press by the committee clerk. Nor did the attorney general take note of the fact that after the initial furor over Hoover's accusation against the Berrigans, the FBI widely distributed printed copies of Hoover's earlier testimony before the House Appropriations Subcommittee, which contained the same accusation.

In the Shogan interview, Mitchell said that Hoover's pre-indictment allegation had caused the government not the slightest problem with the Berrigan case.

Whether or not the Internal Security Division, which was liberally populated with ex-FBI agents, had tried to please the bureau with its handling of the Berrigan matter, the case was of major importance to the division as it emerged from its cocoon of inactivity.

The division, after its respected amiable but unaggressive boss, J. Walter Yeagley, had been eased upstairs to a District of Columbia court post, had quickly become the cutting edge in the attorney general's attack on what he regarded as the prime threat to national security — domestic radicals. This was in sharp contrast to the division's low profile during the Kennedy and Johnson years. Court rulings which found key laws enforced by the division to be unconstitutional and the fact that Communist witch-hunting had gone out of public favor combined to convert the once bustling division into a bureaucratic backwater.

When Nicholas DeB. Katzenbach and Ramsey Clark were running the Justice Department, they considered either eliminating the division or at least returning it to the rank of a section within the Criminal division from which it had been elevated during the Eisenhower Administration. But they abandoned both ideas for fear of the political reaction, particularly among the really powerful on Capitol Hill such as Senator James O. Eastland of Mississippi, whose Senate

Judiciary Committee had so much influence over the Justice Department.

From a peak of ninety-six lawyers in 1956, Internal Security's strength had dwindled to forty-two when Yeagley accepted the court post in the fall of 1970. To replace him, President Nixon named Robert C. Mardian as assistant attorney general for Internal Security, and from that point on the division began to add lawyers. Mardian was a hard-driving conservative from Pasadena, California, who had worked in Mr. Nixon's campaign office in Washington in 1968 and who had been an even more prominent figure in Barry Goldwater's Presidential campaign four years earlier.

At the outset of the Nixon Administration Mardian served as general counsel for the Health, Education and Welfare Department, where civil rights lawyers soon recognized him as their prime nemesis. He played a major role in drafting Mr. Nixon's March, 1970, statement on school desegregation, an anti-busing, pro-neighborhood school stance that the Supreme Court repudiated in part the next year. He also was instrumental in discontinuing the tactic of cutting off federal funds to school districts that refused to desegregate.

Once the civil rights swords at HEW had been effectively sheathed, Mardian moved to the Executive Office Building to direct the Cabinet Committee on Desegregation, which was chaired by Vice President Agnew. The unit was formed after President Nixon's March, 1970, policy statement to help Southern districts work out the problems of desegregating. The theme was federal cooperation, not coercion.

With that job well underway and with the Administration increasingly wary over the activities of domestic radicals, Mardian moved to the Justice Department as head of Internal Security.

Almost immediately the Berrigan case became a top priority item within the rejuvenated division. When Hoover first publicly mentioned the alleged conspiracy in his Senate testimony, the investigation was under the direction of the Criminal Division. With Mardian aboard, it was transferred to Internal Security, which was to take over all matters with subversive overtones.

Although doubts about the Berrigan case had been expressed

elsewhere in the department, none was heard in Mardian's division. Two days after the indictment was returned, Mardian insisted that Hoover's Senate testimony had not prodded the government into bringing the indictment.

"There were no political considerations whatsoever," he told a newsman. In fact, Mardian suggested, the case could have been much broader if Hoover had kept mum. "There's goddamn no telling what we would have if Hoover hadn't talked," he said. "We depended on informants, and they shut up after he testified. We wish he had lied if necessary, anything to not talk about the case."

Although Mardian expressed unqualified confidence about the case when discussing it with persons outside the Justice Department, he had reservations about a crucial aspect of it — the reliability of Boyd F. Douglas, Jr. Mardian was concerned in particular that Douglas had kept copies of the correspondence between Sister McAlister and Father Berrigan in hopes of selling the material to a national magazine.

According to one source, Mardian considered designating Douglas a "national security figure" so that the FBI could use wiretapping or bugging devices to monitor the ex-convict without its eventually becoming a matter of public record. If Douglas had been a suspect in a criminal investigation, the department could have obtained a court warrant to use eavesdropping devices against him. But Douglas was no suspect, and under the law the warrant would have to become a matter of public record eventually. This would have revealed the government had doubts about the chief source of its information. No prior court permission was required to tap or bug in national security intelligence-gathering, however, where the information was supposed to be collected for preventive, not prosecutive, purposes. The attorney general had to personally authorize each national security surveillance after concluding that the information which might be obtained was essential to the protection of the government. Both Mardian and Mitchell had frequently asserted that the use of electronic eavesdropping without a warrant in such national security matters was limited and tightly controlled.

Mardian later scoffed at the suggestion that he had considered using electronic surveillance to safeguard against Douglas' selling the priest and nun's correspondence to a magazine. He insisted that national security wiretapping was so limited and tightly controlled that there would have been no way to use it against Douglas. Mardian said he might have said "in jest" that Douglas should be bugged, but that he did not recall even that.

The Internal Security chief conceded he was concerned about Douglas' keeping out of trouble before the case came to trial. As a result, Douglas was openly tailed periodically and told that he was being kept under surveillance.

When the FBI learned that Douglas was having sexual relations with two married women, a Justice Department official, who declined to be identified, said the FBI was instructed: "Tell him to keep his prick in his pants—or we're going to stop supporting him."

Mardian kept his concern over the reliability of Douglas confined to the security of his office and those officials closely associated with the case. Publicly the government gave not the slightest indication that it had second thoughts about any aspect of the case.

On February 8, a day short of four weeks after the indictment was returned, the six defendants and seven co-conspirators got together for the first time—at their arraignment. The proceeding was dominated by security measures dictated by the Justice Department. Defendants, attorneys, spectators and newsmen all had to show identification when they signed a register at the entrance to the building, had to obtain a pass for the eighty-seat courtroom, board the lone elevator permitted to stop at the courtroom floor, be examined by a metal-detecting device, and turn over purses and briefcases for a more thorough search by security persons.

So stringent were the precautions that at one point the combined corps of General Services Administration, FBI, deputy federal marshals and local and state lawmen prevented Eqbal Ahmad and one of the defense lawyers from entering the courtroom—much to the delight of Ahmad.

"He doesn't have a pass," said the federal agent who stopped Ahmad from entering the courtroom.

"He can't get in," said another agent who, like his companion, was carrying a walkie-talkie.

"I am a defendant," said Ahmad. "I am delighted over the difficulties."

He finally convinced the agents, and they let him in.

Mary Cain Scoblick, wife of the defendant, Anthony Scoblick, asked reporters in the corridor outside the courtroom what had prompted the heavy security force.

"They have nothing to fear from us, certainly," she said. "I wish they wouldn't look so tense and nervous."

She claimed that newspaper accounts of the tightened security would "mislead the ordinary reader, like you or me, into thinking, 'What kind of people are they, if they're that dangerous?' "

James Gerrity, the affable GSA manager of the federal building, noted that two bomb threats had been received the day of the arraignment. A search of the building proved the threats to be bogus. Gerrity insisted that the Justice Department, not the court or his agency, was responsible for the security steps.

During a break in the proceedings, Ahmad was involved in another mixup, but one that left him more anguished than amused. In the lobby of the aging Penn-Harris Hotel, catty-corner from the federal building, Ahmad asked a newsman to accompany him to his room. Shutting the door, Ahmad disclosed in a hushed voice that one of his co-defendants had lifted the handcuffs carried by a deputy federal marshal. He opened his dresser drawer, reached in back and drew out a brown paper sack containing the handcuffs. He was careful not to touch the stolen government property.

"I am dealing with children," he said. It was a complaint the East Asian agnostic had issued earlier about his involvement with the Catholic radicals and one he would repeatedly voice in exasperation.

"Would you see that these get back to the government?" Ahmad pleaded with the newsman, who later turned them over to the Harrisburg defense lawyer, J. Thomas Menaker. Menaker immediately conveyed them to the marshals who already had begun a search for the missing handcuffs.

At the arraignment, defense attorneys urged Judge Herman to ease travel restrictions on all defendants, except Philip Berrigan, the only one behind bars.

Glancing at the government prosecutor, Guy Goodwin, Herman said: "I didn't ask the government about this. I'm sure you oppose it."

Goodwin did argue against it, but the judge lifted the restrictions partially, permitting the defendants to travel to the cities of other defendants and lawyers in the case.

The arraignment provided the first public glimpse of Philip Berrigan since he had been transferred to Danbury six months earlier. The priest, in mufti, stood before the bench, his hands thrust into his back pockets. Judge Herman asked whether he had time to read the indictment.

"Ample time," Berrigan replied without smiling, but drawing smiles and nods from supporters in the spectator's section.

Each of the six defendants entered a plea of not guilty. As Philip was led out, movement friends who had not seen him for at least six months pressed toward him and called, "Phil, Phil."

He turned, grinned and flashed the V-sign for peace. Mary Cain Scoblick shouted a farewell. "You be good now, Phil. Don't get into any trouble."

About a week before the arraignment, Judge Herman had warned J. Thomas Menaker, the defendants' resident counsel in Harrisburg, that he was considering clamping a gag rule to avoid pre-trial publicity. The judge showed Menaker a news clipping that he said the government had sent him. The clipping reported "political statements" by the defendants.

Menaker said he told Herman that he thought the defendants had the right to make such statements and pointed out that the case had begun in the press with Hoover's 1970 accusation.

" 'What do you mean?' " Menaker recalled the judge had asked. " 'I don't know anything about that.' "

The lawyer was dumbfounded that the publicity Hoover's testimony generated had escaped Herman's attention.

Only hours before the arraignment, Herman told Menaker he wanted to limit the right of witnesses and defendants to make statements to the press, but Menaker said he told the judge that he had no right to do that. "He said he would wait and see," Menaker said.

Despite the concern the judge expressed over pre-trial publicity, the defendants and co-conspirators—minus the

Berrigan brothers—held a press conference after the arraignment at the Harrisburg YWCA, a block down Walnut Street from the courthouse. The session had the atmosphere of a post-election meeting that candidates traditionally hold where supporters, who far outnumber the newsmen, shout their approval of everything the principal has to say.

Elizabeth McAlister, whom one press admirer described as having "a long Irish face and a voice like rain on the roof," spoke for the group. Borrowing a page from the draft board raid trials—the Catonsville Nine, the Milwaukee Fourteen, the Flower City Conspiracy—she tried to use the occasion for explaining what motivated the movement and for enlisting support for the cause.

The prepared statement she read proclaimed that the thirteen defendants and co-conspirators were innocent of the government's charges, but said some of them had destroyed draft board records to resist the war. The group statement accused the government of lying to its citizens and of "crimes against humanity."

"We ask our fellow citizens to resist this war by refusing to fight, refusing to pay taxes, refusing to cooperate in any way. Finally, we reaffirm our dedication to a world without violence—that violence which for so long has ravaged so many lands, so many souls."

The defendants took questions but avoided direct answers to those dealing with the facts of the case. Ahmad dominated the Q and A period, often supplementing answers by other defendants. He suggested that newsmen ask more embarrassing questions at Presidential press conferences and fewer "at a conference such as this."

Two weeks after the arraignment, the government's case underwent a radical change as Guy Goodwin, whose talents seemed to blossom behind the closed doors of a grand jury room, was replaced by William S. Lynch. Lynch was regarded by lawyers in the Criminal Division where he served as one of the department's most able prosecutors.

The forty-four-year-old attorney was head of the organized crime and racketeering section, a prestige post under an Administration that had placed unprecedented resources in the war against the underworld syndicate. There was resistance within the department to assigning Lynch to the case. His boss, Henry E. Petersen, the number-two man in the Criminal Division, did not want him to leave organized crime, even temporarily. Petersen held preliminary discussions about taking the case as a specially appointed prosecutor with Washington attorney William O. Bittman. A former Justice Department lawyer, Bittman had won convictions against Teamsters President Hoffa and Robert G. "Bobby" Baker, onetime secretary to the Senate Democrats and protégé of Lyndon Johnson. But Petersen's superiors told him that no outside counsel was wanted on the case.

Petersen reluctantly joined in the decision by Deputy Attorney General Kleindienst, Internal Security's Mardian and Will R. Wilson, head of the Criminal Division, to ask Lynch to take the assignment. Lynch reviewed the case file for five days, including a cold February weekend at his Alexandria, Virginia, town house.

Lynch closeted himself in a carpeted basement room and was interrupted only occasionally by his four children or his wife going to and from the washer and dryer. He was appalled by what he read. He searched in vain for credible evidence that would tie to the case Daniel Berrigan, whom the indictment had listed as an unindicted co-conspirator. He could find only hearsay. Lynch discovered that potential evidence of lesser violations—the plotting of draft board raids—had been ignored as Goodwin concentrated solely on substantiating the bombing-kidnap conspiracy that Hoover had trumpeted in his Senate testimony.

After studying the file, Lynch told his superiors there was a case to be prosecuted, but not the one drawn up by Goodwin. There was an unspoken understanding that it would be a prosecution Lynch would construct, not a salvage operation for the creation Goodwin had left behind. If his superiors had insisted on the case structured by Goodwin, which seemed to echo the charges made by Hoover, Lynch was prepared to recommend against prosecuting. He had no desire, he told associates, to be laughed out of court.

Lynch was named deputy assistant attorney general under

Mardian so that the case would bear the stamp of the Internal Security Division. It was clear from the outset, however, that he would return to his organized crime section post in the Criminal Division once the case was completed. Three young lawyers were assigned to assist Lynch — William Connelly, Phillip Krajewski and Joe Tafe. Tafe later was replaced by Paul Killion. All were Roman Catholics, a fact that Mardian and others in the department insisted was pure coincidence. Another Catholic U.S. attorney, S. John Cottone, also assisted Lynch. Actually, the assignment of an all-Catholic prosecution team was an attempt to head off accusations of anti-Catholicism. Fears inside the department of such accusations had been fed by a quip Goodwin had made earlier in the case when he emerged from the grand jury room.

"What shall we call you, Mr. Goodwin?" asked a newsman who was not sure of the lawyer's title.

"You can call me your eminence," Goodwin shot back without a smile. The line was picked up by columnists and carried throughout the nation.

A calm appeared to settle over the case as Lynch took command. From time to time during the rest of February, developments outside the Harrisburg courtroom would make the case a matter of news. In mid-February, Federal Judge Edward W. Day dismissed indictments in Providence, Rhode Island, against Stringfellow and Towne charging they harbored Daniel Berrigan. The judge ruled the indictments were too general and failed to properly specify offenses. He threw out the indictments "without prejudice," which meant new ones could be brought. But a year later, the Justice Department had not tried again, and a spokesman said there were no plans to do so.

In March there was another event that would become entangled in the case — the theft of files from a small FBI office in Media, Pennsylvania. The incident received little attention from the press when the night-raid on the unattended, "resident" office took place. But a few weeks later, the raiders, who called themselves the Commission to Investigate the FBI, distributed reams of documents which they had copied from the purloined files to mass circulation newspapers. The newspapers carried front page stories on the documents, including some startling excerpts that were never intended for public consumption.

Among other things, the documents detailed FBI success at infiltrating college campuses with informers who reported on professors as well as students and its attempt to recruit for intelligence-gathering purposes teenagers bound for a Moscow visit.

The FBI document that exceeded all the hundreds of others in its impact was an internal memorandum that proposed actions to intensify the "paranoia" that there was "an FBI agent behind every mailbox." The peace movement contended the documents verified excesses they had long accused the FBI of.

Hoover, colleagues said, was livid. For a period he insisted he would close all small, resident offices across the nation, but aides finally convinced him that this would cripple the bureau. While refusing to comment on the practices the documents revealed, the FBI launched a massive investigation of the Media raid.

Catholic radicals, many of them close to those involved in the Harrisburg case, became prime suspects. The Harrisburg grand jury and others as well began to ask questions about the raid. But by the time the Harrisburg case went to trial, no one had been charged in the investigation. The raid probably drew more attention than any other single antiwar raid on draft boards, U.S. attorney offices and other federal facilities.

The air of calm that enveloped the Berrigan case in March of 1971 resulted partly from an extraordinary act by the man who was supposed to be the target of the kidnap plot, Henry A. Kissinger. On March 6, Kissinger met in the White House "situation room" with three of those named by the indictment as co-conspirators—William Davidon, the forty-four-year-old Quaker and physics professor at Haverford College; Tom Davidson, the twenty-five-year-old son of the Episcopal bishop of Western Kansas; and Sister Beverly Bell, the forty-four-year-old nun who participated in a demonstration outside Lewisburg Prison to protest what was happening to Philip Berrigan inside the prison.

The three antiwar activists talked for an hour and a quarter with the man they were alleged to have conspired to kidnap. He began the discussion by apologizing for the widely publicized quip about the indictment that he was said to have made, speculating that "sex starved nuns" were behind the plot. He said he had been misquoted. The national security expert and his guests spent most of the time discussing how the Vietnam war could be ended, the question of individual responsibility for the conflict and war and peace in broader terms.

Another peace-advocate acquaintance of Kissinger had set up the meeting, figuring that a dialogue could only make things better. Brian McDonnell, whom Kissinger met in 1970 when the Philadelphia man fasted for thirty days in Lafayette Park across Pennsylvania Avenue from the White House to protest the Cambodian invasion, brought Kissinger and the three in contact.

Such communication, Kissinger said later, was an attempt "to transcend the bitterness of the public dialogue" about the war. The guests praised their host's willingness to listen.

"He is an excellent listener," said Davidon. "He never took advantage of the weaknesses in our presentation. But that personal humanity, that subjective concern, have to be considered part of the picture in which he is part of a decision-making system which is grossly brutal."

Davidon characterized the session as "bittersweet."

"There we were, accused of wanting to bomb, sitting with a man whose policies had brought about a bombing that was actually going on as we talked. I was talking to a man who considers mass murder in certain circumstances justified. I told him I thought the war had no legitimacy."

CHAPTER NINE

Superseding Indictment

Teams of FBI agents fanned out in the Boston, Philadelphia, Washington and New York areas at mid-morning on April 15, shattering the calm that had settled over the investigation since William S. Lynch had replaced Guy L. Goodwin as chief prosecutor.

The agents served subpoenas signed by Lynch on more than twenty-five persons, most of them linked to the Catholic Resistance through draft board raids or Harrisburg Defense Committee work. Several of the witnesses were ordered to testify before the grand jury at Harrisburg on April 20 when it was scheduled to reconvene for the first time since February 12. The others were subpoenaed for succeeding days.

The move, which government attorneys privately conceded was an effort to broaden the conspiracy indictment to include draft board raids and possibly other illegal activities, was immediately blasted by defense attorneys as a continuing "fishing expedition" and an attempt to salvage a case that rested on flimsy evidence. It also apparently was aimed at snaring in the conspiracy net other members of the East Coast Conspiracy to Save Lives, the group Hoover had accused of hatching the kidnap-bombing plot. So far only one member of the group—Joseph Wenderoth—had been indicted. Among the witnesses subpoenaed were two other members—Sister Sue Davis, thirty-two, of Washington, D.C., and John Finnegan, twenty-three, a former Penn State University student who refused induction in 1969. Federal marshals also accompanied a third member—John Theodore Glick, twenty-one—from the Ashland, Kentucky, federal prison camp, where he was serving an eighteen-month sentence for his part in the Rochester draft raid, to the federal building at Harrisburg for possible testimony before the jury. Others subpoenaed as witnesses included Richard Drinnon, the Bucknell history professor; William Gardiner, twenty-two, a Bucknell student active in antiwar efforts; Mr. and Mrs. Abraham Diamond, Eqbal Ahmad's parents-in-law; Paul Bernard Couming, twenty-two, of the Boston Eight, whose conviction on a draft charge for refusing to accept alternative service as a conscientious objector was under appeal; Jack Hayden, twenty-two, of Chicago, a member of the New York Eight; Theresa McHugh, twenty, of Philadelphia, a coed at Temple University who worked in a Catholic community center in a black ghetto; Dr. George McVey, forty-two, a Rochester dentist, and his wife, Suzanne, who was expecting their sixth child momentarily; Claudette Piper, twenty-nine, of Boston, a member of the Boston Eight and associate director of RESIST, a Cambridge-based organization that raised funds to support antiwar efforts and that helped distribute to the press and others copies of documents stolen in the raid on the FBI office at Media, Pennsylvania; Anne Mentz, twenty-six, a member of "We The People," a group that took credit for a draft board raid in Philadelphia; John Robert Swinglish, twenty-seven, of Washington, past president of the D.C. chapter of the Catholic Peace Fellowship and one of seven members of "The Brothers and Sisters," a group that took credit for a draft board raid in New Haven; and Anne Walsh, twenty-eight, a former nun and a member of the New York Eight.

As the first witnesses trudged into the federal building, one of the defendants, Tony Scoblick, began a fast on the building's cold concrete steps. Wrapped in a blanket in the freezing weather, the smiling Scoblick looked like anything but a man charged with plotting a kidnap and bombing. He joked and laughed with friends and newsmen, but his smile faded briefly at one point and, dark eyes gazing into the distance, he said, "I guess I could laugh myself all the way to a life sentence."

To anyone who would take one—newsmen, court officials, or passing pedestrians—Scoblick handed out a brief mimeographed statement identifying himself as a member of the Harrisburg Six and saying he would continue to fast and walk around the courthouse to protest the continuing grand jury investigation. "I encourage you to see for yourself," the statement said, "if you would endure the ordeal that peacemakers must suffer in the name of justice."

The "ordeal," according to several witnesses, included FBI harassment through constant surveillance and frequent questioning of relatives and friends of suspects. In interviews with reporters, the witnesses complained of what were known as "open tails," the constant, overt following of subjects in attempts to unnerve them. Theresa McHugh of Philadelphia said she had been under surveillance for a year. Her mother complained that the FBI had called her with questions concerning her daughter two or three times each week for a year.

The Temple coed, along with other witnesses, including Couming, Drinnon, and the Diamonds, scheduled to testify as the jury resumed its hearings, filed motions to quash their subpoenas on grounds they were issued to gather evidence in support of existing indictments, an illegal use of the grand jury.

Burton Caine, a Philadelphia attorney representing Theresa McHugh, filed an affidavit with the motion saying that Joseph Tafe of the Internal Security Division had telephoned him and threatened to subpoena her if she did not submit to an interview. In the affidavit Caine said that the Justice Department attorney told him the coed had participated in a draft board raid in Philadelphia in February, 1970, and that when he asked Tafe the connection between draft board raids and the grand jury's investigations, Tafe replied that "the Harrisburg grand jury wanted a total picture of the activities of people involved in the alleged plot to kidnap Henry Kissinger."

Judge Herman refused to quash the subpoenas, but his action only compelled the witnesses to appear, not to testify. And if government attorneys thought they had had a problem of balky witnesses earlier, the new batch proved to be even more difficult. For one thing, practically all of these witnesses, unlike some of the earlier ones, were dedicated members of the Resistance or strong sympathizers who would risk jail rather than cooperate in what they considered to be an unjust and oppressive investigation. Also, the indictment returned three months earlier had solidified the Resistance's opposition to the government.

The first witness scheduled to testify, Paul Couming, a short, baby-faced draft resister, refused to testify on legal grounds, including self-incrimination. Couming, who wore a perpetual smile, passed around a statement which vowed "non-cooperation with any branch of the United States government, including the judicial system, prior to an international war crimes tribunal held to hold both the U.S. Government and individuals accountable for their unhuman use of their position and power to crush the population of Vietnam."

The Diamonds, Eqbal Ahmad's in-laws, an elderly and conservatively dressed Jewish couple who looked strangely out of place among the denim- and khaki-clad peace activists, also refused to testify. They accused the government of harassing them. Government attorneys, they said, were aware that they had no information relative to the investigation, but subpoenaed them anyway.

As the grand jury session wore on, with one witness after another refusing to testify, other witnesses, along with attorneys and newsmen, waited in the federal building corridors, some standing and others sitting on the floor.

Eventually, after the court granted them immunity at the government's request, the Diamonds reluctantly testified. But afterward they said in a prepared statement: "We have no information of any sort concerning the allegations of the indictment, or any other subject that the grand jury is investigating, and we have so stated to the grand jury. We would have preferred to stand on our First and Fifth Amendment rights, with so many of the other witnesses. However, because of the attendant tensions we are unable to carry on this struggle. We wish the best of luck to those who will continue to resist this unlawful action."

The government also secured an immunity order for Paul Couming, but he still refused to testify. Lynch promptly drew up an indictment alleging criminal contempt and the jury dutifully indicted Couming.

During a recess in court proceedings, another balky witness, ex-nun Anne Walsh, took four snapshots from her pocketbook and stared at them silently. The pictures showed North Vietnamese civilians allegedly killed in Hanoi by American bombing raids. Suddenly she strode across the room to Lynch, thrust the photos in front of him and said, "This is what the movement is all about."

One of the pictures, she said, was of a twenty-eight-year-old pregnant woman. The body was sprawled grotesquely on the ground. "This woman is the same age as I am," she said, "only she is dead."

Dressed in dungarees and heavy white knit sweater, Anne Walsh looked like an earnest teenager pressing a point on an elder she regarded as hard to penetrate. Lynch, clad in conservative gray suit, white shirt and dark, striped tie, was like a stern, but sympathetic father. "I want to talk to you as a human being—one human being to another," she told him in the almost empty courtroom, her eyes moist and reddening. "Here is how lives are destroyed, people crushed. This is what it is all about."

Lynch, replying in a crisp, professional, only-doing-my-job tone, said, "I don't have any special insights into the problems of the war, of the ghetto, or of the country. But we have laws and we have to uphold them. And we have to keep dissent in legal limits."

But Lynch, who was more comfortable dealing with professional criminals than with idealists who would violate the law and risk punishment to make a point of protest, obviously had mixed emotions about the ex-nun. He did not want to see her go to jail for refusing to testify and told her so. "You hold the key to the jail," he said gently. "All you have to do is testify, to tell the truth."

She shook her head, near tears. "I can't," she said. "My conscience won't allow me."

Later, she was called before Judge Herman for a civil contempt hearing. The judge, having already indicated his patience with recalcitrant witnesses was wearing thin, was unsmiling. She told him that she thought the grand jury itself was in contempt of court, that several jurors had read magazines or newspapers while she cited constitutional reasons for refusing to answer questions. "All right," Judge Herman said, "you've got it on the record. I have no alternative but to hold you in contempt of the court's order."

About noon two days later—on April 30—the sounds of

women laughing in the grand jury room could clearly be heard in the hallway outside. It was a sure tip-off that the jurors had completed their work, at least for the time being.

The jurors, eleven women and ten men, all white, mostly middle class and middle aged, filed quickly into the courtroom and took their seats, obviously anxious to get through with the formalities of presenting the indictments so that they could leave in time for the noon meal. The foreman, J. Stanley Hoffman, handed a stack of documents to Judge Herman. They included criminal contempt indictments against John Swinglish, Anne Mentz and Joe Gilchrist. And to no one's surprise, a superseding indictment in the conspiracy case.

If the superseding indictment was the result of a fishing expedition, the conspiracy net had landed a small catch indeed compared to the catch the government had proudly produced in the original indictment of January 12. In effect, Lynch had thrown back Guy Goodwin's original catch—or at least had submerged it beneath a pile of draft board raid allegations. No longer were any of the defendants charged with conspiring to violate the kidnap statute, which carried maximum punishment of life imprisonment. Now the charge was violation of the general conspiracy statute, punishable by a maximum of five years.

Lynch had structured the indictment in such a way that the government would not have to prove either the kidnapping or the bombing allegation in order to obtain a conviction on the overall conspiracy charge. Draft board raids would be enough for conviction on the overall charge.

The conspiracy count listed six illegal objectives:

(a) to violate Title 18, United States Code, Section 1361 by willfully injuring and committing depredations against property of the United States, to wit: files, records, books, papers, documents and other personal property of the Selective Service System and other Federal agencies, causing damage in excess of $100 to said property;

(b) to violate Title 18, United States Code, Section 2071 by willfully and unlawfully removing, mutilating, obliterating, and destroying certain files, records, books, papers, documents and other things of the Selective Service System, an agency of the

United States, filed and deposited in a public office of the United States;

(c) to violate Title 50 App., United States Code, Section 426 (a) by willfully and knowingly hindering and interfering with the administration of the Military Selective Service Act of 1967, and the rules and regulations made pursuant thereto;

(d) to violate Title 18, United States Code, Section 844 (f) by maliciously damaging, destroying, and attempting to damage and destroy by means of an explosive, personal and real property, owned, possessed and used by the United States and departments and agencies thereof;

(e) to violate Title 26, United States Code, Section 5861 (d) by willfully and unlawfully possessing firearms, that is, destructive devices consisting of dynamite, plastic explosives, primer cord, and detonating devices which would not have been registered to them in the National Firearms Registration and Transfer Record.

(f) to violate Title 18, United States Code, Section 1201 by unlawfully seizing, confining, inveigling, kidnapping, abducting, and carrying away and transporting in interstate commerce a person for ransom, reward and otherwise, in violation of Section 1201 of Title 18, United States Code.

The first three objectives dealt with draft board raids, of course, and the fourth and fifth concerned the tunnel-bombing plot and the sixth, the kidnapping allegation. The indictment specifically mentioned draft board raids in Philadelphia; Wilmington, Dover and Georgetown, Delaware; and Rochester, New York, and added, "as well as other parts of the United States."

The new indictment added two defendants, Mary Cain Scoblick and John Theodore Glick, who was already serving time for the Rochester raid.

The indictment dropped as co-conspirators the Reverend Daniel Berrigan, Paul Mayer and Tom Davidson. Those keeping tab on J. Edgar Hoover's original accusation could subtract one and add one. Now only one Berrigan was in the case, but Glick joined the Reverend Joseph Wenderoth as the second member of the eleven-member East Coast Conspiracy to Save Lives to be indicted.

Sister McAlister and Philip Berrigan also were charged with separate counts of smuggling communications in and out of the Lewisburg prison, he with four such counts—one more than in the first indictment—and she with three, the same as before. Also, for the first time Eqbal Ahmad was charged with smuggling communications. He was charged jointly with Sister McAlister on one count of attempting to illegally mail communications to Philip Berrigan and was jointly charged with her for attempting to send a "threat" to kidnap Kissinger. The smuggling of letters to and from federal prisons is a common occurrence, but never before had anyone been prosecuted for it. Prisoners caught for such offenses, if punished at all, were disciplined by the prison administration. Each letter-smuggling charge was punishable by a ten-year sentence and the "threatening-letter" charge by a five-year sentence.

In a controversial move, Lynch also attached to the indictment the full texts of the two Berrigan-McAlister letters written in August which raised the political kidnapping question. Defense attorneys contended the attachment of the letters was calculated to prejudice prospective jurors. They argued that the government should have cited in the indictment only those portions of the letters dealing with the alleged conspiracy.

The Justice Department contended that it was "usually the practice" to include letters in an indictment that alleges mailing of threatening communications. The first indictment had not described the letters as threatening communications, though Lynch used that description in the superseding indictment.

Although Lynch had salvaged but little of the case originally structured by Goodwin, the Justice Department tried to persuade the press and public that the case had merely been broadened to include additional allegations and defendants.

Newsmen covering the case in Harrisburg converged on Lynch as soon as court adjourned and pressed for an explanation of the new indictment. He, Cottone and two other government attorneys, Phillip Krajewski and Joe Tafe, assured newsmen that the superseding indictment was "substantially the same" as the original indictment. When reporters persisted in asking for a comparison, Lynch dropped "substantially the same" from his comparison, implying the indictments were the same.

And in Washington, the Justice Department press aide, Robert L. Stevenson, had summoned reporters to pick up copies of the new indictment and a five-page press release. It was, he said, another twelve on a scale of ten. Whatever the indictment's news rating, the handling of it by the Justice Department was a case of misleading the press and public. For there was no explanation about the change in the charge which meant a drastic reduction in punishment.

The press release featured the kidnap-bombing allegation in the first paragraph despite the fact it had been submerged beneath other allegations in the new indictment: "Eight persons were indicted by a federal grand jury today on charges of plotting a series of acts and anti-war vandalism leading to the kidnapping of Presidential Advisor Henry Kissinger and the blowing up of the underground heating systems of Federal buildings in the nation's capital."

Projecting a picture of a broader and perhaps stronger charge, the release continued: "Attorney General John N. Mitchell said a 10-count indictment was returned . . . superseding a seven-count indictment returned on January 12, 1971. The new indictment names two additional defendants and removes three previously named co-conspirators. Three additional counts are set forth in the indictment as well as 13 new overt acts. Two of the three counts are based on letters containing threats to kidnap Kissinger."

"It has been reported in the press that the Government's case depends heavily on Boyd Douglas, an informant," a reporter said. "Does this new indictment mean the case no longer hinges on Douglas?"

"No comment," Lynch snapped.

"Haven't people already been convicted for the Rochester raid which is mentioned in this indictment?" asked another reporter.

"There was no conspiracy charge in Rochester," Lynch said, "and we're alleging a conspiracy here."

Copies of the Justice Department's press release on the superseding indictment were passed out in Harrisburg by Cottone and in Washington by Press Aide Stevenson. Wire service reporters working under deadline pressure in both cities rushed to phone in reports that reflected the inaccurate picture projected by the release. And because of the extensive use of Associated Press and United Press International, their accounts were the ones most Americans saw in newspapers or heard on radio and television.

If the Justice Department had succeeded in misleading most of the news media and thus most of the American public, a few newsmen who had closely covered the case and were not under deadline pressure finally discerned the substantial and highly significant change in the indictment. It was extremely difficult to detect. It lay in the omission of a citation of a statute at the end of a string of alleged overt acts. The original indictment, after listing twenty-two overt acts, declared: "All in violation of Title 18, United States Code, Section 371 and 1201 (c)." Section 371 is the general conspiracy statute while Section 1201 (c) is the kidnap statute. The second indictment, after listing thirty-five overt acts, declared: "All in violation of Title 18, United States Code, Section 371."

Late in the evening of the day the indictment was returned, John W. Hushen, director of public information for the Justice Department, finally confirmed that the maximum punishment involved indeed had been changed—from a life sentence to five years. John Wilson, the information officer who wrote the news release, later said he did not learn of the change in the punishment provision until "too late" to include it in the release.

While the government propagandized the two indictments as "substantially the same," the defendants viewed the second one as proof of their earlier charges that the kidnap-bombing allegation rested on flimsy evidence. As for destruction of draft board records, at one time or another all of the defendants except Ahmad and Elizabeth McAlister had publicly claimed responsibility for such actions. Moreover, they informed their attorneys that if they testified in the case, they would admit any such allegations that were valid.

A week after the second indictment was returned, Internal Security Chief Robert Mardian, in a conversation with two newsmen, defended the Justice Department's handling of the case. He said the first indictment carried too harsh a penalty for the government to expect a conviction.

"But the grand jury did it, not us," he said, crediting the

grand jury with a great deal more independence from the prosecutor than grand juries normally show. "When they came back with that first indictment, I held my head in my hands and asked my attorneys why they didn't explain all the ramifications of the conviction to the jurors. I realized a trial jury would be hesitant to convict with such a stiff sentence. It would be like California's vehicular manslaughter law which has resulted in zero convictions because jurors say, 'There but for the Grace of God, go I.' It's the same with California's law against marijuana which carries a ten-year sentence."

Mardian said the government attorneys fully explained the reduction of punishment from life to five years in getting the jury to vote for the superseding indictment. "And now," he said with a smile, "we also have a hell of a lot more proof. The connection between the draft board raids and the rest of the conspiracy will be established clearly at the trial."

The Justice Department attached the Berrigan-McAlister letters to the indictment, he said, "because that's what department regulations call for—in cases directed from Washington. If we hadn't, or if we had released only a portion of the letters, the press would have said you're taking it out of context. I didn't want to release the letters. But regulations say you have to. I thought it would tell the defense what we know. But now I've learned they can get it in a motion for discovery of evidence anyway."

When the defendants arrived at the federal building in Harrisburg on May 25 for arraignment on the new indictment, a press staffer for the Harrisburg Defense Committee was on hand pointing out the cast—prosecutors, defense attorneys, defendants and witnesses—for television cameramen. But they missed two of the key figures who had been brought from prison, shackled and under heavy guard, and escorted into the building through a back entrance. Philip Berrigan, gaunt and wearing a loose-fitting plaid sport coat, a dingy white shirt, narrow red tie, and baggy trousers, looked fatigued. So did John Theodore Glick, clad in a yellow sport shirt and khaki trousers. Once unshackled and led into the courtroom, however, their eyes brightened and they smiled and exchanged the V peace sign with other defendants and supporters.

Ahmad was the first defendant called by the court to enter a plea. Wearing a dark gray suit and looking very much the Asian scholar, he strode briskly to the bench, looked up at Judge Herman and began reading a statement that said while he had pleaded not guilty to the first indictment, he had been able to understand its allegations and believed that "we needed only a modicum of judicial fairness to prove our innocence."

"Today, three months and seventeen days later, I have been recalled to this court to be arraigned for a second time under a new indictment whose terms I do not understand. Furthermore, I am deeply disappointed that the court has so far failed to stop the government's irregular and extrajudicial behavior which predicated the production of this new indictment."

Ahmad went on to accuse the court of failure to "restrain the government from its lawless behavior" and said he was "unable" to cooperate with such proceedings and therefore was refusing to enter a plea. Herman had listened intently, but he curtly told Ahmad he was making a speech instead of pleading and the court would follow its legal obligation and enter a not guilty plea for him.

Ahmad turned and walked slowly from the bench. The court called Philip Berrigan next. He, too, carried a prepared statement and told the court, "I cannot relate to this indictment." He denounced the document as "a potpourri of false charges, absurd allegations" and as "a piece of legal pathology supporting our military pathology in Southeast Asia." But Judge Herman, acting on government objections that such statements were out of order during an arraignment, cut the priest short, declaring he would enter a plea of not guilty for him.

Each of the other defendants followed suit, refusing to plead and attempting to read statements, but Judge Herman stopped them and entered pleas in their behalf. He permitted their statements to become part of the court record, however, apparently because of his regard for the legal expertise of a defense attorney, Leonard Boudin, who assured the judge this was "proper."

Lynch, still wearing the hat of chief of the Justice Department's Organized Crime and Racketeering Section, characterized the defendants as "more dangerous" than organized criminals and argued against reducing their bail. The comparison with organized criminals came after Defense Attorney Addison Bowman urged Judge Herman to exercise broad discretion in ordering government disclosure of evidence, implying the defendants should have more access to the evidence than defendants in "cases such as organized crime." Lynch retorted that the defendants faced "a very serious charge" of conspiring to kidnap, bomb, and destroy government records, and, with heavy sarcasm, he added:

"Thus, we do not have here, your honor, as Mr. Bowman would imply, a situation of several poets and an assistant professor of humanities inadvertently running afoul of the intricacies of the security law. We have a charge here of a well-planned, well-concerted action over a period of time by individuals who are extremely flexible because they decide what is or what is not violent as it suits their definition. I raise the question, your honor: Which is the more dangerous, since Mr. Bowman has addressed himself to this question—organized criminals who perpetrate their crimes out of greed, or these people who are charged here with violating the law because they reject society's definition of the law and criminality? If we think about it . . . really the group that we classify as organized criminals probably show a great deal more restraint because they violate the law insofar as they seek to further their own greedy ends; whereas, the crime charged here is basically a crime of people who would overthrow, who would violate the structures of the order of society in which we live. So I, for one, your honor, do not think this crime charged and these defendants charged with this particularly . . . do appear to deserve the generous discretion of the court, as Mr. Bowman feels."

Judge Herman agreed that the defendants should be treated "just like any defendant," but he decided that under the new indictment the defendants were entitled to a drastic reduction in bail. He noted that the defendants had always appeared "when wanted by the court." And, casting a sober glance at Tony Scoblick, who invariably was in the courtroom or on the federal building steps, the judge said dryly, "Mr. Scoblick appears whether he's wanted or not." Scoblick joined in the laughter that followed, but the judge did not crack a smile.

Judge Herman slashed bonds for Scoblick and Fathers Wenderoth and McLaughlin from $25,000 to $5,000 and released Scoblick's wife Mary on her own recognizance. He reduced bail for Ahmad from $30,000 to $10,000 and for Sister McAlister from $25,000 to $10,000.

Through the Harrisburg Defense Committee, the defendants also handed out a joint statement declaring,

> We have been presented with a new indictment in which the government backs down from its original charges of conspiracy to bomb and kidnap. It seeks to disguise this defeat by a pre-trial release of possible evidence. This new indictment combines in a single count six separate allegations of different conspiracies. To this conglomeration, it is impossible to plea. We have grown accustomed to our government disguising changes in the Vietnam war with lies, euphemisms and diversionary side shows. Public attention has too often been diverted from reality by false explanations and antiseptic language. The American people are told half truths—or half lies—about the Tonkin Gulf Incident, about extending the air war to North Vietnam, about the so-called secret war in Laos. . . . The U.S. Government has lost the Indochina war many times, and each loss has brought forth denials and escalation to a new war. So too, instead of acknowledging the implausibility of the original kidnapping and bombing conspiracy charges, they now try to bury them in a general assault upon resistance efforts.

Brisk pre-trial legal sparring continued, meanwhile, with both sides showing increasing frustration. An attorney for Dr. George McVey, whose wife, Suzanne, had been excused as a witness because of her advanced pregnancy, argued that McVey should not be compelled to testify because the grand jury ostensibly had already completed its investigation and further questioning would be unnecessary. But government attorney William Connelly, urging that McVey be held in contempt because he refused to testify after being granted immunity, told Judge Herman "the grand jury will continue to sit and there is a possibility additional indictments will be returned." McVey, who showed up in court wearing a "Vacuum Hoover" button on his plaid sport coat, became the tenth witness to be cited for contempt. Judge Herman postponed sentencing of him and other witnesses, however, until the case of Sister Jogues Egan could be finally adjudicated.

Ramsey Clark made his first court appearance in the case when he unsuccessfully sought to persuade Judge Herman to conduct a pretrial hearing on whether electronic surveillance had tainted the prosecution. Drawing on his own experience as attorney general, he contended the government had been vague and equivocal in its response to the defense motion for disclosure of wiretapping and bugging in the case.

He said that as attorney general he had frequently encountered difficulty in determining whether the FBI had used electronic devices. Sometimes, he said, the government suffered "deep embarrassment" by assuring the court there had been no such surveillance only to learn during the course of a trial that there had been.

The rhetoric by opposing attorneys during arguments on pretrial motions became so sharp at times that Judge Herman had to admonish both sides, although he more often called down the defense. At one point, when Paul O'Dwyer, the garrulous Irishman, bitterly assailed J. Edgar Hoover in an argument over pretrial publicity, Judge Herman snapped, "Well, we're not trying Mr. Hoover here."

"Yes, we are, Judge," countered O'Dwyer, arguing that Hoover's public comments about the alleged conspiracy, together with the government's handling of the case, had prejudiced the public against the defendants and made a fair trial impossible.

O'Dwyer's adamant arguments, sometimes based as much on emotional appeal as on law, not only antagonized Judge Herman and the prosecuting attorneys, but caused an uneasiness at the defense table. Once the scholarly Leonard Boudin, upon addressing the court following an O'Dwyer diatribe, smiled and said softly, "Now for the legal aspects."

Boudin was tough minded and outspoken, too, however, and he argued that Lynch and Cottone should be held in contempt for creating a "polluted atmosphere" by attaching the letters to the superseding indictment. He argued that the letters might even be inadmissible as evidence at the trial and that in any event, they were prejudicial, especially to defendants who were not parties to them.

Lynch's face flushed with anger. He denounced the defense motion and arguments as "improper" and said, "I object to it very seriously."

On another defense motion, attorneys argued that the government had improperly characterized the letters as "threatening." Never before, they argued, had a communication been considered threatening when it was sent to anyone other than the person allegedly threatened.

Lynch, warming to the courtroom battle, called the defense argument "a dazzling display of shoddy scholarship" and said it was "predicated upon a misconception of the law which is a curious amalgam of disjointed hearsay, conclusory allegations, innuendo, argument, impugning of motives and an apparent abysmal lack of knowledge of criminal practices and procedure."

Judge Herman, who also appeared to be irritated by the defense attack on the prosecution, denied the motion. Joseph Wenderoth, in priestly attire, including clerical collar, sat in the courtroom frowning. "What a weak fish," he muttered.

Far from the courtroom scene, the government's star witness was making news again even though the government had not yet acknowledged he would provide crucial information for their case. The Philadelphia *Inquirer* quoted Boyd Douglas as saying that he had been motivated by patriotism and would reveal what he had done during the trial. The newspaper reported it interviewed Douglas by telephone, but did not explain how contact was made. However, Douglas, still in close contact with the FBI, was known to have been in touch with his half-brother, Jack Weckman, who was working as a printer for the *Inquirer*.

The *Inquirer* quoted Douglas as saying,

The purpose of breaking my silence is to unequivocally state that I am an American who believes in the democratic system and does not condone violence and subversive destruction of our present form of government. I sincerely hope the American people realize legalities surrounding the Berrigan case dictate guarded publicity at this time. Therefore, my immediate defense of recent accusations by those presently under indictment is impossible.

Actually, except for saying Douglas had duped them, the defendants had made no accusations against him. On the contrary, all except Ahmad had expressed sympathy for him, telling reporters that they should not make him a scapegoat, that he was only a tool of the government and that he had been robbed of his dignity and self-respect by being turned into an informant on his friends.

Ahmad saw things in a much different light. Once, after hearing that Joseph Wenderoth had said, "After all Boyd is a human being and we don't want to see him destroyed," Ahmad blanched and said, "I tell you I am dealing with children. The government is destroying Boyd Douglas and he is helping the government try to destroy us. And they are worried about him!"

The defense attorneys, who had belatedly begun an investigation of Douglas' background, took a hard line on the matter. Terry Lenzner, the chief investigating attorney, said privately, "Douglas is a slimey character and a lying bastard. He must be destroyed on the witness stand despite the feelings of some of the defendants and co-conspirators."

Lenzner, thirty-two, a stocky former Harvard University football team captain, had been named director of legal services for the Office of Economic Opportunity in 1969. But the Nixon Administration fired him after he refused to curb the legal services program support for controversial suits brought against the government by the nation's have-nots.

Although Douglas still lived in the underground the FBI operates for key informants whose security concerns them, he surfaced briefly during the hot, humid afternoon of July 15 in his old hometown of Creston, Iowa. He was there for the funeral of his father, who had died of a heart attack at the age of fifty-six, three days earlier.

FBI agents had taken no chances on security, thoroughly examining the funeral parlor and the cemetery before the funeral and instructing the funeral home not to release information about the services to newsmen if they inquired.

Bearded and wearing a suit and dark sunglasses, Douglas was accompanied by several FBI agents and an attractive young woman who was not identified. They sat apart from relatives of the deceased.

Three agents driving a yellow Chevrolet Capri with Wisconsin license plates drove Douglas and the girl from the funeral parlor to the cemetery for graveside services. Douglas showed little emotion, but at one point he briefly embraced a middle-aged woman at the graveside. Among the wreaths was one of carnations from Douglas with a ribbon marked "Dad."

As the services ended, a lone reporter at the scene tried to interview Douglas, but agents quickly escorted the informant to their car and sped away.

In an interview afterwards, Douglas' aunt, Mrs. Maxine Cederburg, said she had not seen Douglas at the funeral or if she had, she had not recognized him. She called Douglas "the black sheep of the family" and said "he was nothing but a heartache for my bother and now my brother's through with him."

Douglas quickly dropped from sight again after the funeral and defense attorneys, unable to locate him, filed a motion asking that the court require the government to produce him for questioning in preparation for a defense of entrapment. The motion noted that the government itself had now filed a bill of particulars which repeatedly linked Douglas to the case. The defense claimed the government's document showed that its case rested "in large part" upon information supplied by the ex-convict, branded by the defense motion as an agent provocateur with a long history of mental instability who had been described as "psychotic" by the government's own doctors. Dr. Wolfram Reiger, who served as the prison psychiatrist at Lewisburg when Douglas was there, was quoted as saying Douglas was a "pathological liar."

Philip Berrigan, who had been brought to the courtroom at Harrisburg for arguments on the motion, whispered to a reporter during a recess, "Boyd and I were good friends. We said goodbye to each other the day I left Lewisburg to go to Danbury. I just feel sorry for him, that's all. I feel sorry for him."

The fiery Terry Lenzner, feeling no such pity, argued strenuously that Douglas should be produced so he could be questioned by defense attorneys, subjected to a mental examination and exposed as one whose "fabrications" had led to the indictment. He called Douglas a repeated offender who was "incapable of understanding the difference between truth and falsehood." And he said the government, by providing a "hiding place" for Douglas, was interfering with "the defense's ability to seek the truth." Lenzner even suggested that the government might be coercing Douglas.

Lynch, agitated once more by defense charges and insinuations, labeled Lenzner's argument "hutzpah," which he described as "a New York expression for gall," and said it was exceeded only by the "nonsense" of the defense arguments on electronic surveillance.

Lynch's vituperation included a heavy mixture of sarcasm. "Mr. Lenzner in his tour de force attack on Mr. Douglas mentioned that Douglas was a repeated offender," Lynch said. "That could be said of a number of persons being prosecuted in this case. Repeated offenses do not affect mental competency."

Lynch also submitted an affidavit saying he had spoken with Douglas about the defense motion and that Douglas said he did not want to be interviewed by defense counsel. "I asked him if he had any objection to my providing defense counsel with his current address," Lynch continued. "He stated most emphatically that he did. He stated that he knew that if defense counsel were made aware of his whereabouts, he would be harassed by newsmen as well as by people associated with the defendants in this case. I then advised Mr. Douglas that the government would do its best to respect his desire to maintain his present anonymity."

Judge Herman, noting that Douglas "is going to be here as a witness and subject to substantial cross-examination," denied the defense motion.

Although Lynch gave no sign of it during pre-trial arguments, he apparently found prosecuting the case an odious task. In October, while pre-trial motions were still being heard, he expressed that feeling to Will Wilson, who said he "strong-armed" Lynch into taking the case. Wilson had just resigned under pressure as head of the Justice Department's Criminal Division because of his ties to a figure involved in a Texas banking scandal and Lynch was bidding him farewell. "I have only one bone to pick with you," said Lynch, half smiling, but nonetheless serious. "Giving me that Berrigan case."

During a break in the court proceedings, Elizabeth McAlister, Joe Wenderoth, Neil McLaughlin and Tony and Mary Scoblick posed smiling, arm in arm, on the federal building steps, a water fountain with a huge marble eagle in the background. Lynch, Cottone and other government attorneys strode by, scowling, as news cameramen had a field day. "They do have a thirst for publicity," Lynch remarked.

In and out of the courtroom Lynch ridiculed the defendants for seeking publicity and the press for giving it to them. And, in the courtroom during a recess, Philip Berrigan decried the publicity Lynch's attachment of the letters to the superseding indictment had generated concerning his relationship with Elizabeth McAlister. "It's all blown over now, I guess," he said. "Liz had to take the brunt of it as usual. You just feel like you live in a goldfish bowl and are so helpless."

Rapid-fire, he answered a series of questions on a variety of subjects a reporter threw at him while he was briefly unguarded:

"I'm working in the education department of Danbury prison now, but doing practically nothing. Dan and I say mass twice a week, but the prison authorities do not let other prisoners come to the mass. . . .

"Kissinger is very bright, but very wrong. Nixon is smart and the China trip might defuse the peace movement, if it ever was fused. . . . The Republicans probably will win again. . . .

"The war is still going on, it's just a little more computerized now. The killing is more impersonal. . . .

"I don't regret anything I've done. I think the Resistance has had some impact on the war. . . .

"When they brought us down here from Danbury, they had us locked together, leg irons and chains around our waists. We stopped for a piss call and I asked, 'Can't you just unlock us for this?' And the guard said, 'No, you can do it, go ahead.' It just makes you goddam mad. It's so unnecessary."

While continuing its investigation of the Harrisburg defendants, the Internal Security Division also was busy probing other violations attributed to war resisters. Three of these cases worked against the Resistance members as they scurried about the countryside trying to drum up public support and legal defense funds.

One involved the bombing of the Senate side of the nation's Capitol on March 1, an act that outraged many Americans and reminded them that one of the charges in the Harrisburg case was that the defendants conspired to blow up underground heating systems in federal buildings in Washington. Although the FBI seemed to be at a dead-end in its investigation of the Capitol bombing, and no one had linked antiwar radicals to the explosion, the suspicion lingered that they were behind it. And the American public was not known for differentiating between radicals who turned to violence and those who had had a reputation of non-violence as in the case of the Harrisburg defendants.

In two other cases the FBI had much better luck and struck a crushing blow to the Catholic Resistance. On August 21, acting on an informant's tip, agents arrested twenty-six members of the Resistance following a draft board raid in Camden, New Jersey, and police in Buffalo acting on the same tip arrested five others after a raid there. The FBI's trap at Camden, which caught several raiders red-handed in the selective service office, was so well planned that as agents moved in they illuminated the federal building with floodlights set up earlier. A defense attorney commented, "It is an ambush, not an arrest." The five suspects at Buffalo—three men and two women, shoeless, their faces blackened with charcoal—also were caught at the scene.

This time the FBI had actually caught many of the suspects in the act of committing a crime. And this time the informant was no Boyd Frederick Douglas. He was a civic leader and an ex-Marine with an honorable discharge, Robert William Hardy, thirty-two. Hardy, who turned in his own pastor, the Reverend Michael Doyle, thirty-six, pastor of St. Joseph's Pro-Cathedral Church, commented, "I don't think anybody has a right to break the law."

Among those arrested were several with close ties to the Berrigans and to other Harrisburg defendants. They included John Peter Grady, one-time co-chairman of the Catonsville Nine Defense Committee; the Reverend Peter D. Fordi, thirty-four, a

Jesuit priest and member of the East Coast Conspiracy to Save Lives; the Reverend Edward Joseph Murphy, thirty-four, a Jesuit who served as coordinator of the New York office of the Harrisburg Defense Committee; the Reverend Edward McGowan, a Jesuit also with the Defense Committee in New York; and John Robert Swinglish and Paul Couming, both under indictment for criminal contempt in the Harrisburg investigation.

The arrests at Camden were a heartening victory for the FBI after its frustrating experience with the Harrisburg case and the theft of FBI documents in Media, Pennsylvania. Although the FBI still had made no arrests in the Media case, it felt it had snared one of the participants in John Peter Grady, the man it labeled a ringleader of the Camden raid. The FBI quoted its informant in the case, Robert Hardy, as saying that Grady told him he had participated in the Media raid.

Because of the need for large amounts of money for bail and defense funds, the Camden and Buffalo cases drained off money that might have gone to the Harrisburg defendants. But that was not their only effect. Although some members of the Resistance applauded the efforts at Camden and Buffalo, Eqbal Ahmad viewed the cases as bad news all the way around for the Harrisburg defendants.

"My fear at the moment," he said privately, "is we are being hurt more by our friends than by our enemies. Those cases have been a blow to us in every respect—politically, legally and financially. Why did they do it? They should stop those draft board raids. There was a particular moment in the antiwar movement when they were useful. But repeating the ritual over and over is of no value."

On November 26, a year after Hoover's original accusation and seven months after the second indictment, the Justice Department was still building its Harrisburg case. It added yet another unindicted co-conspirator, John Swinglish, the Navy veteran indicted earlier for criminal contempt at Harrisburg and arrested in the Camden draft board raid.

In December, 1971, R. Dixon Herman, natty in a checked sport coat, sat in his huge office on the ninth floor of the federal building and talked of the defendants' penchant for publicity and of the attorneys who would be trying the case before him the following month.

"I don't know why the defendants would be concerned about pre-trial publicity," Herman told one of the authors of this book. "Most of it they have generated and it has been favorable to them." Commenting on a motion by the Scoblicks to be declared paupers so that the government would pay the fees and expenses of defense witnesses, he said: "I read in the press where the defendants had plenty of money. I don't know whether they have a big slush fund or what." (Defendants who are not declared paupers must pay a daily witness fee of $20, plus $15 per-diem and transportation costs for each defense witness. In a lengthy conspiracy case involving many witnesses, this can add up to considerable amounts of money.)

Briefly, the judge sized up several of the attorneys in the case. He called Lynch "very sharp," but mentioned no other government attorney. He said, however, "I question whether the defense attorneys can match Lynch's trial experience." The judge praised Clark for his articulate courtroom manner and described Boudin as "very good from an appellate standpoint," but dismissed O'Dwyer as "a politician."

The case would be the biggest courtroom challenge that the sixty-year-old judge had ever faced. With his solid establishment background, Robert Dixon Herman was a sharp contrast to the radical defendants. A biographical sheet he made available to newsmen listed his membership in the Veterans of Foreign Wars, the American Legion, the Navy League (a World War II Naval officer, he served in the South Pacific), and disclosed that he was a thirty-three-degree Mason.

Named to the federal bench at the end of 1969, Herman was the protégé of a retired Republican boss in Dauphin County— M. Harvey Taylor. " 'Dix' is one of my boys," Taylor said on the eve of the trial. "We made him county solicitor."

Herman was born in Northumberland County, about fifty miles north of Harrisburg, September 24, 1911. He graduated from Bucknell in 1935 and Cornell Law School three years later.

He was appointed county solicitor after he was defeated in his bid for reelection to the Pennsylvania General Assembly in 1950 when there was a mild uprising against Taylor. With seven years as solicitor, Herman was elected to the county court and reelected to another ten-year term in 1967. He gained the reputation of an understanding and considerate judge in juvenile cases.

Herman had the prime requisite for appointment to the bench by President Nixon: He was a self-described "strict constructionist," a judge who preferred to rule on precedent rather than on an independent interpretation of the Constitution. This prompted one Harrisburg lawyer to conclude that Herman was "somewhat over his head" in the Berrigan case. "There are highly complex issues here—wiretapping, conspiracy law—and you can't deal with them all just by looking up precedents."

The Reverend Henry Raab, pastor of the Harrisburg Second United Church of Christ, where Herman was an elder, described the judge as a great churchman and a great American. "Both these things rank high in his loyalties," the Reverend Mr. Raab said. "And by that I mean he would speak and act in whatever way would be best for his country."

The specter of prejudicial publicity so bothered Herman that he seriously considered barring the press altogether during the questioning of prospective jurors.

"Stories listing the names of jurors might subject them or their families to harassment," he explained during an interview.

Asked if the defense might agree to such a plan, he said: "Oh, hell, no. The defendants wouldn't be interested in excluding the press. They want all the publicity they can get and know how to get it, too."

As the trial date approached, the Justice Department once more added to its case, amending its answer concerning co-conspirators and overt acts. The amendment, filed January 4, added Sister Sue Davis of Baltimore, a member of the East Coast Conspiracy to Save Lives, as an un-indicted co-conspirator.

CHAPTER TEN
The Trial Begins

"All rise, please!" croaked George H. Brocha, the grim-faced little eighty-one-year-old bailiff R. Dixon Herman had brought with him from state court after being elevated to the federal bench. Judge Herman, just as grim-faced, his black robe flapping, strode briskly to the bench.

"Oyez, oyez, oyez," intoned Brocha, a J. Edgar Hoover look-alike, whom visiting newsmen nicknamed "the toy bulldog." His eyes cocked to the fluorescent lighting panels that practically covered the ceiling of the windowless courtroom. Brocha barked: "All manners of persons having *aught* to do before the *honorable* judge now holding the *federal* court in the *middle* district of Pennsylvania *will* draw near, *give* their attendance and *they* shall be heard. God save the United States and *the* honorable court. The court is now in session, Judge Herman presiding."

Because of Brocha's colorful style and his emphasis on certain words, the defendants usually smiled, as they did now. But the atmosphere was a little stiffer than usual and the smiles quickly faded as Judge Herman, his bald head furrowed, took his seat. It was January 24, 1972, more than a year since the first indictment, and preliminary court proceedings were finally over—the trial was getting underway.

A stark and sterile courtroom, it provided nothing that might make a juror's mind wander from the case. Wall-to-wall soft, green, deep-pile carpet, walls twenty feet high, the bottom third walnut-paneled and the top two-thirds in a color scheme variously described by newsmen as conspiracy or oppressive green or muddied yellow ochre, raw umber, muted chartruese, tired algae or millpond scum. Straight-back wooden seats like church pews in the public section, with 40 spectators crammed on one side and 40 members of the news media on the other side. The only wall ornament a clock over one of the four doors, its modern face flush on the wall. The public section only one-third the size of the entire courtroom, prompting several visiting law students to comment that modern courtroom architecture seemed designed to make the court itself appear more powerful and to discourage public attendance at trials.

Judge Herman had granted a motion to John Theodore Glick to represent himself, then had severed Glick's case so that he would be tried separately at a later date. Thus the case that was labeled the Harrisburg 6 after the initial indictment, and the Harrisburg 8 after the superseding indictment, was now known, at least in newspaper headlines, as the Harrisburg 7.

The Scoblicks were declared paupers under another motion Herman granted so that some of their defense expenses would be paid by the government. Most of the defense expenses were being paid by the Defense Committee, a nationwide group comprised largely of volunteers that raised funds through solicitation and sponsoring various events, including appearances by the defendants. The Harrisburg Defense Committee raised about half a million dollars of which, after all expenses connected with the trial were met, but $20,000 was left to cover the costs of the appeal.

As local counsel, Tom Menaker, member of a wealthy corporate law firm, represented all the defendants. Father Berrigan was represented by Ramsey Clark, Terry Lenzner and the Reverend William Cunningham; Sister McAlister by Clark, Cunningham, and Paul O'Dwyer; Father McLaughlin by Father Cunningham and Lenzner; the Scoblicks by Clark and O'Dwyer and Leonard Boudin and Boudin's associate, Diane Schuler; and Ahmad by Boudin, Lenzner, O'Dwyer and Schuler.

Both William Kunstler and Addison Bowman had played secondary roles in the early stages of the case, but had left the defense team long before the trial. Kunstler's departure had been a sure sign that the defendants had opted for a trial on the legal issues, and were not planning to use the trial as a political forum for antiwar views.

The chief prosecutor, of course, was William S. Lynch and he would so dominate the government's case that his first assistant,

Connelly, a young assistant U.S. attorney from Ohio, would be left with little to do beyond examining several peripheral witnesses and making an argument to the jury.

The first task would be crucial—the search for a fair and impartial jury with enough intelligence to understand the complicated conspiracy case. Although in federal court the voir dire—the examination of prospective jurors—normally is a routine procedure conducted by the judge, Herman not only permitted attorneys to ask questions, but gave the defense exceptional latitude in examining members of the venire concerning their own background and views on the Vietnam war and the background and war views of their relatives.

Menaker and other Harrisburg attorneys who knew Herman felt he was being extremely tolerant with the defense because he wanted to demonstrate that the defendants were getting every opportunity for a fair trial and because he wanted to protect the court's record against possible reversal in case of a conviction. They pointed out it was also a way of trying to dispose of the war issue before the presentation of evidence so that the case could be heard on its legal merits.

With defense attorneys exploiting Herman's leniency to the fullest, the empaneling of twelve jurors and six alternates at Harrisburg loomed as a long-drawn-out process. The judge allotted the defense a total of twenty-eight peremptory challenges—four for each defendant—and the government a total of six. This meant a panel of forty-six had to be qualified before the attorneys would exercise their peremptory challenges in selecting the jury.

Herman asked prospective jurors several standard questions. The first day he excused thirty-eight persons from the 144-member venire because of fixed opinions, underscoring his own comments to the venire that the case had been "surrounded for a long time by a vast amount of publicity."

As the questioning proceeded, however, it became obvious that the lack of knowledge about the case was a greater problem than the amount of publicity. Many of those summoned for jury service said they never read newspapers and had never heard of Henry Kissinger. The comics, sports pages and women's news were by far the most popular sections for those who said they did read newspapers. During a recess, Eqbal Ahmad said, "My God, I think we would just settle for jurors with enough intelligence to know what a conspiracy is and to be able to understand the defense we put up."

Lynch found little fault with any member of the venire who got by Herman, but it was another matter for the defense.

Clark, looking more like a small-town lawyer than a former attorney general in his dark suits, white, button-downed shirts, narrow ties, Argyle socks and loafers, led off for the defense in his low-key, Texas drawl. He asked a series of questions designed to determine the military or federal employment background of any member of the panel or of the panelist's spouse, children, parents, brothers and sisters and even in-laws.

Herman disqualified many members of the venire because of extensive military or government background. In fact, the judge would never have approved as a juror a man with a role as active as his own in veterans' affairs—the VFW, American Legion and Navy League.

Menaker, clad in dark, tailor-made suits, followed Clark, letting it sink in on prospective jurors that a Harrisburg attorney was on the defense team, asking with obvious knowledge about the schools and churches they attended and the details of their employment. He originated a question that frequently tipped off the defense to prejudices of prospective jurors who otherwise had appeared to be fairly open-minded. "Several of the people who may appear as witnesses in this case have long hair and beards and wear unconventional clothing," he would say. "Do you have any strong feelings about such people? Could you give their testimony the same weight as the testimony of a clean-shaven FBI agent?"

Several of the jurors who expressed strong feelings were excused, but the question's greatest value was in uncovering prejudices to set the stage for further examination or to at least mark a prospective juror for probable elimination by peremptory challenge. Several who said long-haired people were all right as long as they were clean and neat and did not "smell bad" got strike marks on the defense's jury list.

Lenzner and O'Dwyer followed Menaker, usually bearing down on questions that had seemed to indicate bias, O'Dwyer sometimes to the discomfort of the other attorneys and defendants because his aggressive manner seemed to unnecessarily antagonize some of the prospective jurors.

And Boudin mopped up, dominating the courtroom with penetrating questions about war views and other possible prejudices against aliens and priests and nuns, and frequently persuading Judge Herman to disqualify prospective jurors. Boudin often bulldozed ahead in his questioning, ignoring objections by Lynch even though sustained by Judge Herman, and occasionally turning to admonish the prosecutor like a father talking to an unruly child. "Ah, ah, ah," Boudin would say, holding up his hand to shush the prosecutor, "don't interrupt me."

Lynch, arms outstretched, a posture he would constantly assume throughout the trial, would object. But Herman did little to stem the tide of Boudin's questions.

The exhaustive defense examination exposed considerable prejudice. Some of the prospective jurors recoiled at the idea of priests and nuns or an alien being involved in antiwar protests. It was like having the Silent Majority under oath, suggested *Time* magazine's Champ Clark, cataloguing some of the comments:

—The Bible says there will always be wars and rumors of wars, and I guess we'll always have them.

—I'm an open-minded man. I belong to the old patriotic organization of the country—The Patriotic Order of the Sons of America. I have belonged to it for forty-four years, and I haven't missed a meeting in twenty-four years. I lean toward the patriotic idea of supporting the government of the United States. I think it would be very wrong if I didn't stand up for my government.

—This country should never have been involved in the war. I support President Nixon's plan to end the war. But I would be prejudiced against "activities" to end the war.

—If antiwar demonstrators are clean . . . I have no objections to them. But if they look like they just came out of a rag bag . . . well I wonder. But even if they're not clean, they have thoughts and feelings, and I would as soon take their word about something as anyone else's.

After eleven and a half days of questioning that Boudin

described as the most exhaustive ever permitted in a federal court, the forty-six-member panel was filled.

With its extensive questioning and lopsided advantage in peremptory challenges, the defense wound up with a younger, more liberal and better educated jury than it had anticipated. It consisted of nine women and three men, including a Catholic opposed to the war and the mother of four conscientious objectors. Altogether, three of the jurors expressed antiwar views while the other nine were ambivalent or expressed no opinions. Most said they knew little or nothing about the case and seldom kept up with national news. Although most of them voiced support for the right of peaceful protest, two expressed reservations about an alien's right to protest the war.

The only Catholic, Miss Frances J. Yacklich of Cornwall, a printing firm bookkeeper, called the "war a big waste." Eqbal Ahmad had smiled at the comment but the smile faded when she said she did not believe aliens "should get involved" in antiwar protests.

Another juror, Mrs. Patricia L. Schafer of Etters, a pretty housewife in her thirties who said she belonged to no church, expressed similar reservations because she had lived in Thailand with her husband, a civil engineer, from 1967 to 1969, and as a guest of that country "didn't feel I had a right to criticize its policies."

Both Miss Yacklich and Mrs. Schafer had been permitted to remain on the forty-six-member preliminary panel after saying they could follow Judge Herman's instructions that Ahmad was entitled to same rights as American citizens.

The other jurors:

—Harold C. Sheets of Harrisburg, an accountant in his fifties, a Methodist and a graduate of the Wharton School of Finance at the University of Pennsylvania, who expressed no views on the war. He was to be elected foreman.

—Mrs. June L. Jackson of York, a Protestant and mother of three, wife of a World War II Navy veteran. She held a degree in pharmacy, but no longer practiced. Her first husband was killed in service in World War II. She expressed no views on the war.

—Ann V. Burnett, twenty-two, of Harrisburg, a county

welfare worker, with three years of college, majoring in philosophy. She said, "In some ways I feel the war is necessary and in others was unnecessary; one reason I might want it to continue would be to prevent invasion of this country."

—Robert Foresman, forty-five, of Lewistown, a state fire-school instructor, a Lutheran who said his wife and three children were Catholics. He studied a year at Bucknell University and served in the Army just after World War II had ended. He called the war "improper" and said, "I am absolutely convinced it was a mistake." When he first read about the alleged conspiracy, he said, "I thought the whole thing was kind of funny, the idea of a bunch of priests and nuns zipping off with Henry Kissinger."

—Mrs. Pauline E. Portzline of Mifflintown, in her forties, wife of a plumbing and heating contractor. A son-in-law was killed in Vietnam and a brother served in the Army there. She listed no church affiliation. "I wasn't too much opposed to the war at first," she said, "but in the last few years I've been against it."

—Mrs. Nancy Leidy of Carlisle, twenty-one, a petite bride of four months and secretary in the state health department. A Methodist, she voiced an opinion common to many of those called for possible jury service—the inevitability of war and an ambivalance over whether the United States should have waged all-out war or withdrawn. "I can't say I hate war," said Mrs. Leidy. "We will always have war, but I'd like to see our men come home. Maybe we could have followed a different policy—either total involvement or withdrawal, none of this half-and-half business."

—Mrs. Kathryn Schwartz of York, wife of a retired engineer, member of the conservative Brethern in Christ Church and mother of four conscientious objectors, who said she had no views on the war.

—Mrs. Vera P. Thompson of Carlisle, about forty-five, the only black, a member of the African Methodist Episcopal church, a stock clerk with a carpet company and wife of a store manager who was a veteran and an American Legion member. She expressed no views in the war.

—Mrs. Jo-An E. Stanovich of Harrisburg, a Protestant in her twenties, wife of a welder at Bethlehem Steel, with no views on the war.

—Lawrence A. Evans of Dillsburg, in his late fifties, a stocky, stern-faced supermarket owner, a Lutheran and father of six. He said he would like to see the war over but felt it was "being handled as near right as possible." He said priests and nuns should be more involved in social protests.

Lynch had used his six peremptory challenges to strike from the preliminary panel a young black woman who told the judge she had overheard several members of the venire say the defendants "must be guilty"; a man who said he considered Ramsey Clark to be a "great American"; two women who opposed the Vietnam war; a booted, twenty-four-year-old ex-Marine with Jesus-style hair and beard, who wore a neck-chain and gold cross; and a black who headed the civil rights unit of the Pennsylvania Health and Welfare Department.

Comments to the press by the civil rights official, Robert C. Baltimore, and by several other persons who were struck from the preliminary panel left little doubt that as exhaustive as the voir dire had been, some prejudice infected the forty-six member panel, especially against Ahmad.

Baltimore's comments, published by several newspapers, indicated the jury itself may have been contaminated by prejudicial remarks. He said one and probably two women selected as jurors had engaged in a conversation about the defendants the day before the empaneling of the jury. He said they had treated as a joke Judge Herman's instructions not to discuss the case.

"This one group of ladies just kept talking about it," said Baltimore, who was an Air Force pilot in World War II. "Most of the talk was about an alien opposing the government. Second, they talked about priests and nuns and said they should not be involved in something like this. And third, they talked about the case and said there must be something to it if the government indicted them."

At defense attorneys' request Herman called Baltimore into his chambers for questioning. But the judge concluded there was no substantial evidence of contamination and took no further action.

Boudin filed a motion for a separate trial for Ahmad on grounds members of the venire had "evidenced a strong bias against this defendant because of his alienage, race, religion and color." Other defendants joined in the motion, declaring that if they were to be tried jointly with Ahmad, hostility toward him would deny them a fair trial. Judge Herman denied the motion.

Of the six alternates seated, four voiced opposition to the war. The number-one alternate, Mrs. Rosemary A. McGuinn, a Catholic and secretary at the Navy supply depot, had told the court, "I do not wish to sit in judgment of these priests and nuns." She would get her wish—all twelve of the original jurors would sit throughout the trial.

Over defense objections, Judge Herman ordered the jury sequestered throughout the trial to insulate it "from any extrajudicial statements and such matters which might interfere with their ability to render a fair verdict." Defense attorneys had argued that sequestration during a lengthy trial would cause emotional problems that might influence the jurors' deliberations and that by the time the government ended its case, the jurors would be anxious to go home and inclined to resent a lengthy defense presentation. During voir dire, Clark impressed upon each juror that the defense vigorously opposed sequestration.

Herman's broad sequestration order rigidly restricted visits by relatives and friends of the jurors at the Penn Harris Motor Inn where the jurors were housed. Marshals escorted the jurors to and from their rooms and censored all newspapers and magazines, removing any reference to the trial and any "articles relating in any way to crime, criminal or civil litigation." The order banned all talk shows and news-type shows on television and all TV programs dealing with law enforcement, which were numerous in a Nation preoccupied by law and order. Specifically banned were *The FBI, Adam-12, The D.A., Dragnet, Owen Marshall, Perry Mason, O'Hara, U.S. Treasury, Sarge, Mannix, Cannon, The Mod Squad, Cade's County, Hawaii Five-O,* and the lawyer segment of *The Bold Ones.*

The day the government began presenting its case Eqbal Ahmad arrived early in the courtroom and spotted Francine Du Plessix Gray, author of *Divine Disobedience,* sitting in the middle of the press section. He literally ran across the courtroom, scurried by several amazed reporters and hugged and kissed Mrs. Gray, a slim and elegant blonde. She responded in kind. It was a showing of affection common to people in the movement even if some members of the press seemed taken aback that one of their own (she was covering the trial for the *New York Review*) would be embracing a defendant in the courtroom.

The defendants were forever hugging and kissing friends attending the trial, to the irritation of traditional Catholics like Lynch and Cottone. "I'm not used to seeing nuns and priests kissing," said Cottone. "I've always known them to be restrained, even with their relatives."

Also early to arrive, as usual, were Philip Berrigan and Elizabeth McAlister, sitting side by side facing the jury across the room, their straight-back chairs along the wall to the side and rear of the L-shaped defense table. Each day deputy marshals would transport the priest to and from the Dauphin County jail in handcuffs and chains and escort him into the courtroom ten or fifteen minutes before the court convened. The nun often would be the only one there to greet him. The deep affection there was obvious, as they talked and smiled, and their eyes met and hands touched. Some of the defendants' supporters had expressed fear that the jury might be prejudiced by the sight of a priest and a nun on such personal terms, especially in light of the passages of affection in the letters the government would introduce in evidence. But that never inhibited Father Berrigan and Sister McAlister. In fact, their close relationship was to be cited by their attorneys as part of the defense.

The priest usually wore a dark suit or sport coat and a solid white or blue shirt and narrow tie. She wore bright knee-length dresses, sometimes with a large metal cross dangling from a neck-chain. Both spent a lot of time scribbling notes on the trial and sometimes exchanging them.

Joseph Wenderoth and Neil McLaughlin, both wearing clerical collars and sweaters or sports coats, usually sat together. So did Anthony Scoblick and his wife Mary Cain Scoblick, he clad mostly in ill-fitting, outmoded clothes as befitted a court-declared pauper and she in short dresses, her blond hair straight or tied with a ribbon in a pony tail.

Ahmad sat off to the side, scribbling notes for the defense attorneys, at times turning and winking at members of the press.

With his dark complexion and one eye that never seemed to focus properly, he was perfect for the role Leonard Boudin said the government picked for him—"foreign devil" in an internal security case.

Boudin contended that the government knew Ahmad was hanging in the case by a thread, that there was no evidence linking him to draft board raids nor any substantial evidence linking him to any law violation. But the FBI wanted Ahmad prosecuted, Boudin argued, because he had directed the underground network for Daniel Berrigan. Moreover, he said, the government knew that even if Ahmad's eventual acquittal was a certainty, the mere presence of a "foreign devil" might help convict the other defendants.

Lynch had made it clear to newsmen that he considered Ahmad a central figure and that he looked with disdain on all the defendants. While he had taken over the case reluctantly, he had psyched himself to the point that he seemed to loathe the defendants. During recess, he would use his favorite expression—bullshit!—followed by a crack like, "They're a bunch of burglars."

But in his opening statement to the jury, the prosecutor was relatively dispassionate, outlining in fifty minutes what the government hoped to prove over the next several weeks and leaving no doubt the case would rise or fall on Boyd Frederick Douglas, Jr. and the letters he smuggled between the priest and the nun he knew as Phil and Liz.

The government, Lynch said, would show that Philip Berrigan was the leader of a group of individuals, including the defendants, who "took very strong exception to certain governmental policies" and hatched a conspiracy in January, 1970, to commit a series of illegal acts the thrust of which was to disrupt governmental activities and to focus and exploit and magnify news media coverage of those activities."

The first illegal acts—the February 6 raids on three Philadelphia draft board offices—were followed by a February 14 meeting at Independence Hall at which Joseph Wenderoth and Theodore Glick and other members of the East Coast Conspiracy to Save Lives surfaced and took public responsibility for the raids, Lynch told the jurors. "We expect to also show," he said, "that the Scoblicks also were involved and that Phil Berrigan was in on the planning of it." The meeting, he said, was arranged by William Davidon (an unindicted co-conspirator).

Lynch scorned the "lofty purposes" proclaimed by the draft board raiders and said, "They planned—to use one of their words—to 'escalate' their activities by planning destruction of certain underground heating pipes in Washington."

"In fact," said Lynch, alluding to a crucial point in the bombing allegation, "we expect the proof to show that Father Joseph Wenderoth and Father Philip Berrigan entered in early 1970 these underground tunnels with the intent of casing or assessing the feasibility of this particular activity. . . . Their actions were meticulously considered and involved a great deal of pre-planning."

The plans were disrupted on April 22, Lynch said, when Philip Berrigan was captured, but were resumed a short while later when the priest became acquainted with another inmate at Lewisburg prison, Boyd F. Douglas, Jr., who was studying at Bucknell University under a special study-release program. "Mr. Douglas," said Lynch, "in the course of his studies came to know Professor Richard Drinnon who was acquainted with Philip Berrigan and through the professor Mr. Douglas met Philip Berrigan."

The priest "almost immediately" recruited Douglas as a courier, Lynch said, and thereby kept his power to advise his followers outside the prison while they in turn kept him apprised of their plans and activities.

The government's account of how Douglas became an FBI informant was disclosed for the first time by Lynch. He said it occurred in early June after Associate Warden Robert Hendricks confronted the convict with information about the contraband letter referring to "Pete" found in Berrigan's cell. Hendricks then accompanied Douglas to Professor Chenoweth's office on the Bucknell campus, Lynch said, and the convict took from his briefcase the copy of the May 22-23-24 letter from Father Berrigan to Sister McAlister—which he had copied on his own. The letter, Lynch said, was turned over to FBI agents who arranged with Douglas to keep them advised of further activities between Father Berrigan and the Catholic Resistance, including any more letters he might smuggle between the priest and Sister McAlister.

At Father Berrigan's direction, the prosecutor continued, Douglas contacted Sister McAlister and they devised a plan to smuggle messages and to set up mail drops in Lewisburg and New York. Over the next four months, he said, Douglas transmitted fourteen letters from the nun to the priest and ten letters from him to her, always furnishing the FBI with copies. Many of the letters, he said, included descriptions of draft board raids and plans for future raids.

Neither the jurors nor anyone else in the courtroom had seemed especially interested in Lynch's description of draft board actions. After all, with the exception of Eqbal Ahmad, the defendants had pretty well identified themselves with such activities. But the talk of bombing tunnels had caused the jurors to lean forward and now they did again as Lynch told of the allegation that gave the case international notoriety and packed the courtroom's press section.

"About August nineteenth," Lynch said, hesitating and scanning the faces of the jurors, "Boyd Douglas received a telephone call from Sister McAlister and she said that she had sent 'a very hot letter' and it had been sent to Patricia Rom, who was a librarian at Bucknell University. Sister McAlister advised the letter was quite important and under no circumstances should it fall into the wrong hands. . . . Now the plan as proposed, was simply the kidnapping of Henry Kissinger."

Sister McAlister also told Douglas, Lynch said, that he would be receiving a telephone call from Eqbal Ahmad. At that, Ahmad, sitting off to the side of the defense table next to a black deputy marshal, shook his head and Boudin jumped up to object. Ordinarily, attorneys do not interrupt opening statements, but Boudin had been especially sensitive about the allegation because Ahmad had vehemently denied ever hearing of Douglas before Hoover's statement, much less talking to him on the telephone. Herman, overruling the objection, declared, "Mr. Lynch says he has evidence of it and I have to assume he'll put up something."

Lynch assured the judge evidence would be forthcoming, then told the jury that Ahmad telephoned Douglas and told him he was aware of the letter suggesting a plan to kidnap Henry Kissinger and "was very much interested" in Philip Berrigan's views.

It made little sense that a man of Ahmad's background and suspicious nature would be talking about a kidnap plot to a convict—especially on a telephone. But if the government could prove that he had, it might well convince a jury that the mention of kidnapping in the letter was more than fantasy. And it would tend to substantiate Lynch's contention that Ahmad was mastermind of the kidnap plan.

Moreover, if the government could put Fathers Berrigan and Wenderoth in the heating tunnel, as Lynch promised, then the allegation of a joint kidnap-bombing plot would take on more serious proportions.

Lynch spent most of his opening statement on draft board raids and outlining Douglas' informant role, but concluded by emphasizing that Douglas would testify that Fathers Wenderoth and McLaughlin repeatedly told him that the kidnap-bombing plans were in effect. After "publicity about the plans," Lynch said, carefully avoiding specifically mentioning Hoover's Senate testimony, "everybody—so to speak—headed for the woods."

After that, Lynch said, Father Wenderoth told Douglas, "It's better that no one say anything to anyone about anything" and later Sister McAlister told Douglas "he was no longer a part of the plans, he was suspected of leaking information."

"This indictment followed," Lynch said.

In a brief rebuttal of his one-time subordinate, Ramsey Clark told the jury, "You have an opportunity to do something for your country for justice, for truth and in this case for history." He said the indictment had been brought to "justify something J. Edgar Hoover had done," adding, "The government's charges are false. It charges conspiracy. Of course, we know Henry Kissinger was not kidnapped. He is alive and well in Peking."

Rather than telling the jurors what the defense might hope to prove to refute the government's evidence, Clark told them that in weighing the prosecution's evidence, they should consider the source and the government's motive in bringing the case.

The case, he said, depended upon Douglas who had been indicted the first of many times ten years earlier for impersonating an Army officer—"an impersonator all his life." He described Douglas as "unstable" and said he had twice attempted suicide.

"You'll have to watch Boyd Douglas, see him, judge him," Clark drawled. "I think he is a very sad person and I think you'll find he's been in trouble all his life. The United States government, in all its majesty, didn't deem to tell you this morning, but he's made lying a way of life, and it hurts me to have to say that."

As for the Phil-Liz letters, Clark asked the jurors, "Have you ever written more in letters than you know, to comfort a loved one, to help a friend in distress?" He suggested that a person writing to a prisoner she cared about would be inclined to stretch the truth in order to boost his spirits and assure him the cause for which he went to prison was still being pursued.

Clark described the draft board allegations as the "most devious" part of the charges and pointed out that they had not been mentioned in the first indictment. Some of the defendants had been involved in the draft board raids, he said, but they acted out of individual conscience and not in a conspiratorial manner. He described them as "gentle people" who, while they might be driven to discussing violent tactics because of their abhorrence of the Vietnam war, would never conspire to bomb or kidnap or commit any other act that might endanger human life.

Although attorneys' statements and questions are not evidence, as Judge Herman frequently reminded the jury, they can be crucial to the jury's understanding of the issues, especially in a complicated conspiracy case that involves politically motivated crimes and charges of prosecution for political purposes. In this case, both Lynch and Clark had framed the issues well.

Had the defendants, as Lynch charged, decided to escalate their antiwar activities and join in a conspiracy to kidnap and bomb? Or had they merely discussed the possibility of such acts and had the Justice Department decided to prosecute them on those charges anyway in order to protect the reputation of J. Edgar Hoover?

The Justice Department knew it could have had a much more clean-cut case and a better chance of conviction had it confined the second indictment to a plot to raid draft boards. Moreover, the sentence would have been the same and Ahmad was the only defendant it would have had to drop. But the Justice Department instructed Lynch to preserve the kidnap-bombing allegations of the original indictment.

Dragging deeply on a cigarette during a recess, Lynch acknowledged to a newsman that he was proud of the way he had wrapped the kidnap-bombing plot in a blanket of draft board raids. "It's not a bad indictment, is it?" he said, grinning and flicking ashes from his cigarette.

"Is it true," a reporter asked, "that the jury could return a guilty verdict if it found there was a conspiracy to raid draft boards, but no conspiracy to bomb or kidnap?"

"That's right," said Lynch.

"And all we would know," the reporter asked, "is that the jury found them guilty of a conspiracy that included bombing and kidnapping as well as the raids?"

Lynch, still grinning, nodded affirmatively.

In four days, Lynch put up more than a score of witnesses, including FBI agents and Philadelphia police officers, to testify about the Philadelphia draft board raids of February 6, 1970, and about Father Wenderoth and Ted Glick and other members of the East Coast Conspiracy to Save Lives surfacing at Independence Hall and claiming credit for the raids. Their testimony developed little that was new or exciting and the defense did little cross-examining.

Then came Robert L. Hendricks, former associate warden of Lewisburg Federal prison, a stocky, middle-aged man. He testified that after a guard brought him the letter confiscated in Father Berrigan's cell, he confronted the priest and told him that he knew the identity of the "Pete" in the passage, "I will try to hunt down Pete later to see if he has the news or has brought news." Actually, Hendricks said, at the time, he was under the impression "Pete" was Pete Brown, a part-time prison staffer who taught at Bucknell. "That was the only Pete I knew," Hendricks said, "but when I completed my conversation with Philip Berrigan I knew Pete was Douglas."

He went on to describe how he had taken Douglas to Bucknell to get the copy of the May 22-23-24 letter Douglas had smuggled out for Father Berrigan and how he and Warden J. J. Parker had then conferred with a bureau official in Washington and called in the FBI to talk with Douglas. He testified briefly on direct examination, adding little to Lynch's account of the incident in his opening statement. But cross-examination was a different matter.

Clark, who as attorney general had jurisdiction over the Bureau of Prisons, pressed Hendricks on the question of the bureau's cooperation with the FBI in using a convict as an informant, especially one with Douglas' record. He asked Hendricks if during his twenty-six years with the bureau he "did not know it was always the firmest of policies never to permit any prisoner to act as a government informant?"

Lynch objected and Judge Herman sustained him, but Clark persisted, claiming the government had violated a standing policy in order to indulge in discriminatory prosecution. Herman finally rebuked him for "a highly improper" action and said, "Mr. Clark, you're not going to testify—if you want to make a statement, come to the sidebar [bench]."

"If a question is put and disallowed," Herman said in one of several instructions to the jury during Clark's cross-examination, "you must completely disregard that question and must not speculate on what the answer might have been."

How completely jurors disregard such questions, however, is problematical. And Clark pressed on.

Did Hendricks know that Warden Parker opposed the use of Douglas as an informant? Was Hendricks familiar with Douglas' psychiatric record? Did he know of Douglas' suicide attempts? Did he know of Douglas being caught with a hypodermic needle?

Lynch, objecting to each question and popping up and down in exasperation, finally said, "Your Honor, will you instruct the jury that the answer is the evidence, not the question?"

"Yes," said Herman, who had sustained each objection, "I instructed them this morning."

Clark attempted to delve into the FBI's working arrangement with the Bureau of Prisons that permitted a man of Douglas' record to continually violate prison regulations. But Hendricks, pleading ignorance, was not very helpful. He said the only thing he knew about it was that Douglas cooperated with the FBI and continued to bring letters in and out of the prison.

Asked if he knew Douglas had an apartment in Lewisburg, he said, "No sir, I don't believe he did."

"You did not know that some of the guards at the prison lived two blocks from that apartment?" Clark demanded. "You did not know that?"

Hendricks said he did not believe it. And to other questions, he said he did not believe Douglas had had access to money, liquor and telephones, all in violation of prison rules.

Clark, expressing disbelief, continued:

Q. Did you know he traveled to Williamsport thirty miles away?

A. I do not believe that he did.

Q. Did you know that he was being paid by an agency of the government?

A. I do not believe that he was.

Q. Did you know that he purchased a car before he left the prison?

A. I do not believe that he did.

If the defense had problems getting anything from Hendricks, the prosecution had an even more difficult time with its next four witnesses—Jane Hoover and Betsy Sandel, Douglas' old girl friends from Bucknell, and Bucknell librarians Patricia Rom and Zoia Horn. All were extremely reluctant to testify. They smiled at the defendants and defense attorney Tom Menaker, who had represented them during the grand jury investigation. At Lynch's request, Judge Herman had granted them immunity and ordered them to testify at the trial or face imprisonment for contempt of court.

Now a Boston University law student, Jane Hoover, clad in a bright orange mini skirt, testified slowly, her hands clasped in her lap. She told of transcribing the letters for Douglas and when Lynch asked if she could identify Sister McAlister, she pointed to her and smiled.

Asked about any discussions of destroying draft board records during the picnic at Professor Chenoweth's house she said, "There were discussions about the Vietnam war and how bad it was and how it should be protested and about destroying draft board records as an alternative for people who were committed to protest the war."

Lynch pressed her on whether Father Wenderoth or Father McLaughlin had discussed draft board raids, but she said, "I couldn't say." He showed her a copy of her grand jury testimony and she said, "It seems that last January I had a vague memory that they discussed draft board raids."

Questioned about other meetings, she said they involved academic discussions or she didn't recall or "It was a very social occasion—it wasn't even what you call an academic discussion."

Cross-examined by Terry Lenzner, she was a willing witness. Upon first meeting Douglas she said, "He told me he knew Father Berrigan in Lewisburg prison and that he was a great man and he gave me Father Berrigan's book, *Punishment for Peace*, and said I should read the book and it'll make you think about things."

"What did he say he was in prison for?" asked Lenzner.

"He said he was with a group of friends in California and they had a plan to blow up trucks carrying napalm, but got caught because somebody got nervous and went to the police."

She also told of Douglas' arranging for her to meet Sister McAlister in New York and Lenzner asked, "Why did you go there?"

"Well," Jane said after hesitating, "it was a personal thing . . . Boyd asked me if I would marry him and I was taken aback."

Lynch jumped up, objecting, "Your honor, this goes far beyond the scope of direct examination." But Herman overruled him and Jane continued: "He told me that he had cancer and six months to a year to live and he showed me a letter that was supposed to be from a doctor and I was very nervous and upset and didn't know what to do. I felt some sympathy for him. He said Sister McAlister would be a good one I should talk to."

Knowing the next question would be disallowed, Lenzner rushed through it. "Did he ever tell you he was engaged to a girl who had blond hair like you?"

"Yes," Jane said, with Lynch objecting and Herman sustaining him.

As the attorney who headed up the defense's investigation of the government's case, Lenzner knew far more about it than any other member of the defense team and he was intent upon discrediting Douglas even before the informant took the stand. In staccato fashion he ran through a series of questions to emphasize Douglas' role as a provocateur:

Who organized a luncheon which Fathers Wenderoth and McLaughlin attended in Lewisburg? Well, Boyd did. Who arranged the picnic at the Chenoweths'? Boyd said he did. Who arranged the luncheon meeting in July? Boyd did. Was he continually encouraging you to get more involved in activities against the Vietnam war? Yes, he used to say to me and my roommates and my friends and other students that we should be willing to commit ourselves and go further than demonstrating and signing petitions. Did he tell you he was an expert in explosives? Yes. Did he describe how he could wrap explosives around a tree and blow a tree into a stump? Yes.

Finally, Lenzner paused and asked, "Did Sister McAlister ever ask you to participate in draft board actions?"

"No."

Lowering his voice, Lenzner slowly asked the same question about each defendant (except for Ahmad who had never met Jane) and got a "no" each time. Suddenly, Lenzner's voice boomed:

"Did Boyd Douglas ever ask you to participate in draft board actions?"

"Yes," she said.

Several jurors looked surprised and murmurs rippled across the press and spectators' areas. "No further questions," Lenzner said, walking slowly back to the defense table.

He had left little questioning for other defense attorneys, but Boudin asked a key one about Douglas' stated plans for using explosives. "He said he knew a lot about explosives because of his experience in the Army," Jane said, "and when he got out of prison he wanted to be involved in meaningful acts that would entail his using explosives . . . he said that when he got out of prison he would become involved in a big action in Washington, D.C."

Although Jane Hoover's testimony may have disappointed the prosecution, it was vital in linking up the Phil-Liz letters and in corroborating the holding of various meetings that Douglas would testify about.

Betsy Sandel, wearing a sweater and slacks, proved even less cooperative, but the prosecution needed her testimony, too, for she was a link in sending the "kidnap" letter from Sister McAlister to Father Berrigan.

Like Jane, Betsy recalled most meetings as "social events" and when Lynch showed her her grand jury testimony about one meeting and asked if she had testified there was a discussion about draft board actions, she said, "That very well may have been my testimony then, but I don't recall it now."

She hesitated and bowed her head for long periods after some questions, her long red hair hiding her face from the judge on her right side and the jurors on her left side.

After she repeatedly said she could not recall Fathers Wenderoth and McLaughlin discussing the draft board actions, Lynch handed her a document and said, "Would you look at pages forty-two and forty-three of the grand jury testimony. Was anything said about civil disobedience?"

"I don't recall."

"Did Father McLaughlin say anything about it?"

"I don't recall much of the conversation at all."

Lynch finally handed Betsy a copy of the "kidnap" letter:

Q. Have you seen that before?

A. Parts of the letter look familiar.

Q. Is that the letter you copied for Boyd Douglas? Do the parts that look familiar to you look like the parts you copied for Boyd Douglas?

A. I can only say the passages look familiar but I can't say the whole letter looks familiar.

Q. Are the passages of the letter that look familiar to you the passages you copied for Boyd Douglas?

A. Yes.

On cross-examination, Lenzner led Betsy through the same set of questions he had asked Jane Hoover concerning Douglas' role as a provocateur and got the same answers.

"Did he tell you he was engaged to a girl named Nancy Williams," Lenzner asked as Lynch jumped up, objecting, "and she had red hair like you?"

Although Herman sustained the objection and the question was of doubtful relevancy anyway, the picture of a convict conning coeds at Bucknell University while serving as an FBI informant seemed to unsettle some of the jurors, especially several of the women, who exchanged glances.

Patricia Rom, another link in the "kidnap" letter chain, acknowledged turning over to Douglas a sealed envelope marked "Boyd" which was enclosed in another envelope sent to her by Sister McAlister in August of 1970. But she said she had lost a note that was enclosed to her from the nun thanking her for helping with a meeting at Lewisburg.

"Tell us as completely as you can what the note said," Lynch said.

"All I can remember about it," she replied, "is that she . . . had enjoyed being here, she enjoyed meeting the people here and she thanked me for my part in the hospitality. And she said could I please give the enclosed to Boyd Douglas."

When Lynch persisted in questioning her about the whereabouts of the note, defense attorneys objected that he was cross-examining his own witness. At a sidebar conference Herman agreed to stop the line of questioning, but told defense attorneys, "I will say that these last witnesses are very evasive and forgetting things that they apparently testified to in the grand jury and . . . I am thinking very seriously of allowing the grand jury minutes to be admitted into evidence." He said, "These last two witnesses, at least the first one, are evasive . . . very close to being guilty of perjury."

Cross-examined by Lenzner, Patricia Rom said that Douglas talked to her about being a demolitions expert. "Did Douglas ever tell you if you wanted to get involved in some action he could put you in touch with the right people?" Lenzner asked.

"Yes," she said.

Zoia Horn, who had left Bucknell and was now living in Turlock, California, refused to testify. Called to the witness stand out of the jury's presence, she attempted to read a statement saying she could not in good conscience cooperate with "this black charade," but Judge Herman cut her short.

Defense attorneys tried to save the librarian from a contempt citation, declaring that her testimony was peripheral anyway and that they would stipulate for the record that if she took the stand her testimony would be the same as it had been before the grand jury. But Lynch, angry over the government witnesses' reluctance to testify, declared, "My experience with the witnesses from Bucknell University—Rom, Sandel, Hoover and Horn—is that their testimony does not exhaust their knowledge of the issue. Miss Horn takes a position that she is above the law, that she does not choose to give testimony."

Herman ordered her jailed for contempt until she testified or for the duration of the trial.

"Call your next witness," said Judge Herman.

Lynch turned to a deputy marshal standing to the jury's left, near a door used by witnesses, and said, "Mr. Douglas." All eyes turned to the door. The deputy stepped outside. Two other deputies took up positions at the door, two others walked over to guard the door used by the defendants across the room, and two others stationed themselves at the main entrance at the back of the courtroom between the press and spectators' section.

CHAPTER ELEVEN

Mr. Douglas Takes the Stand

Boyd Frederick Douglas, Jr. walked stiffly into the courtroom, his dark eyes glued on Lynch. The prosecutor waved him to the witness stand. Avoiding all other eyes he strode to the stand and raised his right hand. Sworn by Deputy Clerk Richard Bowen to tell the truth, he said softly, "I do," then sat down, carefully adjusting his wide lavender tie and unbuttoning the coat of his much too-tight gray, pin-striped suit. He wore a pink shirt and black buckled shoes—and a wedding band. Pudgy, with a double-chin, he was clean-shaven, his razor-cut, collar-length hair held by spray in semi-mod style. Those who knew him barely recognized him, not because of his style and dress but because of the weight he had added. "He must have put on thirty pounds," whispered Joseph Wenderoth.

Still ruggedly handsome despite the extra weight, Douglas was cool and calm, but obviously feeling his way in his latest role as a witness. Philip Berrigan tried to catch the eye of his former prison mate, but Douglas looked only at Lynch.

"Mr. Douglas," Lynch began, "in 1970, the early spring and summer, where were you?"

"In Lewisburg penitentiary," Douglas said in a barely audible voice.

To the rear of the prosecution table and facing Douglas sat two stocky, middle-aged men in white shirts, narrow ties and dark business suits—FBI Agents George Menzler of FBI headquarters in Washington and William Anderson of the Philadelphia office. Both agents took notes as he testified.

In a low monotone, Douglas briefly told of arriving in Lewisburg in January, 1968, of winning a settlement against the government in connection with the medical experiments, and of attending Bucknell University and meeting Professor Richard Drinnon. He could not testify about anything specific that Drinnon had told him because the professor was not a defendant or co-conspirator and his conversation would be disallowed as hearsay. But Lynch elicited from Douglas testimony that the first time he ever heard the name Philip Berrigan was in a discussion with Drinnon. Some time after, Douglas said, he informed Drinnon that Father Berrigan and David Eberhardt had arrived at the prison.

He then contacted Father Berrigan at the prison, he said, and told him that Drinnon had asked him to do anything he could for the priest. "Phil Berrigan told me," Douglas continued, "is there any way that you could get a message out or possibly make a phone call to a friend of mine?' So I told him, well, I think I could get a letter out for you if that is what you like. So I told him I would meet him the next morning in the mess hall prior to my leaving the penitentiary for the university. And he said he would give me the letter at that time."

The next morning, Douglas said, the priest gave him two letters to give to Drinnon—one addressed to the professor and the other to Sister McAlister. He said he read both letters and the one for the nun was of "a personal nature." A week later, he said, Drinnon gave him a letter "of a personal nature" from Sister McAlister to Father Berrigan and he read that one, too, before taking it into the prison.

When he gave the letter to Father Berrigan, Douglas said, the priest told him that he was a member of a group called the East Coast Conspiracy to Save Lives that had tried to recruit Drinnon to help raid draft boards. "He told me at the time," Douglas said, "that due to Professor Drinnon's not becoming involved in this action—because he was writing a book on the American Indians—why, he did not fully trust Professor Drinnon. So he told me—he said he would like to set up a mail drop and that way alleviate [sic] Professor Drinnon completely."

Douglas told of ingratiating himself with Father Berrigan by acting "quite sympathetic" to the idea of draft board raids and by telling the priest he was hostile to the government because he received "numerous scars" as a result of medical experiments and had been rejected for a parole he expected to get when he settled the damage suit against the government. He said the priest then "brought out the fact to me that he had looked at several different projects around the country."

"Was there a particular project he talked about?" Lynch asked.

"Yes. This was the destruction of the utility system in Washington, D.C."

Q. Tell us about that, what he said about that?

A. Well, he told me that he had been in this system along with another individual.

Q. What do you mean he had been in the system?

A. He had been down in the tunnel system itself with another individual. He said it was the complete utility system, and it carried conduits in the system. He said he had been down there posing as an electrical engineer. . . . He said he had no problem in gaining access to the tunnel, that several GSA people in the tunnel raised no question to them when they were down in the tunnel.

Q. Did he tell you where he had gotten access to the tunnel?

A. Yes. He said he had been down through the tunnel, through the entrance in the Forrestal Building. He said that to destroy these . . . utility pipes in Washington itself, would be the utmost impact upon the United States Government, if they were destroyed and destroyed right. I told him at that time that I had some experience in explosives while I was in the service.

Q. Was that accurate?

A. No. I had no experience.

Douglas testified that both Father Berrigan and Father Wenderoth told of going into the tunnels wearing uniforms identifying them as engineers with the Robb Electric Company. Lynch later would bring out that ROB is an acronym for Regional Office Building and that engineers in ROB-7 of the Health, Education and Welfare Department near the Forrestal Building wore uniforms emblazoned "ROB Engineer." The prosecutor considered this a vital point of corroboration for Douglas' testimony that the priests had told him they had inspected the tunnels.

Douglas told of using a number Father Berrigan furnished to telephone Sister McAlister in New York and arrange with her to use the name and address of Sister Judith Savard in New York for a mail drop. He then met with Sister McAlister in Lewisburg, he said.

"She just came back from the penitentiary," Douglas said, "and she told me how well Phil Berrigan looked. She also said, 'Phil was telling me you have a very interesting trade.' "

After Sister McAlister's reference to his "interesting trade," he said, "I told her, 'Oh, you mean my experience in the Army as a demolition expert?' and she said, 'Yes.' "

Sister McAlister, he said, told him Father Berrigan suggested he use the code name "Pete" in the clandestine communications network.

Douglas was now speaking louder and showing more self-assurance on the stand, even glancing occasionally to his right front trying to pick out the defendants without meeting their eyes. But his face was like a mask, large, brooding eyes gazing, out of focus, an apparent effort to see but not be seen. His head was rigid and his lips barely moved when he answered questions.

"Incidentally," Lynch said, "do you see Philip Berrigan in the courtroom?"

Douglas' head did not move, but his eyes shifted to the defense table. Father Berrigan, sitting to the rear of the table raised his hand. "Would you point him out please?" Lynch asked. "Raising his hand," said Douglas, his eyes back on Lynch. Asked to point out Sister McAlister, he said, "Sitting next to Philip Berrigan."

Douglas was a polished, well-rehearsed witness, a professional in his new-found role. He hardly missed a chance to put the defendants' names before the jury. Asked to point out Mary Cain Scoblick, he said, "The one with the striped blouse on sitting next to Sister McAlister." Anthony Scoblick "has the blue suit on—he is talking to Joseph Wenderoth." Neil McLaughlin was the one "in full clerical attire" sitting next to Scoblick.

"When they visited you were they wearing clerical garb?" Lynch asked.

Douglas hesitated several seconds, then said emphatically, "This is the first time I have ever seen them in it."

Asked if he could explain why he had made and kept a Xerox

copy of Father Berrigan's May 22-23-24 letter to Sister McAlister, Douglas solemnly replied:

"Yes. . . . I became concerned about the goals of these people, also the fact that everyone I met at that time had been in the clerical field. I am Catholic and I am a product of a very strict Catholic upbringing. I knew that it would be only a matter of time before the institutional authorities realized that I was carrying out contraband material for the defendant. I became concerned about what I was hearing from Father Philip Berrigan in regard to the destruction of the tunnel system. . . . I knew that it was only a matter of time since I have spent seven years of my life in prison; that there was *no way* that I could continue to take letters from the institution and bring them back in without being detected by the prison authorities. . . . I knew that I would eventually be apprehended for this and I felt that if I had enough evidence to produce at the time, that the authorities would believe in what I was telling them in regards to my conversations, and also in regards to the letters; and they would realize the threats of these people to the United States government."

"Not 'these people,' " Judge Herman gently corrected Douglas. "You are talking about Philip Berrigan."

"I made that mistake, your honor," Douglas blurted out, "because I knew the story."

O'Dwyer and Boudin both popped up, Boudin declaring, "That is provocation."

"No, no," said Herman irritably. But Boudin demanded he admonish the witness. The judge insisted he had admonished Douglas not to say "these defendants" or he "knew the story." But Herman told the jury, "I am sure it is inadvertent that he said it."

It was not much of an admonishment, but it was as close as the judge would ever come to admonishing a witness who would increasingly offer more information about the defendants than he was asked for, while remaining evasive or unresponsive in his replies to cross-examination.

At the end of the day's court session, after testifying for less than two hours, Douglas hurriedly left the federal building in a car full of marshal's deputies, his face hidden by a newspaper to prevent news photos. He returned in the same manner the next morning, with the deputy wheeling the car into the building's underground garage past a mob of cameramen. It was a routine that would be followed throughout the trial.

Just before the next day's session began, Eqbal Ahmad stopped by the press section and whispered, "We are going to have a bombshell for you in a little while. We have found out Boyd Douglas was trying to blackmail the government."

At seven o'clock the previous night, Lynch had turned over to the defense a copy of a sensational letter Douglas had written to an FBI agent on October 3, 1970, requesting $50,000, tax-free, and other favors, to help secure evidence in the case. The defense, charging that the government, in compliance with a court order to disclose records, had made an "eleventh hour disclosure," moved that the court delay further examination of Douglas until the prosecution turned over the records, including all FBI payments to Douglas. But Herman denied the motion and Lynch resumed the questioning.

Douglas testified that one evening in late May or early June he met Philip Berrigan in the prison mess hall and the priest told him "that his cell had just been shaken down by an officer and that there was a letter discovered in his cell. I asked him at the time, I said, well, did you say anything about me in the letter. He said no, he said I mentioned Pete in the letter, but he said I don't think the authorities there can figure it out, and that was the end of the conversation."

Several days later, Douglas said, Associate Warden Hendricks confronted him and he gave Hendricks a copy of Father Berrigan's May 22-23-24 letter. He said he later met in a picnic area near the prison with FBI Agents Delmar Mayfield and Philip Morris and they questioned him about his courier role and informed him that smuggling letters was a violation of federal law. Later, he said, Mayfield told him that the U.S. attorney's office had declined to prosecute him for smuggling letters, but that the FBI wanted him to continue working with Father Berrigan and his friends and to report to the FBI on their activities, including any other letters he might smuggle. He said he agreed to cooperate and asked for nothing in return.

Douglas had so warmed to his role as witness now that when

Lynch asked a question it was like pushing a button on a tape recorder. The prosecutor asked him if Father Berrigan had told him anything about "rap sessions" on draft board raids.

"Philip Berrigan told me," Douglas said looking at the ceiling, then droning on in a monotone, "that they would go about it by having several people that had been involved in some type of civil disobedience, and they would have get-togethers with students on campus. They would go into several sessions—in fact, it may take twenty to thirty sessions before any member of the group decided that they were ready to break into a selective service office. They would start out the conversation, well, someone in it that had already been in the draft board would start the session out, and they would continually discuss our involvement in South Vietnam or Asia, and normally it was done with the most hopeful activists on any campus. After they had discussed this with the individuals that they had at the session they would be able to pretty much pick out the individuals that they thought might participate, and they would continue these sessions until they had enough individuals to go into a draft board or do some other type of civil disobedience."

Douglas not only testified to numerous conversations with Father Berrigan, but frequently implicated the priest in the alleged conspiracy through the conversations of other defendants. Douglas himself had much closer contact with Father Berrigan than did any of the defendants, of course, meeting with him on an almost daily basis in prison. So it seemed odd that any of the defendants would have mentioned to Douglas that Father Berrigan was particularly anxious about a project, as Douglas testified when asked about a conversation with Father Wenderoth.

"He told me that he had been contacted by Elizabeth McAlister," said Douglas, "that Elizabeth McAlister advised Joseph Wenderoth and Neil McLaughlin about the destruction of the tunnel system in Washington, D.C., and that Philip Berrigan was most anxious to get this under way. Joseph Wenderoth stated to me that he thought it would require approximately fifteen people. All these people would be taken from actions, or all these people would be participating in the destruction of the tunnel system would have already been involved in some type of civil disobedience. He said he had been in the tunnel itself . . . posed the best I can recall, as some type of an engineer. He said this—Joseph Wenderoth—that I understand you are a demolition expert. I said, yes. He said at that time he was trying to obtain blueprints of the tunnel system itself. He said that there was an elevator operator in the Capitol building that would be involved in this project."

Judge Herman asked, "Is this still Wenderoth or McLaughlin talking?"

"Wenderoth," said Douglas, but eagerly volunteering, "they both seemed delighted." The judge ordered the remark stricken.

A moment later Douglas volunteered that Father McLaughlin "was delighted over the breaking in of the selective service offices in Delaware."

"Don't say he was delighted," Herman corrected gently, "just say what he said or how he said it or something of the sort."

Boudin, always anxious to emphasize J. Edgar Hoover's connection with the case, got the chance after Lynch asked Douglas when he had turned over to the FBI a list of telephone contacts in the movement. Douglas said, "Between June and the time Mr. Hoover made his statement."

Boudin bounded to his feet and headed toward the witness, cupping his hand to his ear.

"Could I hear that last answer?" Boudin said, "I think I missed the last name. Between June and what?"

"Now, your honor," Lynch said, "I suggest Mr. Boudin knows full well."

"No, I don't," said Boudin, smiling. "As a matter of fact, I did not hear the name. May I hear that?"

"Mr. Hoover," said Douglas.

Boudin, by far the most entertaining attorney of the trial, frequently emphasized points by pleading poor hearing. Or if testimony was going particularly well for the defense, he would amble about the courtroom, in the jury's sight, smiling puckishly, his thinning gray hair askew, his spectacles pushed atop his head. Because of a heart condition, he had the court's permission to move about when he felt it necessary and he took full advantage of it.

"That's bullshit, that theatrical stuff Boudin's doing," Lynch told newsmen. But it was effective, not only in underscoring points, but in establishing a rapport with jurors who otherwise might have looked disdainfully on a scholarly Jewish lawyer from New York who had grilled them at considerable length during voir dire.

Lynch, realizing Douglas' provocative role in the alleged conspiracy could hurt the prosecution, elicited testimony not only that gave a reasonable explanation for provocative acts, but that tied Father Berrigan into the acts. Concerning the picnic at Chenoweth's house, for example, Lynch inquired, "Did you have anything to do with the setting up of this little get-together?"

"Yes," said Douglas, "as far as asking Professor Chenoweth if it would be all right if we used his home for the meeting . . . it was at Philip Berrigan's suggestion. He had met Professor Chenoweth and he thought that the professors, if they were not willing to actually become involved in some type of civil disobedience, that at least they would take some type of risk factor in letting them use their homes for discussion of a political nature."

With Douglas on the stand to identify the Phil-Liz letters, Lynch now introduced as evidence the first one Douglas had turned over to the FBI, the May 22-23-24 letter from Father Berrigan to Sister McAlister.

The prosecutor began reading the letter to the jury. As he droned on, Douglas, for the first time looked at the jurors, who were now watching Lynch. The witness' eyes swept down the front row of six jurors and three alternates, then down the back row. What he saw were puzzled expressions, for the cryptic passages of the letter had little apparent bearing on the conspiracy charge. Laced with chit-chat, the letter included general suggestions for antiwar activities, such as one that students "should shut down ROTC and begin to zap Sel. Service in college and university towns." But little about draft board raids and nothing about bombing or kidnapping.

Through agreement with defense attorneys, Lynch had excised from this letter and others many of the expressions of personal endearment, especially those of a sensuous or passionate nature that had so titillated Douglas. Defense attorneys had argued the passages were irrelevant to the case and would cause unnecessary embarrassment to Father Berrigan and Sister McAlister. Perhaps, but they also would have bolstered the defense contention that the letters that contained descriptions of illegal activities were the distorted products of two people in love, one trying to spread a little sunshine and the other reassuring himself that he had not gone to prison in vain and was still fighting the good fight.

Enough personal passages remained in some of the censored letters, however, that Lynch's reading of them to the jury embarrassed both the priest and the nun. The defense, of course, was concerned that the personal references could cut the other way, perhaps prejudicing the jurors who might be offended by a love relationship between a priest and a nun.

The importance to the case of the first letter Lynch introduced was that it was smuggled by Douglas prior to his becoming an FBI informant. Lynch's predecessor in the case, Guy Goodwin, had not even seen fit to include it in the first indictment. But Lynch, overlooking nothing, added it to the superseding indictment as a smuggling count against Father Berrigan because he knew it was the one letter where the priest could not plead entrapment.

The prosecutor's task now, as he introduced one letter after another, was to corroborate passages in the letters with Douglas' testimony—or vice versa. And Lynch did a masterful job.

Lynch read the letter of July 6 from Father Berrigan to Sister McAlister in which the priest mentioned "untouched areas" of several states and said that "the district is still the elusive golden fleece" and that "the subterranean project in the district . . . should have priority for the winter of '70-71."

Douglas testified that Father Wenderoth, in discussing the tunnel project, "told me that in the winter months of 1970-71, this project would be completed—in those months." He said the priest told him to tell Father Berrigan "that they were working on the project, and that it would be carried out as planned, and as per his instruction."

"Whose instructions?" Lynch asked.

"Philip Berrigan's instructions," Douglas said, "in the previous letter, that the District of Columbia is still the 'golden fleece.' "

On its face the corroboration seemed sound enough, but in the courtroom corridors during a recess several supporters of the defendants said the way they figured it, a con man like Douglas would read such passages in a letter and then shape his testimony to fit the letters and please the FBI. "It's terrible what they are doing to that blob up there on the witness stand," said Mary Drinnon, wife of Professor Drinnon. Father Wenderoth, finding it difficult to accept the fact that a man he had befriended had turned on him, said, "After that performance, I really do feel sorry for him."

Defense attorneys were hardly feeling sorry for Douglas, of course. They complained that he was testifying like a programmed computer. But they admitted that overall he was making an excellent witness.

In his testimony and in letters he wrote that were introduced in evidence, Douglas borrowed key phrases from the Phil-Liz letters—and did not always interpret them correctly. For example, he repeatedly referred to the "inner circle" as being the defendants and perhaps a few other persons allegedly involved in a conspiracy. But in the letters the priest and nun referred to the "inner circle" as relatives or friends who knew of the pair's close relationship.

Evidence showed that after Sister McAlister wrote Father Berrigan that "S.S. things are boot camps for something else," Douglas wrote Professor Drinnon he planned to be in "something more involved than S.S. boards, but they are only boot camps at present anyway."

Through Douglas' testimony or that of earlier witnesses, all of the defendants except Eqbal Ahmad had been linked in one way or another, although peripherally in some instances, to draft board raids or the alleged tunnel plot.

Lynch finally reached Ahmad's name for the first time in reading Sister Elizabeth McAlister's remarkably detailed letter about the Delaware draft board raids. "Tonight we're going to try to see Eqbal," Lynch quoted one letter, hesitating on the name, "and pick his brain." That was all there was to it, but Lynch let it sink in on the jury that at last Ahmad's name had entered the picture.

For Father Berrigan and Sister McAlister, the reading of the letters proved exceedingly painful, not only because of the personal passages, but because of some things they wrote that criticized their friends and even implicated them in the alleged conspiracy. Although Sister McAlister was forever writing about "picking Eqbal's brain," and of his great help "behind the scenes," Father Berrigan was ambivalent about the Pakistani. One time he would write, "delighted with Eq," and the next he would lump him and Douglas Doud, the peace activist and former Cornell professor, with a group of spineless liberals. He once wrote:

> The peace liberals are sumpin—enough to make a mainliner of a person. But if you've got Doud and Eq your score is high. They want scenes where conditions are posh, where floodlights are on and publicity secure, and where there's no danger. All of them have been through surgery— getting a hose-pipe for a backbone when they were kids. Helps flexibility—bobbing and weaving with issues.

Ahmad, smiling as Lynch read that passage, later told newsmen that Father Berrigan had apologized to him for the criticism and explained that he had not really known him. "I think he is a fine man," Ahmad said, "and I can understand how under the circumstances of being in prison he might have written something like that."

Father Berrigan's anguish over hearing his criticism of a friend and co-defendant read aloud in the courtroom was compounded by the passages praising the man who had betrayed him, the witness then on the stand.

"The local minister with portfolio," Lynch quoted one letter, "has emerged as the best thing hereabouts since polio vaccine." Douglas was "no less than providential" and "our chargé emerges in a truly astounding fashion—he's thinking movement—will be one of our best people."

The personal passages were so embarrassing that even some of the more callous members of the press corps felt as though they were peeking at someone's private mail. Both Father Berrigan and Sister McAlister stared at the floor as Lynch read such passages as the priest saying he was "longing for the fleshpots of

Egypt" and the nun replying: "So you're longing for the flesh-pots of Egypt after yer [*sic*] long fast. Could philosophize and say, like the Jews, there is no possibility for you to turn back to them. But know this, that they're traveling by a slightly different route and they'll be awaiting you at journey's end in the Promised Land."

During a recess, Sister McAlister, shaking her head and whispering, "I feel like a roomful of peeping toms is looking at me," stepped into the corridor for a smoke. Her hands trembled as she asked a reporter for a match. When he suggested, "Cigarettes will kill you," she said, "Sometimes you would just as soon be killed if it would be quick."

Personal anguish and invasion of privacy notwithstanding, the legal question about the letters was their relevancy to any conspiracy to kidnap Kissinger or blow up heating tunnels in Washington. Some of the letters did indeed corroborate Douglas' testimony about draft board raids. But so far there had been nothing about kidnapping and only cryptic references such as "elusive golden fleece" or "subterranean project" that might be linked to the alleged bombing plot.

For the most part, the reading of the letters had been deadly dull, so dull that Scoblick and Father Wenderoth went to sleep after the reading of the first few. Finally, Ahmad nodded. Then at least three jurors closed their eyes. Two newsmen went to sleep and were awakened and admonished by U.S. Marshal John Buck. Eventually he also dozed.

Except for testifying briefly in between the reading of each letter to establish that he had received the messages and passed them on to either Father Berrigan or Sister McAlister, and to perhaps link some phrases to illegal acts, Boyd Douglas also paid little attention to the reading. He slumped in his chair and used the time to steal glances at the defendants or to study the jurors' reactions.

But Lynch was now leading up to the kidnap letters and Douglas straightened up. Yes, the witness said, there had come a time when he received a pre-arranged telephone call at the pay phone of a laundromat from Sister McAlister.

"She told me she had sent a very hot letter to the address of Patricia Rom," Douglas said. "I asked her if she sent it to the

Bucknell University campus and she said no, she sent it to her home address. She told me that when I received the letter, that I should read it thoroughly. If I thought there was any chance that I might be apprehended inside the penitentiary with the letter that I should just read it, memorize it and destroy the contents of it and then relay this information to Philip Berrigan."

The following day, he said, Patricia Rom gave him a sealed envelope marked "Boyd" that she said she had received from Sister McAlister and then the nun telephoned again and "told me that she would like to have comments of Philip Berrigan as soon as possible. She also told me that Eg would like to talk to me in regards to the letter. She said within a couple of hours Egg-Eggball Ahmad will call you at this number in the laundromat."

Lynch had reached the critical point in the case against Ahmad—two telephone calls that Douglas contended Ahmad made to him. Both calls allegedly dealt with Sister McAlister's "kidnap" letter and were the basis for all three of the charges against Ahmad—conspiracy, smuggling a communication and sending a threatening communication. Boudin demanded and won the right to cross-examine the witness in the jury's absence.

The government could not legally link Ahmad to Sister McAlister's "kidnap" letter, for whatever it might be worth, unless it could show some positive act by him in furtherance of the alleged conspiracy. And Boudin, in the absence of the jury and the witness, pointed out that other than the telephone calls, the government had stipulated in a memorandum to the court that it expected to prove only three other acts, all innocent on their face—Ahmad's delivery of Father Philip Berrigan's prepared speech at St. Gregory the Great Church on the day of the priest's capture; a midday meeting with Sisters McAlister and Egan at Ahmad's apartment; and a record of telephone calls made from the Weston, Connecticut, home of Ahmad's in-laws to Sister McAlister's residence. That was all the evidence, except for letter references to "picking Eqbal's brain" and his helping "behind the scenes," that the trial would produce against Ahmad.

Douglas, cross-examined in the jury's absence, said that after talking to Sister McAlister he returned to the laundromat two hours later and received a call. He said a man's voice "said this is Eqbal. He said that he was in the presence of Elizabeth McAlister. He said that I understand that you have received the letter of Elizabeth McAlister's in regards to the Kissinger kidnapping. I said yes. He said to me, 'I would like to discuss this with Berrigan or at least discuss it with you prior to Berrigan's transfer to Danbury so that I can get his comments on the letter.' "

The following day, Douglas said, he returned to the laundromat expecting to receive a 4 P.M. call from Sister McAlister. Instead, he said, when he answered the phone it was the same man identifying himself as Egg or Eggbal and saying, "I'm calling you because Elizabeth McAlister could not make the call that she previously arranged. She will call you later."

Douglas said the FBI played a tape recording of Ahmad's voice for identification on April 15, 1971—eight months after the alleged telephone conversations, three months after the first indictment in the case and two weeks before the superseding indictment. Douglas said it was a tape of Ahmad's voice on a radio program. He said the voice, the only one on the tape, had "a distinct foreign accent" and he could recognize it as the same voice he had heard in August, 1970. In other words, Douglas was identifying the voice of a man he never met on the basis of a one-minute telephone conversation matched against a tape recording eight months old.

On January 24, 1972 (the day the trial started), Douglas said, an FBI agent played a second tape and he was able to pick Ahmad's voice from among several voices on the tape. It was a tape of a February 12, 1971, press conference of Ahmad, Scoblick, Sister McAlister, and Fathers Wenderoth and McLaughlin. When the tape was played, with the jury still absent, newsmen and spectators agreed with defense attorneys that Ahmad was heard identifying himself and saying he was from Pakistan. But Judge Herman agreed with the prosecution that Ahmad did not identify himself.

In any event, the FBI's identification was so flimsy that Judge Herman eventually agreed to strike it from the record and to direct a verdict of acquittal for Ahmad on the charges of letter smuggling and sending a threatening letter.

Boudin argued that Ahmad should also be dropped from the conspiracy charge, and that testimony about the telephone calls should be stricken. But in a heated counter-argument Lynch declared: "Not only could reasonable men find that that was Eqbal Ahmad on the phone, but it would take an act of irrationality to say that it was anybody else other than Eqbal Ahmad on that phone."

During a recess newsmen asked Ahmad if he were relieved that the judge had dismissed the letter charges, reducing his possible maximum sentence from twenty to five years. "I had no damn business being in this case in the first place," said Ahmad. "I never even knew about Boyd Douglas, and the charge that I was the author of the letter written by Sister Elizabeth McAlister was so goddamn spurious it had to be taken out."

After the jury returned to the courtroom, Douglas repeated his testimony about the telephone calls, adding that during the first call "Egg said he would like to have the kidnapping done around Christmas time."

The date was at considerable variance with the indictment, which alleged the tunnel explosion was scheduled for Washington's Birthday of 1971 and the kidnapping slated for the following day. In fact, the only other evidence about a specific time for either the bombing or kidnapping was testimony by Douglas. He testified that during a stroll on the Bucknell campus on July 16, 1970, the day demonstrators went to Lewisburg to protest prison treatment of Father Berrigan, he asked ex-nun Marjorie Shuman, an un-indicted co-conspirator in the case, if a date had been set for the tunnel explosion. Douglas said she replied, "Yes, we will do it on Washington's Birthday in February of 1971." He said he then asked Father Wenderoth, "Why that date?" and the priest replied that it would mean government buildings would be deprived of heating during the coldest month of the year.

The jurors listened intently to Lynch's reading of Sister McAlister's letter proposing the kidnapping of "someone like Henry Kissinger" and to the note she enclosed with it to Douglas saying "the enclosed is dynamite and I mean it."

Douglas testified that after getting Betsy Sandel to transcribe the letter and taking a copy to Father Berrigan, he discussed the contents with the priest.

Said Douglas: "Berrigan told me that I should get in touch with Joseph Wenderoth and Neil McLaughlin, that this plan should be carried out after the destruction of the tunnel system itself. I told Philip Berrigan I did not see how this can be done without the use of a gun. Philip Berrigan agreed that it could not be done without the use of a gun but that possibly we could use blanks instead of having it loaded with real bullets. I told Philip Berrigan at that time that I was sure I could obtain a gun for use in the kidnapping if it was requested of me. Philip Berrigan further stated that . . . the operation would involve the use of several cars, many different locations in which to hide Henry Kissinger. Philip Berrigan also said that it would have to be considered by the people that would be recruited for the project, that a very severe sentence might be given as a result of such a kidnapping."

Father Berrigan then gave him his letter of reply to Sister McAlister suggesting that the kidnapping be "tied into the D.C. fiasco," Douglas said, and he sent it to her through Sister Grace Marie Russell. Douglas explained that Sister McAlister had changed the mail-drop address from Sister Judith Savard's for fear Sister Savard's mail was being checked by the FBI.

Both of the "kidnap" letters were so tenuous in many respects and so filled with apparent fantasy in others that solid corroborating evidence would be needed to give them credence. Douglas did his best to provide it.

He said that a few days after taking out Father Berrigan's reply, he met the priest in the prison library and took notes of their conversation on a piece of paper. "Philip Berrigan told me," Douglas said, studying a piece of paper Lynch handed him, "that he wanted several things made known to Joseph Wenderoth and Neil McLaughlin in reference to the destruction of the tunnel system and also the proposal of kidnapping Henry Kissinger. He gave me a list of these events and the plans. I wrote them on this piece of paper. They are approximately twelve to fourteen different things."

The piece of paper, from a page of Douglas' Bucknell

University notebook, would become a critical and hotly disputed piece of evidence. Defense attorneys objected that he should not be permitted to look at it while testifying and Judge Herman instructed him to try to testify without referring to it.

Douglas, gazing over the jurors' heads, hesitated, then said: "I can remember that he wanted me to tell Joseph Wendorf [for some reason for the remainder of the trial he referred to Wenderoth as Wendorf and Scoblick as Scolbnick] to get a map from Patricia Chanel's brother in reference to the design of the tunnel system. He wanted me to obtain explosive handbooks so that these could be distributed to other members of the group. He wanted me to make sure of the dimensions of the tunnel. He wanted me to see if there could be trucks stolen from the Washington, D.C., area, utility trucks. He wanted me to try and make sure no one was injured if at all possible. He wanted me to train someone else in the use of explosives, as he said that I might be involved on both of the projects and that I would be a key factor in their group and that if I was apprehended, due to my past background, I would surely receive the most severest of all the group's sentences. He told me I should set up a maildrop for Joseph Wendorf. He said that both of the projects should be coordinated with Elizabeth McAlister. Also, Elizabeth McAlister and a John Swinglish should be able to recruit the necessary people involved. He said I was to determine myself what types of explosives I should use. That is about all I can recall without the paper that I made my own notes on from this meeting."

With Judge Herman's permission, Douglas then referred to the paper and said that notes on the ROTC and Drinnon meant that Father Berrigan had told him to "get someone in the area, possibly Professor Drinnon, to see if something couldn't be done" about destroying the ROTC building at Bucknell.

Also, Douglas said, Father Berrigan "told me that the people for both these projects should be able to get some approximately 150 people that had been involved in some kind of civil disobedience in the past. He told me he was counting on me when I was released from the federal penitentiary to make sure these projects would be completed."

Of the many conversations Douglas testified about, that was the only one he claimed to have taken notes on. He said it occurred a day before Father Berrigan's transfer to Danbury in late August.

Douglas said that on September 5 he met with Fathers Wenderoth and McLaughlin in the basement of the New Dorm, where Betsy Sandel lived and "I went down each item that I have just testified to with Joseph Wendorf in the presence of Neil McLaughlin." He said he asked Father Wenderoth "if he thought Eqbal could carry out such a plan as the kidnapping of Henry Kissinger. Joseph Wendorf said, yes, he felt that he could, that Eqbal . . . was the most violent one of the whole group. He told me that they were afraid in a way of Eqbal. Joseph Wendorf described to me that his parents had been killed in Pakistan by guerrillas. Joseph Wendorf—when I went into the discussion of asking about the destruction of the tunnel system—he said that he knew it would cost millions of dollars . . . to rebuild after it was blown up."

Douglas testified that he turned over to Father Wenderoth, at the priest's request, two explosives manuals that FBI Agent Delmar Mayfield had secured for him from the Bucknell ROTC. Douglas tried to counter the obviously provocative nature of the act by saying he had asked for the manuals only to "familiarize myself with explosives in case—in case they threw in somebody that knew explosives, as I know nothing about them." He did not relate his securing of the manuals to the statement he earlier said Father Berrigan had made about wanting him to obtain explosives handbooks.

Douglas was near the end of his fifth day on the stand and Lynch was leading him through a wind-up that would emphasize that bombing and kidnapping plans were proceeding after Berrigan left Lewisburg for Danbury. Defense attorneys, impressed by the witness' ability to rattle off names, dates, places and events, feared he would stand up well under cross-examination.

"He's an absolute rock—and a machine," Boudin whispered to a reporter. "I don't know whether we can crack him."

In rapid-fire order Douglas testified that:

—Father Wenderoth returned the explosives handbooks to him and told him he had copied the contents and "plans for the underground tunnel system was still going on."

—Sister McAlister, when she saw him during the colloquy program at Bucknell in September, told him that "they were going ahead with the plans" to kidnap Kissinger.

—Father Wenderoth telephoned him and asked him if he had read a New York *Daily News* article of October 16, 1970, reporting J. Edgar Hoover had briefed Republican leaders on a kidnap-bombing plot involving the East Coast Conspiracy to Save Lives. "I told him that I had not . . . he told me not to worry about it . . . that it must have been an anonymous tip to the FBI."

—Sister McAlister telephoned him and said "not to worry about the article, that everything was going ahead as planned."

—Sister McAlister telephoned and "told me that herself and Jogues Egan were going to Baltimore, Maryland, for a meeting in reference to the K situation and the tunnel system."

Although Lynch produced no letter or other documentary evidence to corroborate Douglas' testimony that kidnap-bombing plans were still being discussed after the "kidnap" letters, the prosecutor did introduce a letter, dated October 28, 1970, from Fathers Wenderoth and McLaughlin to Douglas which said: "Boyd, things are in good shape! We have a small group forming and will probably have something doing within the next few weeks. . . . No feds for a long while; in fact it seems that the phone has not been tapped for at least a month—still we don't take chances!!"

Douglas also testified that on December 5, 1970, about a week after Hoover's testimony, FBI agents took him to a motel in Danville, Pennsylvania, where he went over his information on Resistance activities and signed a long statement. At that time, he said, he also identified photographs of several of the defendants.

During Douglas' sixth and final day of direct examination Lynch hurriedly tried to dispose of the FBI's financial dealings with the informant.

"Did there ever come a time when you requested additional money?" asked Lynch.

"Yes."

"A lot more money?"

"Yes."

"How much?"

"Approximately $50,000, I requested that in writing."

Most of the jurors stared at Douglas during the exchange about the letter. He shot a darting look and weak smile in their direction, then looked back at Lynch and said he had written the letter on October 3, 1970. "And then I had a meeting that evening with the special agent of the FBI [Mayfield]," he said. "And he told me that if my thoughts were along these lines to just forget about it. I told him 'all right' at the time. In fact I thought I had taken the letter back from him. He told me this request would not be considered."

O'Dwyer suggested that Lynch read the letter to the jury and when the prosecutor refused, O'Dwyer declared, "I respectfully object . . . Mr. Lynch has been good enough to read every other letter to the jury. This should be read to them at this time."

Judge Herman declared: "It is Mr. Lynch's case . . . he can read it or not read it." But with the issue now before the jury and O'Dwyer and Boudin both demanding that it be read, Lynch agreed. He began reading at a rate so rapid that the words ran together:

"Molly, Thank the Bureau for the reward and thank you. This will be used for a new car soon. I have never owned a car. Can you get me some expense money for this month. . . ."

O'Dwyer jumped up objecting. "Slowly, Mr. Lynch. I can't hear you. May I suggest, your honor, that this be done in a fashion so that people can understand it."

"Please, please, Mr. O'Dwyer," said Herman impatiently. "He is reading it like every other one."

"No, that is not so," O'Dwyer insisted.

Herman, however, said he did not think Lynch was reading too fast and told him to proceed. Having inadvertently accentuated the letter's contents with an obvious effort to quickly dispose of it, Lynch now read at a more normal pace:

After my cover is gone, I will need an honorable discharge from the Army so that I can settle out West and it will look as though I just returned from Asia, etc. I will obtain a transcript of my grades here at Bucknell at the end of this semester, should I wish to continue at some university out West. I may either continue at a university or go into a small business out West.

Considering what I will go through before and after the trial or trials, I request a minimum reward of $50,000 (tax free). $5,000 be paid me the first week in December, 1970 and the rest at the start of the trial or when things are blown wide open. With this I could start a small business or continue at college. This figure may sound a little high, but considering everything, I feel it is worth it to the government and it will make a life for me. I will do all I can to help the government obtain enough evidence to prosecute these people concerned. However, I don't want to feel that I am just being used. I know these people may not bother me, but the only way I will feel comfortable, is to take some precaution as they are the cream of the Catholic left. This figure doesn't account for expenses between now and the time for the trial.

I can have "no" ties with my family for at least a year and possibly I would never feel safe. At the present time we know only some of the Catholic people that are involved, but it may even involve other types of people in the movement.

It would be much easier to work if I was free of supervision at the end of January. It would be necessary when my cover is gone because only you should know where I am at. Can the bureau do something about that?

Would you please give me something concrete on this letter as soon as possible? Pete.

The letter had been every bit the bombshell that Ahmad had promised newsmen. Several jurors looked at each other and shook their heads. Douglas had slumped in his chair and stared at the floor during the reading of the letter. Now Lynch asked him: "You are the Pete?"

"Yes, I am," said Douglas, still looking down.

"Who is Molly?"

"That is Special Agent Delmar Mayfield of the FBI."

"After this refusal by Special Agent Mayfield of the FBI, did you continue to keep the FBI informed of what you knew was going on?"

"I did."

Lynch switched abruptly to a letter dated November 6, 1970, from Sister McAlister to Douglas thanking him for "the license" and asking, "Is it true that it's only good until December 31?"

Douglas explained that the nun had "requested some type of alias" so that she could visit Father Berrigan and that through an ex-convict in Boston he had arranged for a phony driver's license. If the letter and testimony added little to the case, Lynch had at least moved the trial away from the Molly letter.

About mid-November, Douglas testified, Father Wenderoth telephoned him "that plans for the D.C. action was continuing, that he wondered when I would be getting released. I told him in late December. He told me, 'Fine, we will get together.' "

"Now, did there come a time," asked Lynch, "when you had a conversation with Joseph Wenderoth about other publicity that had occurred in connection with this matter?"

"Yes . . . it was toward the end of November," Douglas replied. "I had received a telephone call from Joseph Wenderoth asking me if I had heard the publicity that was recently announced on all the national networks in regards to the director of the FBI's statement before a—before some type of committee. I said that at the time I hadn't heard it, but soon after that I heard it, and he told me at the time that we should not discuss this over the phone and that we should not be seen in person at all."

After the telephone conversation and about two weeks before being released from prison, Douglas said, he received the following letter from Father Wenderoth:

Boyd, please don't take my panic seriously, quite a experience for all of us.

I feel responsible for you—I don't want to sound paternalistic but Boyd—two weeks to go—!

Things I hope will get back to normal soon. I hope I have called you before this but I feel for all events & purposes things should not be brought up by anyone!!

The Feds are around now & then and what they are doing is pure garbage. They want us to know they are around.

I'm sure Dan & Phil are O.K. Anderson and Goodell in
Wash are looking into some things for them.
See you very soon. Peace, Joe.

Shortly before Christmas, Douglas testified, he met Father
Wenderoth at Baltimore's Friendship Airport and "I asked
Joseph Wendorf at that time in reference to Hoover's statement,
if he had any idea how they could have known these facts. He
told me . . . it was possible they could have had a tap inside the
Federal Correctional Institution at Danbury. He also . . . I said,
'Well, I guess the Washington action is out.' Joseph Wendorf
told me, 'Well, at least for the time it's definitely out. We will
have to wait now and see what happens as a result of this.' "

Douglas then told of meeting Sister McAlister at the Sheraton
Motor Inn in New York on New Year's Day "and she was highly
suspicious that I was the leak."

O'Dwyer interjected that the best evidence of what the nun
had said was a tape recording Douglas had made. But Lynch
said it was "almost undecipherable" and defense attorneys had a
copy if they wanted to introduce it. Neither side introduced it.
The highly sensitive recorder had picked up so much clattering
of dishes and other extraneous noises that the tape was in-
coherent.

"Well," Judge Herman told Douglas, "tell us what she said
that led you to believe she was suspicious. Just as you can recall,
what was said. You met her there by arrangement, did you?"

"Yes," said Douglas. "She told me she had observed an agent
watching her at the Danbury Federal Correctional Institution.
She also told me that during one of my phone conversations
when I was talking to her, that she hung up the phone, and she
had heard my conversation played back to her. She was quite
paranoid in reference to me."

Douglas said, "She also told me that as far as the kidnapping
of Henry Kissinger was concerned, that only the inner circle
people knew about the kidnapping, and that she—"

"You were one of the inner circle, were you?" asked Judge
Herman.

"Yes—that she could name the number on her hands, other
people, that the kidnapping of Kissinger revolved around; also

that she knew the times and places that this plan had been discussed. And she felt none of the other people would have given this information but me."

Douglas testified he told Sister McAlister, "Well, I am sorry you feel that way, and I guess we'll soon find out or time will tell."

After that, Douglas said, the FBI began paying him "subsistence or per diem for travel expenses for relocating in various parts of the United States."

He said he continued to receive the funds until April, 1971.

"How did you sustain yourself after that?" Lynch asked.

"I had a job myself."

"I have nothing further at this point, your honor," said Lynch.

It was now noon of Douglas' sixth day on the stand and Judge Herman suggested that cross-examination begin at 2 P.M. But at a sidebar conference, defense attorneys argued for a recess until the next morning so they could prepare.

Lynch bitterly objected: "Your honor," he said, "they have been talking about Boyd Douglas now for months. The newspapers have been talking about him for a year, and how he was going to be the central part of the Government's case, and how they were going to destroy him on cross-examination. And I submit that they should be made to proceed with the destruction."

Judge Herman agreed to give the defense until 9:30 A.M. the next day, however. Lynch lit a cigarette in the corridor, blew a cloud of smoke and angrily declared: "Just another defense delay—pure unadulterated bullshit!"

CHAPTER TWELVE

Mr. Douglas on Trial

"Has the government given you immunity from prosecution?" drawled Ramsey Clark.

Boyd Douglas, his responses no longer automatic, gazed at the prosecution table as though in deep thought. Finally, he said, "To my knowledge, no."

"Have they charged you in connection with the letters?" asked Clark.

"Have they charged me? No."

It was a critical question. A promise not to prosecute in return for turning state's evidence would strike at the witness' credibility. After a long pause, Douglas said that when he first turned over a copy of a Berrigan letter to the FBI in June, 1970, he was told that he could be prosecuted for smuggling the letter. But he said that a few days later FBI Agent Molly Mayfield advised him that the U.S. attorney had declined prosecution and "if I wanted to cooperate it was up to me, I could assist in the investigation of these people—of the defendants."

Although it did not surface at the trial, Mayfield filed a deadpan report of the session with Douglas quoting him as saying he was cooperating because he disagreed with the goals of the antiwar activists and felt "they are completely dedicated to destroying our country." Douglas, reported Mayfield, was not asking "any favors from the FBI."

Douglas made clear his eagerness to help when Clark questioned him about his confrontation with Associate Warden Hendricks over the letter found in Father Berrigan's cell. "That's when you told Warden Hendricks at that time you'd like to be a double agent, right?" Clark demanded.

"No, I didn't tell him that," Douglas said. "That was his

262

terminology. He said, 'Oh, yes, you'd like to act as a double agent.' I said, 'Yes, if that's the way you want to put it.' "

Trying to discredit Douglas as a double agent, Clark led him, step by step, through a forty-five-minute chronicle of his criminal career from the time he was charged with writing a bad check at the age of eighteen in Belfonte, Ohio. All of the bank fraud cases in several states. Defrauding a hotel in Miami Beach. Larceny in Hong Kong. Bad-check charges in Reno. Armed assault on an FBI agent in Milwaukee. Impersonating an Army officer. Undesirable discharge. Auto theft in Texas and Michigan. Five escapes or escape attempts. Prison violations, including theft, gambling and lying to an officer. The rundown fascinated the jury, and Douglas seemed somewhat proud of his escapades. At one point Clark noted that after Douglas' arrest by the FBI in Laredo, Texas, in 1962 following his deportation from Acapulco, Mexico, a newspaper quoted him as saying he had passed between $50,000 and $60,000 in bad checks.

Douglas acknowledged that the newspaper had quoted him correctly and Judge Herman asked, "Was that true?"

"Yes, it was," said Douglas, with a trace of a smile. He turned to get the jurors' reaction. They were looking at Clark for the next question.

"Larceny in Hong Kong on February twenty-sixth, nineteen hundred and sixty-two?" asked Clark.

"That is correct," said Douglas.

Lynch jumped up, red-faced. "It was sixty-one dollars—that ought to be in it."

"That would be sixty thousand dollars plus sixty-one dollars," said Clark without missing a beat. "Arrested in Reno, Nevada, bad checks, nineteen hundred and sixty-two. Correct?"

"Correct."

It was also correct, Douglas acknowledged, that he had told a series of lies to Professor Drinnon to try to dupe him into thinking he was bitter against the government. He said he falsely told Drinnon that the government had promised him a parole but had failed to grant it and that he felt cheated by the $15,000 settlement of the damage suit growing out of the medical experiments.

Pressed by Clark, Douglas admitted that the government

suspected him of fraud in the damage suit. "You settled your suit against the government after the government accused you of having induced the abscesses, didn't you?" Clark demanded.

"Not to my knowledge," Douglas first answered. But he finally conceded that he had agreed to the settlement after his attorney advised him there were "some suspicions along those lines."

On the alleged facts of the conspiracy case, however, Douglas was proving to be the "rock" Boudin had feared. He stuck to his story and took advantage of every opening to throw in something extra. When Clark asked if he knew that there was nothing Father Berrigan could do about directing a bombing plot because he was in prison, Douglas retorted: "I knew after a period of several months, to my knowledge, Philip Berrigan was highly looked upon by all the members of the Catholic inner circle and anything he said, to my knowledge, would be carried out in due course."

Questions concerning his direct testimony brought replies that sounded like a replay of a tape recording. "You first raised the issue of a gun, didn't you?" Clark asked.

"Yes," Douglas said, "I told Philip Berrigan I didn't see how it could be done without the use of a gun. He agreed with me and said maybe we can use blanks instead of real bullets. I told him I thought that if a gun would be needed, I might be able to obtain one."

When Douglas insisted that Fathers Berrigan and Wenderoth had told him they inspected heating tunnels in Washington to determine the location of generating plants, Clark sought to show that there would have been no need to inspect the tunnels because the location of the plants was a matter of public record and common knowledge.

Clark introduced an Esso Oil Company map of Washington showing the location of the plants serving government buildings. Waving the map at Douglas, he suggested the witness "made this whole thing up."

"I did not make it up," Douglas declared.

"I have no further questions," said Clark. He had examined Douglas less than a day.

Judge Herman recessed the court, and Lynch, grinning,

walked from the courtroom and in a mocking aside told a reporter, "Devastating cross-examination!"

If Clark's questioning on the facts of the case had been less than devastating, the self-portrait he had drawn from Douglas had left the jurors with the picture of a con man who appeared to enjoy the reputation and who had considerable vested interest in the case. And since Douglas' story of the conspiracy seemed unshakable, the defense strategy necessarily would be to concentrate on Douglas' background, his provocative role, his motives for testifying, his acknowledged record of lying, and any discrepancies between his trial testimony and what he had told the FBI or the grand jury.

"Mr. Douglas is not on trial here," Lynch would shout, his face red and arms outstretched. "They're trying to put Mr. Douglas on trial."

But indeed, in a sense, not only Douglas, but the FBI and the Justice Department were on trial. For the motive of the prosecution became more of an issue than the motive for the alleged crime. In fact, Lynch struck only a glancing blow at the defendants' motives, declaring that they had set themselves above the law for what they deemed "lofty purposes."

On the other hand, defense attorneys delved into Douglas' relationship with the FBI, including financial negotiations and arrangements that raised the issue of his motive as the government's chief witness. The defense also sought to prove that the case was brought by the Justice Department only to protect Hoover's image.

Judge Herman permitted extraordinarily broad cross-examination on grounds Douglas was a paid informant. Contrary to usual restrictions on cross-examination, defense attorneys were permitted to examine Douglas on many subjects that had not been raised on direct examination and on subjects that had no apparent relevance to the case. At the same time, however, the judge frequently ridiculed the relevancy of defense questions, suggested that Douglas could not be expected to answer some questions, adopted what defense attorneys complained was a protective attitude toward Douglas, and emphasized to the jury that he was being extremely lenient with defense cross-examination. All of this, defense attorneys charged, overcompensated for the leniency and prejudiced the case against the defendants.

Paul O'Dwyer, replacing Clark as cross-examiner, handed Douglas a long list of FBI payments and asked him to read it. "On eight-eighteen-seventy," Douglas began, "I received two hundred dollars from period seven-one-seventy to seven-thirty-one-seventy. . . ."

O'Dwyer smiled and studied the jury, as Douglas continued reading and the jurors listened intently. The payments totaled $9,278, including $1,500 for information leading to the Rochester arrests. Douglas said the reward came as a "surprise" and partially inspired him to write the "Molly" letter requesting $50,000.

The FBI payments, Douglas said, were used for relocating and living expenses after he testified before the grand jury in Harrisburg. He lived first in a hotel in Omaha where the FBI set him up with an alias, Robert Dunn, and supplied him with a bank charge card, listing as his address a confidential FBI post office box.

But he stayed in Omaha only a brief period, relocating in Phoenix with the FBI's help after an Omaha newspaper ran a story about him which, he said, "described me . . . described my car, which was a nineteen seventy-one Javelin, blue, white top—easy to spot." FBI agents stored his car in Omaha when he moved.

In Phoenix, Douglas got a job at the Motorola plant. His working relationship with Molly Mayfield was so close at the time that the agent actually spent time with him during his honeymoon period going over the evidence in the case in preparation for the trial. Mayfield visited him in Phoenix from February 25 to March 30, 1971, going over FBI reports with him during the evenings and on weekends. Douglas said he married a secretary of a telephone company executive on March 16.

One purpose of the meetings with Mayfield, Douglas said, was to "clear up discrepancies" in verbal reports (302s) he had made as an informant to Mayfield in 1970.

Douglas also acknowledged that he had conferred with Mayfield and another agent about the possibility of becoming a career informant for the FBI. But the continuing questions about his working relationship with the FBI so nettled him that he frequently equivocated when he obviously could have answered a question unequivocally.

He said he told the agent it was "possible" he would like to continue to work for the FBI after getting out of prison on parole. It was true that he told them he would like to deal with only one agent if he became a permanent informant. But it was "possible, yes," that he had in mind a career with the FBI.

Money was never far from Douglas' mind. He acknowledged discussing financial problems not only with the FBI, but with the prosecutor. He said that when meeting with Lynch during trial preparations several months before the trial began, he told the prosecutor he had suffered a $2,000 loss because he had to sell his car quickly after its description was publicized. But he said he did not ask Lynch for government reimbursement for the loss.

"Did Mr. Lynch tell you you wouldn't get it?" asked O'Dwyer.

Lynch angrily objected and declared, "He didn't ask for money. He simply told me about it."

Judge Herman sustained the objection, leaving unanswered the question of whether the prosecutor told Douglas anything about reimbursement.

Douglas denied that he had negotiated with anyone for the story of his part in the case. However, before he left the witness stand he did try to sell the story. Unknown to the defense and therefore the jury, he telephoned William Zeidler of the Harrisburg *Patriot* one evening and talked with him about the possibility of collaborating on the story for a magazine. Zeidler, a thorough, professional trial reporter, found no interest among magazines.

O'Dwyer pressed Douglas to explain what "movement" he meant when he wrote Molly Mayfield that he needed $50,000 because he might "never feel safe" and "we know only some of the Catholic people that are involved, but it may even involve other types of people in the movement."

"The Panthers, the SDS," Douglas blurted out, his eyes suddenly blazing. "All of that to me is considered the movement."

"And *that* is what you felt threatened by?" O'Dwyer demanded.

"I did," he said.

O'Dwyer turned from Douglas to the jury and asked the next question slowly, scornfully chopping the air with his right fist on almost every word: "Catholics, Panthers, SDS, and what not; is that right?"

"And the nuts in this country, yes," Douglas shouted.

Lowering his voice now, O'Dwyer asked, "That is why you needed fifty thousand dollars, is that right?"

Douglas, staring at the floor, said: "I have already testified to that. You have read it yourself."

The defense's thorough investigation of Douglas paid off on several matters that seemed relatively minor on their face, but which went to the heart of his credibility and showed that during his role as double agent he also deceived the FBI. For example, when Douglas denied asking Professor Drinnon for money to pay for telephone calls, O'Dwyer brought out that he not only made the request in writing, but that he was reimbursed for the calls by both the FBI and Professor Drinnon's wife, Mary.

Q. Did you ever ask him for money for reimbursement for calls that you made?

A. I never asked him. He did, or his wife did, give me some money for telephone calls.

Q. And were these the telephone calls for which you have sought reimbursement from the government?

A. Well, I did receive reimbursement from the government, yes.

Q. Did you ever ask Professor Drinnon for fifty dollars to reimburse you for these calls?

A. I did not.

O'Dwyer then showed Douglas a copy of a "Dear Dick" letter telling Professor Drinnon: "I have spent about $50 for calls and if you want to pay part, I will the rest." Douglas acknowledged he had written the letter.

During a recess, Duncan Spencer of the Washington *Star*, chatting with Lynch in the corridor, commented, "Everytime Douglas opens his mouth he looks worse to the jury."

"What did you expect," asked Lynch laughing, "we'd have a bishop as a witness? They've still got the letters to swallow."

Before concluding his first day of cross-examination, O'Dwyer left the jurors shaking their heads at the way Douglas had duped

Betsy Sandel. Douglas acknowledged he asked Betsy to attend the July 6, 1970, demonstration protesting the prison treatment of Father Berrigan.

Q. And did you point out Betsy Sandel as being one of the demonstrators? Did you identify her photograph to the FBI?

A. I am sure I did, if she was there.

Q. And did you describe her as a student at Bucknell to the FBI?

A. The FBI knew that.

Q. Did you describe her to them as a student at Bucknell?

A. Yes, yes, well—well, yes, I did.

Q. Did you ask her to marry you?

Inexplicably, Douglas blushed—Ramsey Clark later called it "an enormous blush"—and covered his face with his hands and laughed. He finally muttered, "Possibly."

"Was it before or after you pointed out her picture to the FBI?" O'Dwyer asked.

"I don't recall," said Douglas, his head bowed.

Juror number two, Robert Foresman, the state fire school instructor, slapped his hand to his cheek, his mouth fell open, and he shook his head. Most of the jurors appeared shocked.

The next morning a man Hoover had accused of helping mastermind the alleged plot showed up in the visitors' section of the courtroom in a black turtleneck shirt, a cross dangling from his neck. He sat in the front row and discreetly exchanged peace signs with Father Berrigan and Sister McAlister before the jury came in.

The appearance of Father Daniel Berrigan who had been paroled because of his deteriorating health caused a minor stir in the courtroom, and when the jury came in and recognized him, there were whispered exchanges. Although there was not the slightest hint of any disruption or demonstration, Judge Herman cautioned defense attorneys at sidebar that the priest could remain only "as long as he is a normal spectator. If any demonstrations start in this courtroom," Herman said, "or if any of this hilarity that begins every once in a while, then I will have a different thought on it."

Douglas, irritable in his ninth day on the stand and third under cross-examination, repeatedly hesitated and looked to

Lynch for help when the questions bothered him. The prosecutor generally obliged with objections, as he did when O'Dwyer tried to pin Douglas down on his activities with the FBI immediately after Hoover's statement.

Judge Herman sustained the objection, but O'Dwyer persisted. "Your Honor," he said, "I want to pinpoint a certain date at which things began to happen. Mr. Lynch in his opening statement said that everybody ran for cover and I want to show that the government was running for cover as of that date. And this is the purpose . . . it is crucial to the case."

O'Dwyer finally asked Douglas whether, after Hoover's statement, FBI agents had asked him to give them any data "or anything in writing" that he had not previously given to them. Judge Herman said Douglas "couldn't possibly know" the answer to the question, but O'Dwyer retorted that "that would be for the witness rather than the court to answer." Douglas acknowledged he could answer it.

"Yes," he said. "I had still in my possession a list of—I don't recall the exact number. I think it was over ten things that Philip Berrigan told me to write down to instruct Joseph Wendorf. This was the period just prior to his being transferred to Danbury in the library of the federal penitentiary."

That was the list of instructions about which Douglas earlier had testified to at such length on direct examination, a critical piece of evidence that went into detail on the alleged kidnap-bombing plot. He said he did not give the FBI the list until a meeting with Molly Mayfield at a Holiday Inn in Danville, Pennsylvania, on December 5—a week after Hoover's accusation and more than three months after he claimed to have written it. Until that time, he said, the FBI had no knowledge of the existence of the list.

Citing copies of Douglas' reports to the FBI, O'Dwyer showed that after the "kidnap" letters and Father Berrigan's transfer to Danbury, Douglas was still impatiently encouraging talk of the alleged plot. O'Dwyer read a Douglas-Mayfield report which said, "Source advised he asked her [Sister McAlister] if she had discussed the letter she had written Father Berrigan with Berrigan yet. She said she had not but for him to be patient, as the plans were for big things and these plans take a lot of work to get organized."

Douglas acknowledged he had also reported to the FBI on November 13 that Father Wenderoth had telephoned and told him, "Don't be discouraged, plans are going forward."

"Were you discouraged, how things were making out?" O'Dwyer asked.

After a long pause, Douglas said, "No, I wasn't."

It wasn't until after Hoover's statement, Douglas acknowledged, that the FBI gave him a tape recorder. He said, "They told me if I wanted to tape-record anybody's conversation with regard to the kidnapping and bombing, I could do it." The Supreme Court had recently upheld the use of recorded conversations as evidence as long as one party to the conversation consented to the recording.

O'Dwyer had spent relatively little time questioning Douglas on the allegations in the indictment and the next cross-examiner, Terry Lenzner, would spend even less. With short, pithy questions, Lenzner bore down on Douglas' provocation role and brought out that on one occasion he had arranged the smuggling of letters from prison without the FBI's knowledge and that another time he had lied to the FBI about smuggling a message.

Lenzner asked Douglas who arranged for his old Lewisburg roommate, Tom Love, to smuggle the writings of several other antiwar activists from Lewisburg Farm Camp and he said, "I told him that there would be some . . . political writings coming out. I told him if he wanted to go out there to pick up the documents, I said the documents would be there."

Douglas said he did not believe he told the FBI about the arrangement with Love because that would have caused "friction" between the FBI and the Bureau of Prisons.

After several routine questions about the demonstration outside the prison at Lewisburg on July 16, Lenzner asked, "By the way, Mr. Douglas, did you bring out statements from Father Berrigan and Mr. Eberhardt in connection with that demonstration?"

"I did."

"And did you once deny to the FBI that you did bring out

statements from Father Berrigan and Mr. Eberhardt?"

"I told them I didn't know anything about it."

"And so you lied to the FBI?"

"I didn't want to cause any friction between the two agencies, so I did not tell them I took the letters out."

Lenzner, suggesting that an extortion plan was the real reason Douglas began copying the Phil-Liz letters before becoming an FBI informant, asked Douglas if he had ever talked to another inmate about "the possibility of getting money out of the Catholic movement."

He said he had not, but Lenzner pressed on: "The idea was to get money from the donors in the movement through extortion?"

"That's a lie!" shouted Douglas, finally using a word the defense had used scores of times in questioning him.

At Lynch's request, Judge Herman instructed the jury that the witness' answers, not the attorney's questions, were important. And the judge said, "I hope, Mr. Lenzner, that you are going to follow this up with evidence." Lenzner said he had already supoenaed a witness who would testify to it.

Lenzner rapidly ran through a series of lies Douglas admitted telling Jane Hoover and Betsy Sandel, then asked: "Were you continually pressuring Miss Hoover and Miss Sandel to get more involved in the movement?"

Sullen and angry now, Douglas lost his composure. "I didn't encourage them, as you were putting it," he exclaimed. "I didn't have an FBI badge there."

"Excuse me, sir?" queried Lenzner incredulously.

"I say," said Douglas, "I didn't have an FBI badge there. I didn't tell them what I was really about, no."

Asked if he had tried to recruit another Bucknell student, Joyce Frederick, for the movement, he said he had. But he said he could not recall telling her his function in the movement was "organization after people were committed to civil disobedience."

Lenzner then introduced a copy of the letter Douglas wrote to Joyce Frederick saying that was his function in the movement. It was one of several letters of a provocative nature that Douglas had written without the FBI's knowledge. The defense introduced them to the surprise and chagrin of the prosecution.

"Mr. Douglas," Lenzner said, referring to the letter, "this reference to someone being close to you that testified for the FBI, that was a lie, was it not?"

"It was."

"And your reference to being totally committed to that movement, that was also a lie, is that correct?"

"Yes."

"And the reference to your giving your life to the struggle and losing your freedom and life in the struggle, that was a lie, was it not?"

"It was."

After two more admissions of lies, Douglas suddenly erupted: "The letter is a lie."

"The whole letter is a lie?" Lenzner asked.

"The whole letter," Douglas said.

Lenzner, reaching for another document, asked Douglas if he had told people on the Bucknell campus he was a revolutionary.

"Telling people on campus that I was a revolutionary?" Douglas replied. "No, I did not."

Lenzner handed Lynch a copy of the *Bucknellian* in which Douglas arranged to have published an article headed "By a Revolutionary." Lenzner later recalled Lynch muttered, "Good God."

Douglas admitted that he had claimed authorship of the article and asked the editor of the *Bucknellian* to print it under the byline, "By a Revolutionary." But the witness volunteered, "That is not mine anyway. That is Philip Berrigan's. That's his writings. He is the revolutionary."

Boudin bounded from his chair: "Your honor, I move to strike that."

But Herman, increasingly irritated by the cross-examination, refused. When Boudin persisted, declaring that Douglas was interpolating remarks rather than responding to the question, Herman declared, "He has done it sometimes before, I have stricken it and I'm not going to strike this."

It was not unusual for Herman to rule one way one time and another way the next time. In fact, attorneys for both sides privately expressed the feeling that Herman sometimes presided more as a mediator than as a judge, trying to give something to both sides rather than ruling in accordance with law and normal court procedures.

Lenzner, who stood impatiently holding another document while Boudin and Herman clashed, asked Douglas if he had ever told people that he was committed to and believed in strategic sabotage.

"No," he replied.

Lenzner then read a letter Douglas had written to Susan Williams of Rochester which said: "This is where I am at politically: a made, totally committed non-violent revolutionary who believes in strategic sabotage."

The letter also said, "There may be an interesting project that would interest you after the turn of the year." This referred to the tunnel system, Douglas testified. Lenzner asked if he were trying to recruit Susan Williams for the tunnel project. Instead of answering the question, Douglas said, "Theodore Glick had called me from Rochester, New York. He knew about the tunnel system."

"Excuse me, your honor," interjected Boudin. "I move to strike that statement . . . because it is, again, not responsive to what Mr. Lenzner asked him."

"It is," insisted Douglas.

The exchange that followed reflected not only a hesitancy to rule that frequently caused Herman to temporarily lose control of the courtroom dialogue, but a hardening of his attitude toward the cross-examination:

Boudin: If Your Honor will hear the question again, Your Honor will see that the witness has added something that is not responsive.

Lynch: Your Honor, I object to Mr. O'Dwyer interrupting Mr. Lenzner.

The Court: Mister who?

Lynch: Mr. Boudin.

Boudin: May I state that I represent clients other than Mr. Lenzner's clients.

The Court: I understand that.

Mr. Boudin: And I have my clients here and I do not think really the interruption is unwise.

The Court: I am not going to strike it.

Lenzner returned to the letter Douglas had written to Joyce Frederick and when the witness said it was of a "personal nature," the attorney demanded, "All that business about your being committed to the movement and the struggle and devoting your life . . . that was all of a personal nature?"

Lynch objected that Lenzner was arguing. Herman agreed, brushing off the letter in the process: "He said all of that was lies to her. He was writing to a young woman and he told her a lot of lies."

Lenzner brought out that in Douglas' signed statement to the FBI on December 5, 1970, he identified the bombing target as the Pentagon instead of the tunnel system. "As I said before there were some discrepancies in the three-oh-twos [the FBI form on which informant information is recorded]," said Douglas.

"But this is a signed statement, not a three-oh-two, sir," said Lenzner. "You reviewed this before you signed it, didn't you? Didn't you go over it carefully with the FBI before you signed it?"

Douglas said: "I don't recall that I went over it carefully with the FBI. I probably went over it. I had to be back at the penitentiary that day and I was in a hurry to get back."

There was never any explanation as to why a convict would be in a hurry to return to the penitentiary or why he "had to be back" when in fact he was under control of the FBI, not the Bureau of Prisons.

"This is information that you gave them and they had typed up and you signed, isn't that correct?" asked Lenzner.

"I did sign it, yes," Douglas replied. "I did sign that statement."

"Are you saying now that that was incorrect?" asked Lenzner.

"Yes," Douglas replied. "Instead of the Pentagon, it should have been the tunnel system."

If that was simply a mistake, as Douglas contended, it is difficult to understand why the FBI did not catch it at the time. All of the other information about the alleged bombing plot, until that point, concerned the tunnel system.

Douglas also admitted that at one time he reported to the FBI that Father McLaughlin had discussed the tunnel project with him over the telephone, but that later he had reported he was mistaken, it was actually Father Wenderoth. He acknowledged frequently confusing the names of the two priests.

But Douglas denied he had ever told Professor Drinnon that "the system must be changed" and that he hoped to participate in "something more involved than selective service boards." Lenzner then read to the jury a letter from Douglas to Drinnon containing those quotes, and Douglas acknowledged he had written the letter.

Still another Douglas money-making scheme was brought out by Tom Menaker, who succeeded Lenzner as the cross-examiner. Douglas said he "quite possibly" had asked Mayfield to help him arrange a $400-a-month phony study of prisons after his release on parole so he could spy on radicals in federal prisons. He acknowledged the proposed study was a cover so he could "contact individuals associated with the East Coast Conspiracy to Save Lives and related matters."

On Douglas' fifth day of cross-examination, Daniel Ellsberg of Pentagon Papers fame and his wife showed up and sat in the front row of the spectators' section, causing a buzz in the courtroom. Ellsberg, whose own trial for conspiracy was scheduled to begin within a few months in Los Angeles, told newsmen he had brought his wife to see Boudin in action and to reassure her that Boudin was a good trial attorney. "Some of her relatives told her that while he was a good appellate attorney, he was not experienced at trials and was an unknown quantity," Ellsberg said.

Boudin, mopping up for the defense, quickly antagonized Judge Herman as well as Douglas by pressing repetitious questions about why Douglas had carried a gun with him in 1966 when he entered a Milwaukee bank on a fraud scheme. Douglas insisted he bought the handgun for hunting purposes, but Boudin pressed on, with Lynch objecting and Herman saying with exasperation, "Sustained, sustained, sustained," and "He is not on trial" and admonishing Boudin for asking a "ridiculous question."

Douglas, openly belligerent and enjoying the judge's put-downs of Boudin, would turn to Herman, carefully addressing him as "Your Honor," and complain, "I have answered that ten times" and "I've told that a hundred times." Once during later questioning, he volunteered, "Your honor, that is not evidence." He was never admonished.

Boudin persisted, however, and finally Douglas said he carried the gun "to frighten someone so they wouldn't apprehend me." The attorney then held up a pre-sentencing statement Douglas had made in federal court at Milwaukee and the witness said, "I know what I told the court. After I was apprehended I knew I had a very heavy sentence I might possibly receive. I told the court at that time I was carrying the handgun on me so that in the case I was apprehended I would shoot myself . . . with that statement I could gain leniency from the court."

Boudin suggested Douglas had lied to the Milwaukee court by saying he planned to use the gun on himself or lied to the Harrisburg court by saying he had planned to use it to frighten someone. But Lynch objected he could have had both plans in mind and Herman said, "He certainly could have both of them," and Douglas replied, "They were both in my mind."

Following a luncheon recess, Boudin asked Douglas if he had talked with FBI agents about the case before returning to the courtroom. He said he had eaten lunch and discussed the trial with his wife in the presence of several FBI agents, but had not discussed the case with the agents. Boudin, suggesting that Douglas was being coached on his testimony by agents, demanded to know what he had said.

"I told my wife a few of the questions that you had asked me," Douglas said. "I told my wife that you spent one hour on the gun issue that had no relevance to the case. I also said that as far as I was concerned, during all of my cross-examination that you had not changed the basis of my testimony here in this courtroom."

Boudin then pressed Douglas on why he pulled the gun in the bank. Douglas snapped: "I was afraid, I was scared. What would you do?"

Lynch objected that Boudin was "getting into a psychological matter" and Judge Herman, instead of citing Douglas' testimony, said: "He was scared and he drew the gun. He had no intention of shooting anybody. He didn't shoot anybody. As far as I know, he didn't put a shell in a chamber. Did you put a shell in the chamber?"

"No, I did not," Douglas said.

On Douglas' sixth day of cross-examination, he occasionally glanced at the number-one juror, Mrs. Vera Thompson, seated directly beneath him, holding a handkerchief to her cheek. Suddenly he turned to Herman, and the judge recessed the court.

"If Your Honor pleases," O'Dwyer said as the door closed behind the jurors, "the record does not reveal what the witness has said to Your Honor, although it was audible to the jury and it was audible to some of us here. And I respectfully submit it should be in the record."

Herman, looking annoyed, said, "Well, I will tell the counsel and everybody here what I thought he said. He said, number-one juror had pain or something like that. And I told you before she had two teeth pulled yesterday, and that she was having difficulty."

"That is right," O'Dwyer exclaimed. "And . . . the relationship between the witness and the court and the fact that the witness has constantly been called upon to appeal to the court from time to time has laid the foundation for the fact that this witness has said to Your Honor . . . that one of the jurors was suffering, something that Your Honor knew and that we know. And I think it is highly prejudicial. I think to permit a witness this liberty is something that is unheard of in jurisprudence."

After an angry exchange during which Herman banged his gavel and threatened to hold O'Dwyer in contempt, the jury returned and Herman told the ailing juror, "Mrs. Thompson, you give me a sign if you have any problems. I didn't see you before, but Mr. Douglas apparently did."

Defense attorneys charged that Herman's comment compounded what they already considered a grievous error. They later filed a formal motion for a mistrial citing eighty-five pages of transcript they said were "merely a sample" of the judge's rulings and remarks "which make it impossible for the jury to deal fairly with these defendants."

Boudin brought out a series of crucial conversations Douglas had testified to at the trial, but had not previously mentioned in reports to the FBI or in grand jury testimony:

—Father Berrigan had told him that Sister McAlister wanted

him to get in touch with Fathers Wenderoth and McLaughlin about the tunnel project.

—Marjorie Shuman had told him that the tunnel project would be on Washington's Birthday and he had relayed the information to Father Berrigan.

—Father Wenderoth had told him to tell Father Berrigan that the tunnel project would be carried out "as per his instructions."

—Father Wenderoth told him at a September 5 meeting in the New Dorm that Eqbal Ahmad was "prone to violence."

Holding Douglas' report to the FBI of the September 5 meeting, Boudin asked, "There is no reference to Dr. Ahmad being prone to violence in this report, is there?"

"I am telling you what Joseph Wenderoth told me," Douglas insisted.

Boudin finally accused Douglas of making false reports, and Herman instructed the jurors that they "must ignore these comments of counsel."

Douglas acknowledged he was reporting several conversations for the first time at the trial. "There is a lot of testimony I have given in this courtroom," he said, "that refreshes my memory when I am testifying."

Boudin also brought out that Douglas got a reward for information leading to the capture of Daniel Berrigan, although at first the informant denied it. Showing him an FBI report, Boudin said, "Tell us whether that doesn't refresh your recollection that in fact you did get two hundred dollars for helping turn in Father Daniel Berrigan?"

Douglas read the report, then said: "I received two hundred dollars. I have no idea what it was for. As far as I knew, it was for expenses. This is the first time officially that I had any knowledge that I was the one that led to his capture."

The FBI was tipped off by passages in two of Sister McAlister's letters that Douglas smuggled which indicated Daniel Berrigan planned to get together with William Stringfellow.

Boudin introduced in evidence three more provocative letters that surprised Lynch, all written by Douglas apparently without the FBI's knowledge, and the attorney used the FBI's own reports to try to discredit Douglas.

Nearing the end of his cross-examination, the lawyer said: "You told us about a number of aliases you have used in the course of your life. Without taking the time of the jury to ask you to repeat those, let me give you a list as appears in the FBI report and ask you whether this is an accurate list: Boyd Frederick Douglas, Jr., also known as Frank Douglas, R. Douglas, Robert Blake, James Brow, William Cook, Meredith Dickinson, Charles Gray, Robert Gray, Captain Robert Edward Gray, Ronald Gray, Frederick P. Gordon, Bob C. Hill, Jr., Robert Hill, Donald Rogers, J. L. Shipley, Dr. James Link Shipley, David Summerville, Carl Strand, James Stranton?"

"I didn't use James Brow, Dr. James Link Shipley, J. S. Shipley, David Summerville, James Stranton," Douglas said in a reply that hardly helped his credibility. "Those names they could have put on there because I signed checks, checks were made out to that name."

"I see," said Boudin; "that will do."

Boudin then introduced an FBI report of Douglas' parole in 1967 which said he had made "a poor social adjustment since being in the Army and certainly has many attributes of a confidence man."

"Your witness," said Boudin, ending seven days of defense cross-examination.

The following morning—Douglas' fourteenth day on the stand—Lynch, apparently intent on giving the defense little excuse for keeping Douglas on longer—took less than an hour on re-direct examination.

Douglas denied that he had ever encouraged Father Berrigan to write of illegal acts in his letters or that he had an extortionist plan in mind when he began copying the priest's letters.

Lynch brought out that Douglas had been hospitalized for a year at the National Institutes of Health after the medical experiments. And yes, Douglas said, he was quartered in the "honor dorm" at Lewisburg federal prison while attending Bucknell University and yes, he did get a letter of commendation from an executive of the department store in Des Moines where he worked from April to December in 1971.

O'Dwyer objected that the defense had not questioned him about his whereabouts since his release. But Lynch, fumbling for words, countered: "The purpose of this ah . . . question was that the defense has been attacking his credibility before nineteen seventy-one and I would like to ah . . . establish the ah . . . ah . . . ah . . . ah sterling character of Mr. Douglas since nineteen seventy. . . . He's been a hard-working, dependable man."

"Come on, Mr. Lynch," O'Dwyer shouted, shaking his fist. "You've hidden him for a year and a half!"

When Lynch concluded his questioning, Ramsey Clark said, "I will stand on my previous cross-examination." Except for a question by Menaker about the name of the bank in Omaha where Douglas had a credit card, defense attorneys, feeling they had destroyed Douglas' credibility, did not further cross-examine him.

During a recess, Lynch told newsmen, "I was very pleased at the way Douglas held up. I was afraid they might tangle him up on dates and events, but they didn't. He told the truth and it stood up."

"So," said Weldon Wallace, the Baltimore *Sun*'s courtly religion editor, "we are left with a vision of a sterling character, a hard-working, dependable man."

"Yes," said Lynch, grinning, "that's the way it should be."

CHAPTER THIRTEEN
The Outcome

For Delmar H. Mayfield, Jr., a husky, solemn-faced, thirty-two-year-old FBI agent, testifying at the conspiracy trial could not have been one of the more pleasant experiences of his career. He could add little to the government's case, but defense attorneys had been anxiously awaiting his appearance, not so much to quiz him about Douglas' letter requesting $50,000, which they had already thoroughly exploited, but to cross-examine him on other financial dealings with the informant.

Lynch questioned the agent for less than fifteen minutes, just long enough for him to testify that he worked with Douglas on the case from the outset and that Douglas had become an informant voluntarily and continued to smuggle Phil-Liz letters, always making copies for the FBI and keeping in close contact with the FBI.

Defense attorneys, however, kept Molly Mayfield on the stand for several hours, grilling him on Douglas' informant activities and on the FBI's financial arrangements with him—past, present and future.

The first "conversation about money" with Douglas, Mayfield said, occurred in late July or early August of 1970 when the informant said he was incurring expenses "and I said fine, I think we can reimburse you for expenses."

Pressed by Mr. O'Dwyer to explain the "expenses," Mayfield said, "Mr. Douglas did not keep an itemized list of expenses nor did I ask him to keep one." But the payments, Mayfield acknowledged, were for services, as well as expenses.

The agent also testified that FBI Director Hoover directed that all of Douglas' outstanding obligations be taken care of before the trial "so he would come to court with no obligations which would prejudice the case."

"What recommendations are you going to make for paying him for services at this trial?" O'Dwyer asked.

Mayfield, apparently surprised by the question, said, "I do not know at this time what recommendation I'm going to make. He has been specifically told he has not been promised anything."

"You did not promise him anything for Rochester and you came through," O'Dwyer exclaimed. "You didn't promise him anything for Dan Berrigan and you came through. Are you prepared to recommend payment to him after his testimony and for services in this case?"

After a long pause, Mayfield replied, "Sitting right here in court at this time I do not know the answer to that question."

O'Dwyer brought out that when Mayfield conferred with Douglas in Phoenix, the informant handed him a letter asking for $200 a month in additional payments for "expanding on the information" he had already given on Father Berrigan.

Lynch objected that O'Dwyer was covering the same ground "ad nauseam."

"Ad nauseam is on your table, Mr. Lynch," O'Dwyer flared.

Lynch appealed to Herman to inform O'Dwyer "his idea of comical remarks are most inappropriate," and O'Dwyer countered, "They're as fair as yours." The judge ignored them both.

Cross-examined by Menaker, Mayfield acknowledged that in November, 1970, he recommended payment of $1,000 a month to Douglas, but Hoover had sent an urgent teletype message that the informant should be paid on a COD basis.

Asked what that meant, Mayfield said, "Collection on delivery."

"Delivery of what?" asked Menaker.

"Information," said Mayfield.

Boudin pressed Mayfield about provocative letters Douglas had written and the agent said he was unaware of them. At one point Mayfield, putting the onus of provocative acts solely on Douglas, volunteered, "I gave him very few directions, I left him on his own."

Quoting the Susan Williams' letter in which Douglas said he believed in "strategic sabotage," Boudin asked, "If you had known Mr. Douglas was writing this letter, would you have retained him as an informant?"

"Yes, I would have," said Mayfield.

Boudin quoted the passage about "an interesting project that would interest you after the first of the year," and asked: "If you had known he sent a letter as provocative as that, would you have still kept him as an informant?"

"Yes, I would have," Mayfield said, "but I would have instructed him to not try to recruit people for anything."

"If Mr. Douglas had attempted to recruit people, you would have regarded that as a highly improper action?" asked Boudin. "Would it have been in violation of his duty to you?"

"It would have been a violation of FBI regulations and a violation of my own personal standards," said Mayfield.

Mayfield, carefully choosing his words and talking slowly in a deep voice, expressed confidence in Douglas, which was hardly surprising. This was by far the biggest case of the young agent's career. And his career could hardly have been helped by lack of confidence in an informant he had nursed along for more than a year.

However, in view of Douglas' extensive criminal record and known propensity for lying, Mayfield's unqualified expression of faith in him put the agent's own credibility as a witness on the line.

Asked if he had not considered it might be dangerous to turn over explosives manuals to a man who had been convicted of a violent crime, Mayfield replied, "I had no qualms whatsoever in handing them to Mr. Douglas. I had complete faith in him."

Boudin shook his head and smiled at the jury, then began bearing down on Douglas' almost constant association with agents during the trial. He asked the agent how often he had seen the informant since the trial began. Every day, usually for an hour or three or four hours, Mayfield said, "but a number of these times I was having dinner with him."

Boudin walked over and put his hand on the shoulder of William B. Anderson, who was sitting to the rear of the prosecution table taking notes. "Did Mr. Anderson ever attend these one to three- to four-hour sessions?" he asked.

Mayfield said both Anderson and Agent George Menzel frequently attended the sessions, but added, "My visits were not to discuss the case or to prepare him for the case."

"Just social visits?" Boudin asked.

"I would characterize them as pretty much so," Mayfield said, never losing his deadpan expression.

"No further questions," said Boudin.

With the prosecution wrapping up its case now, Lynch sought to prove that Fathers Berrigan and Wenderoth had entered the heating tunnels. The government had been so specific on this crucial allegation, charging that the priests entered the tunnels on April 1, that even defense attorneys felt the prosecution must have solid evidence to substantiate it.

Two college students, John F. Millard and Anthony D. Barone, testified that Father Wenderoth, with unindicted co-conspirator, John Swinglish, once initiated "vague discussions" about the possibility of destroying tunnels. And Millard quoted the priest as saying that he and Father Philip Berrigan had been down in a tunnel. The discussion, the students said, occurred in August, 1970, on a mall at Catholic University in Washington, D.C.

But Millard called it "a very vague idea."

Barone, asked on cross-examination, if it was speculative, said, "I would have to say so. There was nothing about plans, they were just asking what we thought about it."

Lynch also called as a witness Joseph M. Joynt, the government elevator mechanic who complained of FBI harassment during the investigation, but he added nothing. He testified that he had met several of the defendants at his mother's house in Silver Spring, Maryland, a Washington suburb. But he denied ever hearing any discussions about blowing up tunnels.

Joynt had said before the trial that FBI agents insisted four or five persons had seen him taking the priests into the tunnel and that he told them, "That's four or five liars you'd better check out." He was not even asked about that at the trial. The defense did not cross-examine him.

FBI Agent Palmer A. Tunstall, a handwriting expert, testified that Father Berrigan and Sister McAlister had written the letters introduced by Lynch, a fact the defense had already agreed to stipulate. O'Dwyer accused Lynch of "putting on a show" by calling several FBI agents to testify about that and other matters already stipulated by the defense, including a fingerprint linking Sister McAlister to the Delaware draft board raids and Father Wenderoth to the explosives manuals.

Cross-examining Tunstall, however, the defense drew out the fact that the agent did not make his handwriting analysis until three days after Hoover's Senate testimony. It was yet another piece of evidence that the investigation of the alleged kidnap-bombing plot did not get fully under way until the FBI director's public accusation.

The day Tunstall testified, March 23, Lynch rested the government's case. In a month's time, sixty-four government witnesses, including twenty-one FBI agents and nine policemen, had testified. But only the testimony of one witness—Boyd Douglas—had been crucial to the kidnap-bombing charge. Without Douglas and the letters, there was not even a hint of a case.

Even the government's evidence on the plot to raid draft board offices had been surprisingly thin. Sister McAlister had been linked through a fingerprint and other evidence, including her own letter. And Fathers Wenderoth and McLaughlin and the Scoblicks had been linked to the Philadelphia draft board raids through the largely uncorroborated testimony of Douglas. There was no evidence, as promised by Lynch in his opening statement, that Father Berrigan was "in on the planning" of the Philadelphia raids.

The government had utterly failed to prove that Fathers Berrigan and Wenderoth had entered the tunnels and Judge Herman was to instruct the jury to dismiss from its mind that crucial part of the bombing allegation.

In the jury's absence, Clark argued for a directed verdict of acquittal, declaring: "I am shocked that the United States government would present such flimsy evidence on such serious charges. If the evidence I have heard in the case had been brought to me when I was attorney general I would not have permitted it to go to a grand jury," which requires a lesser degree of proof than a trial jury.

Lynch retorted, that there was "fairly overwhelming evidence of a conspiracy," and said, "When a man stands up in court and leans on the weight of his former office to make an argument with no analysis of the testimony, I think it is fair to observe that the argument is less than rational."

Judge Herman denied the motion.

The following day reporters, still wondering which defendants, if any, would take the stand, filled the press section early. Eqbal Ahmad earlier had said he was anxious to testify and Boudin had said perhaps all the defendants should take the stand.

When court convened, Ramsey Clark stood up, ostensibly to make an opening statement to the jury on what the defense expected to show. Instead, in a move that stunned everyone except defense attorneys and their clients, Clark declared:

"Your honor, the defendants will always seek peace, the defendants continue to proclaim their innocence—and the defense rests."

Lynch, not realizing at first what was happening, arose to object to the "peace" reference as irrelevant, but upon hearing "the defense rests" sat down, shaking his head. It happened so suddenly that reporters were asking each other for fills on what Clark had said.

The defendants smiled and looked at Lynch as though they had put one over on him. They clearly thought they had. He turned and looked at FBI Agent Anderson and shrugged as though he thought that they may have, too. The prosecutor had been telling newsmen he was anxious for the defense to present its case so that he might have the opportunity to cross-examine the defendants.

In the jury's absence, Lynch angrily accused the defense of "some sort of trickery, some sort of fraud on the court" for resting its case without calling some twenty-five witnesses who had been subpoenaed "from all over the country." Herman also expressed annoyance, but Menaker insisted the defense had not decided to rest until the previous night.

The defendants had made the decision late at night after conferring at Dauphin County jail where Father Berrigan was imprisoned during the trial. Ahmad and Sister McAlister told a news conference that they and Father Berrigan opposed the decision but agreed to go along with the Scoblicks and Fathers Wenderoth and McLaughlin.

Ahmad read a handwritten statement from Father Berrigan saying, "I disagreed with the resting, as humanly and as strenuously as I could. I felt we ought to face squarely the violent absurdity of this indictment (insofar as we could in this suffocating court); that we ought to submit to the requirement of truth, even toward the Nixon administration; that we owed the people an explanation of our lives and resistance."

Sister McAlister, an inveterate note-taker, had recorded the defendants' conference at the prison and said the decision to rest was based on three principal points:

—The government's case "is essentially false and they have been unable to prove it so we should not have to answer it."

—The government would try to use the defense case as a "fishing expedition for future prosecution" of members of the Resistance who had been involved in draft board actions, but had not been prosecuted.

—Judge Herman's denial of two defense motions, one which would have permitted the defense to present evidence of discriminatory prosecution and one which would have granted immunity for defense witnesses. (Judge Herman had held that any evidence of discriminatory prosecution was a legal matter for the courts and had said that while he understood the defense's problem in asking for immunity for defense witnesses, there was no precedent for such a move.)

In her notes on the defendants' conference, Sister McAlister also mentioned they considered resting the case the "ultimate put down of the government" and a recognition that "the courtroom is not a forum to express anything." She wrote: "The rules of evidence, the prejudice of this judge—manifested over and over, and the particular overt violence of this prosecutor make it impossible. The response of silence seems the best response to the illegitimacy of this indictment, of the process of this government."

In a message to the authors of this book immediately after the defense decision to rest, Father Berrigan wrote that if he had taken the stand, he would have testified Douglas had lied to him and that there was no conspiracy. He wrote:

I would have asserted some of the following:

1. One in a maximum security penitentiary is physically and mentally unable to conspire with anyone outside. Anyone questioning that statement ignores the realities of penitentiary life, or is simply ignorant of them.

2. Douglas, by his vested interest in the "plot," imparted to me an exaggerated version of the consciousness of those outside—he lied to me as to their thinking, aspirations, present involvements. By the same token, he lied about my consciousness, giving my friends a distorted picture of what I was thinking. He adopted a triple role, informer, provocateur and entrapper—out of these roles came the "plot" which he presented to the FBI, for a price, of course. (Some day, someone will discover what that price is—most probably it is not $9,200.)

3. Even apart from the above, the "plots" never got beyond discussion, which I understand is protected by the First Amendment.

4. If any conspiracy existed, it was between Douglas and me. And here, no agreement was possible since he belonged to the government.

I would, in short, have tried to testify truthfully and convincingly to the above regardless of the verdict.

Father Berrigan went on to write:

I feel great satisfaction with this trial, simply because I *know* that the principals did the best they could under tremendous pressure and disadvantage. To be convinced, on the one hand, that you have paid a very heavy price to save this bloody nation non-violently and lovingly; and on the other, to receive a reward of indictment, trial, probably conviction and sentence is a very heavy scene. It is the main pressure on one, or on the Community. To hold firm under such burdens; to remain human and balanced; to take legal and tactical

positions requiring some risk and exposure; to put up with jail
under these deplorable circumstances; and for the others, to
deal with audiences, to attend endless meetings, to work with
lawyers until far into the night; to rest a case when defense
might guarantee a better chance for acquittal—all this is
something of an achievement. I think that all of us would want
something different than what happened—I certainly would.
Yet we will nonetheless agree that collectively, this trial has
touched on the remarkable; and even the heroic.

I think it has served a useful purpose, despite the huge
expenditure of money and talent. Perhaps it has done more
than any other event, both in preparation and in trial, to keep
alive the consciousness of the war, its new nature, its con-
tinuity and even intensification, under new and innovative
technological barbarities. (Hopefully, the trials of Angela
Davis; of Daniel Ellsberg and Tony Russo and of the
organizations among them, will continue this trend.)

To carry our hopes—even further, we end the trial with the
best movement organization in the country. If'n we had our
druthers, this network would serve as a mere beginning—to
inculcate non-violent philosophy and tactics, to develop a
reasonable politics of resistance, to educate about nuclear
diplomacy and public justice. We hope that the Defense
Committee network will help deepen roots; to find security in
a life style of resistance; and to hold the reeling oligarchy
accountable for its crimes.

It was all over now except for the arguments and the judge's
charge to the jury. Although jury arguments usually are designed
more to persuade than to enlighten, appealing more to emotions
than to reason, the arguments at Harrisburg had an extra
emotional dimension—the Phil-Liz letters. Both sides used
them, reading passages out of context for their own purposes, a
final indignity for the priest and the nun.

Lynch left the government's opening statement to Connelly,
who described the defendants as a group of highly educated
persons who had escalated their antiwar protests from draft
board raids to kidnap-bombing plans and in the process had
taken advantage of a convict who had never finished high school.

To Connelly, the letters were letters of criminal intent. He cited such passages as "the enclosed is dynamite" and kept referring to Ahmad as the "man behind the scenes" and quoted one passage in which Sister McAlister referred to an FBI agent as "a devious bastard." Walking over to the defense table and pointing out each defendant by name, Connelly finally thundered, "And Philip Berrigan, the priest of peace whose most famous letter is the kidnap letter—a disparagement of true peace—an obliteration of the distinction—even his own—between violence and non-violence. They all found good in Boyd Douglas, but they didn't bring it out. They wanted to use him, they wanted to use his criminal talents. And now they say 'Oh, find us innocent. Damn Boyd Douglas!' I say, don't be a part of that."

To O'Dwyer, they were letters of love. Captivating the courtroom with his Irish brogue, he read: "The best part was seeing you and the old fighting spirit. . . . You know—but you must remember—what you mean to your people. . . . As long as it remains possible to get some words to you, guess we can keep it going."

On and on O'Dwyer read, interpolating as he went, talking of "the fantasies of people" and the need of a man who went to prison for a cause to feel that he was not there for nothing.

After Boudin, Lenzner and Menaker presented their summations, Clark closed with a rundown of the government evidence, declaring: "The case is built on Boyd Douglas and the letters—pure and simple. A man you can't believe and letters that don't say what the government has tried to torture and twist them into saying."

Clark's argument ran so long that Judge Herman called a recess in the middle of it. In the corridor, Lynch, fidgety and anxious to make his own closing argument, remarked: "I'm getting screwed—the jury will already be tired by the time I get to them. It doesn't make any difference anyway—he's not making an impression on them."

The letters, Clark said, "were from two people who cared very much for each other" and it was indecent to have had to read them in public. "Did you hear Paul O'Dwyer read those letters?"

he asked the jury. "If you weren't moved, you're a lot harder than I am. The letters are noble. And this is the first case I have ever seen—and I hope it will be the last—where the government of the United States tries to prove a crime by dramatic readings rather than by evidence."

Clark said Douglas "lied to you more times than you and I will ever know. If you believe Boyd Douglas you'll go to your last day wondering whether you were the most recent of a long, long line of people he has taken in."

When Lynch's turn came he waded in like a boxer, pacing in front of the jury box, gesturing lightly with his left hand at times, slashing with his right for emphasis, ridiculing the defendants and pointing them out by name as he would in an organized crime case.

"Defense attorneys have tried to divert the jury from the facts of the case," said Lynch, quoting an old courthouse saw: "When the facts are against you, argue the law; when the law is against you, argue the facts; and when both are against you, attack the prosecution."

He sarcastically referred to "gentle Sister McAlister and gentle Father Berrigan" and with a sweeping right-hand gesture suggested a passage in the priest's letter about law enforcement officers' attempts to "pick off the gurus" was prophetic: "I submit to you these are the gurus!"

"Now we are told Boyd Douglas has imposed himself on these innocents," Lynch declared, "this very experienced group of burglars. . . . They had him on the stand almost eight consecutive days and they asked him everything: they never, never turned him from the basic truth of what he testified to and what he testified to is corroborated by the letters down to a tee."

Standing at the lectern in front of the jury box, his back to the defense table, Lynch bared his teeth and cited a passage from Father Berrigan's "kidnap" letter: "When I refer to murder, it is not to prohibit it absolutely."

"That really sticks in the craw of the defense," the prosecutor rasped. "They can't explain it. . . . You can look at the New Testament until your eyes go blind and look in the Bible and you'll never find anything saying this is not to prohibit murder.

"A society bent on its own destruction can find no better way to do it than to let each person decide what law to obey," said Lynch, adding that the defendants "have argued basically not for justice but for pardon.

"On all the evidence," the prosecutor concluded, "there is but one conclusion you can rationally draw—that is the defendants are guilty as charged in the indictment."

The jury filed out grim-faced.

The next day Judge Herman delivered his charge. It was so confusing on the conspiracy law's application to the case that there was disagreement as to its meaning among attorneys on both sides. It was so loaded with a summary of evidence against the defendants that it could only be called a hanging charge. Clark said that Lynch himself "could not have done a better job—and didn't."

The confusion centered around the six different statutes cited in count one—the conspiracy section of the indictment. Three of the statues dealt with draft board raids, two with explosives and one with kidnapping. Lynch understood Herman's charge to mean that to convict any of the defendants, the jury would have to find that a conspiracy existed to violate all six statutes. However, Cottone, interviewed jointly with Lynch, said he thought the charge meant the jury would only have to conclude that a conspiracy existed to violate any of the statutes.

"No," Lynch told the U.S. attorney, "that's what I asked the judge to charge the jury, but he didn't do that. He charged them that they would have to find the defendants conspired to violate all six of the statutes."

Defense attorneys called the charge "misleading, contradictory and grossly inefficient." Moreover, they were dismayed that in his extraordinary fifteen-minute summary of evidence, the judge had made critical errors, overlooked evidence favorable to the defense, and had underscored evidence against Father McLaughlin and Mary Cain Scoblick, whose roles in the alleged conspiracy had received scant mention in the trial.

Defense attorneys urged the judge to recall the jurors and instruct them to disregard all comments he had made about the evidence. Instead he recalled them and attempted to rectify mistakes he had made and told the jury to consider as evidence letters introduced by the defense. "Whatever I said about evidence," he concluded, "the facts and the credibility of witnesses are for you to decide."

The jurors began their deliberations on Thursday, March 30. On Easter Sunday, after having deliberated thirty-three and a half hours and having heard, at their request, a second reading of the charge of conspiracy, they reported they had reached a partial verdict. They filed solemnly into the courtroom. Harold Sheets, the foreman, reported they had agreed on count four, but were deadlocked on the conspiracy count and the other eight counts dealing with letters. Count four accused Father Berrigan of smuggling the only letter the government alleged was smuggled prior to Douglas' becoming an informant. The jury found the priest guilty.

But the jury was still baffled both by the judge's conspiracy charge and by the complicated case Lynch had constructed. Normally, conspiracy cases do not involve such diverse goals and therefore are not as complicated. And if multiple statutes are involved in a single conspiracy indictment, they generally are related, as were the first three statutes in the Harrisburg case, all dealing with draft board offenses.

The jury continued deliberating the other nine counts and on April 5, the seventh day of deliberations, Foreman Sheets sent Judge Herman a note:

> The answer to the following question is requested by a juror before closing deliberations—Do we find some of the defendants guilty *if* we have evidence that they have conspired to commit a., b., c., and f., if we cannot find enough evidence that anyone conspired to commit d. and e. in Count I [a., b., and c. were statutes dealing with draft board raids; f. dealt with the kidnap statute; d. and e., with explosives]?

Judge Herman instructed the jury: "I can't say yes, you can do anything, but you may find some of the defendants guilty if you find credible evidence beyond a reasonable doubt that they conspired on counts a., b., c. and f. even if you cannot find enough credible evidence that anyone conspired to commit d. and e."

At last Herman had at least partially clarified his charge on conspiracy—and it was contrary to what the chief prosecutor had understood him to say in the original charge. The judge still had not explained it the way Lynch had requested, that the jury could find some of the defendants guilty if it found a conspiracy to violate any one of the statutes.

But the defense considered Herman's answer to the question ominous. It amounted to "directing the jury to find some of the defendants guilty," said O'Dwyer.

The prevalent expectation among the press and the defense attorneys was that the jury was likely to convict Father Berrigan, Sister McAlister and Joseph Wenderoth of conspiracy charges.

The jury resumed deliberating. Later that day, after a total of fifty-nine hours of deliberation, the jurors filed back into the courtroom, unsmiling, avoiding the eyes of the defendants.

They had another partial verdict: Father Berrigan, guilty of three additional counts of smuggling letters; Sister McAlister, guilty of three letter-smuggling counts.

But the jury was hopelessly deadlocked on the principal charge of conspiracy and on the counts charging Father Berrigan and Sister McAlister with sending a threatening letter.

Judge Herman declared a mistrial on those counts. Defendants and defense attorneys smiled and Ahmad embraced Father Berrigan and Sister McAlister. FBI Agents Mayfield, Anderson and Menzel sat glumly behind the prosecution table. Lynch, just as glum, tried to shrug it off: "Seven out of ten counts isn't bad."

But Lynch knew better. It was a bitter end for J. Edgar Hoover's great kidnap-bombing conspiracy case. Even the *National Review*, which Editor William F. Buckley, Jr., had said was the only serious journal that did not think the case was a lunatic act of Hoover's, called it "the greatest federal fizzle of recent years." The Reverend Sheldon Moody Smith, whom Buckley had described as "just the man to cover the trial," called it "a big, expensive letdown: something like being promised the apocalypse and winding up with a leaky basement."

In Harrisburg, the conservative *Patriot* editorialized that to the government "it must be evident that conspiracy is an elusive charge; that a principal witness whose testimony can be eroded as his motivation is revealed is a very weak reed; and that a faulty case is better left untried than subjected to pitiless media and public exposure." And for J. Edgar Hoover, the *Patriot* continued, "there is a lesson to be learned even this late in life: Don't sound off in public unless you are fully prepared to prove your allegations."

The Los Angeles *Times* said, "The whole affair was surrealistic from the beginning" and the New York *Times* said, "The Harrisburg jurors exhibited more sense and sensibility than the Justice Department, which insisted on prosecuting the defendants for conspiracy in a quixotic scheme that never approached serious fruition."

The letter charges were peripheral issues and not even Father Berrigan and Sister McAlister would lose much sleep over the guilty verdicts. Although letters commonly had been smuggled to and from federal prison, never before had anyone been prosecuted for it, much less convicted. Defense lawyers voiced confidence the convictions would be overturned on grounds of discriminatory prosecution. And they contended, as O'Dwyer had said, there were enough reversible errors in the trial "to free the whole peace movement."

Had there been no love relationship between Father Berrigan and Sister McAlister, there never would have been any such letters—and thus no excuse for the government to bring the kidnap-bombing case. For their letters' references to such suggested activities gave some credence to Douglas' testimony. And under the conspiracy law, it mattered not that the other alleged conspirators knew nothing of the letters' contents. A person who joins in a conspiracy becomes liable for the acts of other conspirators in furtherance of the plot even though he may be unaware of the acts.

The outcome was clearly a legal and political victory for the defendants, and a setback for J. Edgar Hoover and President Nixon's Justice Department. Although the defendants had failed to gain an outright acquittal on the conspiracy charge, the jury had voted ten to two that there was no conspiracy.

One angry man, Lawrence A. Evans, a stern-faced grocery store owner in his late fifties, had led the fight to convict, thus preventing acquittal. His lone supporter was Mrs. Kathryn Schwartz, mother of four conscientious objectors.

Evans made up his mind quickly. Mrs. Vera P. Thompson, the juror with the toothache, told newsmen that as soon as the jurors went into the room to deliberate, "Before we opened the box of evidence, Evans said, 'They're all guilty.' He just exploded out of a clear blue sky."

And Robert Foresman, the state fire school instructor, said Evans started out with a presumption of guilt until proven innocent.

Evans, agitated and outspoken in several interviews with newsmen, said that after the verdict was read in court, "I would have liked to face the press and say, 'I voted guilty on every count and I want the world to know it.' And then I would have liked to turn to and face the defendants and say, 'May God have mercy on your soul.' " He was the juror who had asked the question about whether the jury, in reaching a guilty verdict, would have to conclude there was a conspiracy to violate all the statutes.

Evans, however, as well as Mrs. Thompson and Foresman, said that Douglas' lack of credibility had been crucial in the lopsided vote in favor of acquittal.

Actually, the jury never reached the point of voting on the guilt or innocence of the individual defendants, a point that virtually escaped public notice. It voted ten to two that there was no conspiracy. Jurors first vote in a conspiracy case on whether a conspiracy exists. If the jury agrees there was a conspiracy, then it votes on whether individual defendants took part. But if the jury deadlocks on whether a conspiracy exists, it never reaches the point of assessing individual guilt or innocence. Therefore, a defendant on whose innocence all jurors might agree is deprived of an acquittal—an inherent problem of double jeopardy in the conspiracy law.

Aside from the strength or weakness of the government's case, the use of the conspiracy statute, which Judge Learned Hand had scorned as "the darling of the modern prosecutor's nursery," put the defendants in acute jeopardy. In addition to permitting the prosecution to charge the defendants with a series of diverse crimes under one umbrella, reliance on conspiracy law opened the door to vast amounts of evidence that would have been barred if a substantive crime had been alleged.

Underlying conspiracy law is a kind of Catch 22 reasoning. As Supreme Court Justice Robert H. Jackson put it: "A conspiracy often is proved by evidence that is admissible only upon the assumption that conspiracy existed."

The Phil-Liz letters, as a prime example, would not have been accepted as evidence against five other defendants if they had been charged with the commission of a substantive crime instead of plotting to commit one.

Boyd Douglas' extensive testimony about what one defendant told him about another's conversations also would have been inadmissible hearsay if conspiracy were not the charge.

In a dazzling display of such hearsay, linking four of the alleged conspirators, Douglas testified: "He [Wenderoth] told me that he had been contacted by Elizabeth McAlister, that Elizabeth McAlister advised Joseph Wenderoth and Neil McLaughlin about the destruction of the tunnel system in Washington, D.C., and that Philip Berrigan was most anxious to get this underway."

Hearsay evidence is considered less reliable primarily because it is not subject to testing by cross-examination. The theory in conspiracy law is that hearsay testimony about virtually any act or declaration by a conspirator to further the conspiracy is admissible against every other co-conspirator if independent proof for the conspiracy's existence is given. But in practice prosecutors present hearsay before the independent foundation is laid, as they did in the Harrisburg trial.

The burden of this practice on a jury is heavy. Judge Hand termed it "a practical impossibility for laymen . . . to keep their minds in the isolated compartments" required by the conspiracy rules.

The naming of unindicted co-conspirators also permitted the prosecution to introduce otherwise inadmissible evidence. One example was ex-nun Marjorie Shuman's conversation with Douglas in which she allegedly said that Washington's Birthday, 1971, was the target date for blowing up the heating system.

Only two months before the trial began, the government added—by a bill of particulars, not by grand jury action—John Swinglish as an unindicted co-conspirator. The addition of Swinglish allowed the government to introduce testimony about a discussion of the political kidnappings in South America. The discussion, at an October, 1970, meeting of the Catholic Peace Fellowship, linked none of the defendants. But because a co-conspirator was present where the kidnapping subject was raised, the government presumably considered the evidence to have scene-setting value—to show that such tactics were a matter of discussion among the Catholic peace movement.

Perhaps the most unjust characteristic of being named an unindicted co-conspirator is that the person has no opportunity to present a defense in court. Sister Jogues was enraged when she was so designated and then subpoenaed to testify before the grand jury that continued its investigation after the first indictment. The mention of the name of William Davidon, another unindicted co-conspirator during testimony, was not restricted to the meeting in Weston, Connecticut. He also was linked to draft board raids, but had no way to respond to the allegations.

The injustice was compounded in the case of Daniel Berrigan, who was designated a co-conspirator in the first indictment—six weeks after Hoover named him a ringleader. He was dropped without explanation in the second indictment. The mystery of Daniel's link grew during the trial when there was scant mention of him.

In FBI reports turned over to the defense by order of the court, there was one reference by Douglas to Daniel and the kidnapping plot. The August 29, 1970, report said the informant "also reported Liz had said Phil discussed kidnapping plans with Rev. Daniel Berrigan and 'she said Berrigan was in complete agreement with the plan.' "

Some of these complaints on the inherent injustice of conspiracy prosecutions were registered against the Spock trial during the Johnson Administration and later against the Chicago Seven riot conspiracy and the murder conspiracy charges against Bobby Seale and other Black Panthers in Connecticut. In the Spock matter, then Attorney General

Ramsey Clark brought a case that raised far more troublesome free-speech questions than the Harrisburg prosecution.

But the Harrisburg prosecution had a special quality all its own—the strong evidence that the case never would have been brought had not J. Edgar Hoover made his accusation against the Berrigan brothers.

The dropping of Daniel Berrigan in the superseding indictment because of an acute lack of evidence and the submerging of the kidnap-bombing allegations gave powerful support to the suggestion that the prosecution was strongly influenced by the need of the Nixon Administration to shore up its leading law and order symbol.

A Justice Department official, familiar with the evidence, reluctantly conceded in an interview that if Hoover had not made his accusation, the kidnap-bombing case most likely would not have been brought. At that stage of the investigation, he said, there was insufficient evidence. Declining to be identified, he cited "prosecutorial discretion," the doctrine under which Justice Department resources are devoted to those cases that will do the most public good. The Berrigan investigation was no such case.

However, the official contended it was Hoover's testimony that blocked the department from reaching the point where it could exercise sound prosecutorial discretion in the Berrigan matter. At the time of the testimony, the Criminal Division considered the case "a live one" and had instructed the FBI in a memorandum what points needed to be nailed down. Speculation that Hoover's testimony sought to prod the department into cracking down on the Berrigans by prosecuting can only be supported with the conjecture that the FBI director feared the points could not be nailed down.

Whatever motivated the extraordinary bureaucrat, he dropped his Berrigan bombshell at a time when he and, to a lesser degree, his FBI were under Congressional and news media fire as never before.

Hoover chose to fire back at a target that was not likely to evoke widespread sympathy from the public. The Philip Berrigans and Elizabeth McAlisters and Joe Wenderoths of this nation strike a no more responsive chord with much of the public than do those who break laws for less lofty purposes. Respect for law runs deep in America, and those who challenge it have a hard time convincing most Americans of the justice of their actions.

The Berrigans and McAlisters and Wenderoths turn off the public for another reason as well. They are conscience-stirrers, which may be acceptable when they are saying a rosary or hearing confession, but not when they are trying to turn the nation's attention to a case of collective guilt—the slaughter in Vietnam.

The Harrisburg indictment and trial came at a time when the nation, led by President Nixon, was striving to ignore the killing in Vietnam and America's role in it. Priests and nuns who were willing to risk their freedom in order to drive home America's responsibility did not fit into that kind of calm-the-waters operation.

Hoover gave no sign that he regarded the Harrisburg jury's failure to convict on the kidnap-bombing charge as a setback. Two weeks after the trial, he invited Lynch and his young prosecution team—Connelly, Killion and Krajewski—to his office. U.S. Attorney Cottone was tied up in Pennsylvania and couldn't make it. The visit lasted five minutes, and Hoover was "very complimentary" about the prosecutors' efforts, Lynch recalled later. In the midst of the session, an FBI photographer, following the standard practice of photographing Hoover with his visitors, recorded the event on film.

Hoover wrote Boyd Douglas commending him for his service. But the FBI did not disclose how much Douglas was finally paid.

Four weeks after the trial ended, Hoover died. His body was found on the floor beside his bed, and death was attributed to natural causes—a seventy-seven-year-old heart giving out. The body lay in state in the Capitol Rotunda, and President Nixon delivered the eulogy at the funeral.

On the night before the funeral, a White House staff member called several newsmen to advise them the President had resisted "intense pressure" from his senior aides over the last year to force Hoover to retire. The caller, who insisted on being identified only as "an administration source," told of three meetings where Mr. Nixon rebuffed his advisers' counsel and backed the FBI chief. The anonymous official volunteered that one of the "goofs" that helped turn the White House staff against Hoover was his Berrigan testimony.

"It's an old Nixon principle to stick behind a man when he's under fire," the White House staff member explained.

Attorney General Kleindienst, soon after the Senate confirmed him to succeed John N. Mitchell, decided against retrying the case. No immediate public announcement was made, however, because Judge Herman had still to rule on some post-trial motions. When one of the authors of this book suggested that Kleindienst might decide to try again, the blunt-talking attorney general asked his co-author whether he was "crazy."

Loose ends still remained hanging from the case. Near the end of its 1971-72 term, the Supreme Court rejected the stance taken by the Justice Department in the Jogues Egan contempt case. The court ruled the third circuit appellate court was right in reversing the nun's contempt conviction because the Justice Department would not reveal whether she had been illegally wiretapped until its tardy denial of eavesdropping when the case was appealed to the high court. The justices sent the case back for a hearing on the wiretap question, but it was doubtful the department would pursue the issue because of the decision not to retry the defendants. The Supreme Court's ruling in Sister Egan's case was costly for the department. It established the precedent that grand jury witnesses threatened with contempt for refusing to testify could require the government either to disclose whether they had been picked up on wiretaps or drop the contempt proceedings, a choice prosecutors were loath to make.

The responsibility for the Harrisburg prosecution does not rest entirely on the FBI or its late director. The Bureau of Prisons, headed by a man who had been recognized as a progressive administrator, must shoulder some blame. The prison administration repeatedly stressed its devotion to rehabilitation, but it sat by while the sole Lewisburg convict on a Bucknell study program—the essence of rehabilitation—informed on the campus community as well as the Catholic radicals and broke numerous prison rules.

As former Lewisburg Warden J. J. Parker told Bucknell Professor Gene Chenoweth: "When all the facts come out, it's going to be very embarrassing for the Bureau of Prisons."

The ultimate responsibility lay with the Justice Department hierarchy, and indeed reached all the way to the White House. Assistant Attorney General Mardian underscored his confidence in the case in several interviews. Attorney General Mitchell repeatedly defended Hoover against charges he had prejudiced the matter. When President Nixon was asked two weeks after Hoover's Senate testimony whether he approved of Hoover's pre-indictment accusations, he ignored the fact that Hoover had violated basic constitutional rights and praised the FBI director.

Saluting Hoover's "very great service to this country," and noting that he "generally" approved of the action Hoover took, Nixon said: "The Justice Department is looking into that testimony that Mr. Hoover has given and will take appropriate action if the facts justify it."

The Berrigan case was brought against a backdrop of a Justice Department which had become highly politicized. Four of the nine top Justice Department officials recommended by Mitchell and named by President Nixon at the outset of his ad-ministration came from the ranks of politicians who had lost their last race out. This trend continued during Mitchell's years as attorney general. It was a kind of musical chairs involving justice and politics.

The Nixon Administration rode to office on a series of "law and order" promises, including Mr. Nixon's vow to name a new attorney general as his first order of business. Yet before his first term was over, Mr. Nixon's Criminal Division chief, Will R. Wilson, was forced to resign under a cloud because of his in-volvement with a Texas banker who was at the center of a scandal; the Law Enforcement Assistance Administration, a model for the President's revenue sharing proposals, was wracked by revelations of misspent funds; and the Justice Department's relationships with big business, typified by the

International Telephone & Telegraph Corporation, threatened to become a campaign issue.

The Justice Department's deep-seated concern over subversion, manifested by its claim that the attorney general could, without a judge's permission, authorize wiretapping persons and organizations he deemed domestic subversive threats, also was rejected by the Supreme Court. The justices held that the Fourth Amendment guarantee against unreasonable searches and seizures required that the department obtain a court warrant before it initiated such eavesdropping.

Not all of the blame for the Berrigan case rests with the government, of course. The Catholic left did not come into court with clean hands. Its protest actions—unlawful acts in response to what the radicals regarded as unlawful acts by those in power—did violence to a system of government that could only function if its citizens obeyed the law. Philip and Daniel Berrigan and others of the Catonsville Nine who fled rather than surrender after their court appeals ran out escalated the protest and helped create a climate that would encourage Hoover to overreact. Refusing to accept punishment for their illegal act of protest violated an established precept of civil disobedience, as practiced by Thoreau and Gandhi and King.

With these developments in the background, the Berrigan prosecution took on a discolored hue. It would be wrong, however, to conclude that the investigation and prosecution were simply politically motivated from the start. Justice Department professionals were genuinely concerned over information on the case the FBI had relayed to them before Hoover transformed the case from one of justice into one of politics. Before his testimony there was even thought given to arresting the suspects Douglas had identified on criminal complaints. The year 1970 was a tense time in Washington, with fear of bombings and political kidnappings uppermost in officials' minds.

But once Hoover captured headlines with his Berrigan accusation, the politics became paramount, and the opportunity for an objective, detached exercise of prosecutorial discretion was greatly reduced. Given the fact that J. Edgar Hoover and the Nixon Administration shared a "law and order" constituency, prosecution was virtually assured if even a small amount of credible evidence existed. Mardian, who conceded having periodic doubts during the investigation about Douglas' veracity, became convinced his information was credible in attempting to verify a key point—whether Fathers Berrigan and Wenderoth had told the informer they went into the underground tunnels. Douglas said the priests described entering the tunnels posing as engineers from the Robb Electric Company. But the FBI failed to turn up any such company despite an exhaustive check. Pondering the lack of corroboration, Mardian and his secretary, Wyn Drake, recalled from his service at HEW that ROB was government shorthand for regional office building. HEW had a regional building next to the Forrestal Building and the entrance to the tunnel. To Mardian, this, plus the fact that Douglas knew the approximate dimensions of the tunnel, amounted to dramatic confirmation of Douglas' story. How could Douglas acquire such information unless the priests related it to him?

Lynch, a skilled prosecutor, drew up the most convincing case that could be drawn from the available evidence. How slim it was can be gauged in part from the derisive reaction the case received from conservative as well as liberal journals. It can be argued that the jury's deadlock on the central charge reflected the justness of the American system of jurisprudence. The same observation could be made about the Chicago Seven jury's rejection of the central conspiracy charge and the reversed convictions in the Spock case.

But this begs the question of whether the case should ever have been brought in the first place. The decision to prosecute illustrated how susceptible the career staff of the Justice Department can be to the non-judicious influence of those running the department at any particular time.

History probably will record the Berrigan case as one of the fallouts of the nation's involvement in Vietnam. Opposition to the conflict produced a degree of prolonged resistance to government authority surpassed only by the Civil War in America's history. As a counter-reaction the federal government brought a series of unprecedented prosecutions to put down the resistance.

But in the Berrigan case, there was a special lesson: So powerful had the director of the FBI become that the President of the United States, who frequently reminded his countrymen that he was a lawyer, chose to ignore Hoover's blatant violation of the Bill of Rights. Instead the Nixon Administration prosecuted in a vain attempt to show the FBI director had his facts right. When a nation that prides itself on being a system of laws—not men—permits itself to be so corrupted, the portents are ominous.

Index